Women's Movements in America

WOMEN'S MOVEMENTS IN AMERICA

Their Successes, Disappointments, and Aspirations

RITA J. SIMON
AND GLORIA DANZIGER

New York
Westport, Connecticut
London

Library of Congress Cataloging-in-Publication Data

Simon, Rita James.
    Women's movements in America : their successes, disappointments,
and aspirations / Rita J. Simon and Gloria Danziger.
        p.   cm.
    Includes bibliographical references and index.
    ISBN 0–275–93948–0 (alk. paper). — ISBN 0–275–93949–9 (alk. paper : pbk.)
    1. Feminism—United States—History.   2. Women's rights—United
States—History.   3. Women—United States—Social conditions.
I. Danziger, Gloria.   II. Title.
HQ1426.S478   1991
305.42′0973—dc20   91–8619

British Library Cataloguing in Publication Data is available.

Library of Congress Catalog Card Number: 91–8619
ISBN: 0–275–93948–0 (hb)
        0–275–93949–9 (pb)

First published in 1991

Praeger Publishers, One Madison Avenue, New York, NY 10010
An imprint of Greenwood Publishing Group, Inc.

Printed in the United States of America

The paper used in this book complies with the
Permanent Paper Standard issued by the National
Information Standards Organization (Z39.48–1984).

10   9   8   7   6   5   4   3   2   1

CONTENTS

Women's Movements in America

Chapter 1

WOMEN'S MOVEMENTS: AN OVERVIEW

No mention of women's rights was ever made by the delegates to the Constitutional Convention in 1787, even though at least one of the framers—John Adams, who would become the second president of the United States—had been exhorted by his wife, Abigail, not to "forget the ladies": "Emancipating all nations, you insist upon retaining absolute power over Wives," she wrote in 1776.[1] Women were deprived of property rights, were denied guardianship of their children, were unable to vote, could not sign contracts, and were barred from testifying in court.

Despite the Constitutional Convention's failure to grant legal rights to women, or perhaps because of it, a visible and organized women's movement had emerged by the 1830s. In 1848, that movement brought forth a manifesto, the "Declaration of Sentiments," which for the first time called for a cohesive program of reforms.

But in the 1830s and 1840s, the nation's attention was focused on another issue, one whose moral overtones placed much greater demands on leaders of social change. That issue was slavery. The abolitionist movement was the major social movement of the two decades prior to the Civil War, and it captured the energy and imagination of women who saw injustice and inequality in the treatment meted out to slaves. Rather than continue to pursue their own goals, the leaders of the women's movement threw themselves into the struggle for the abolition of slavery. They joined the speakers' platforms of the male-led and organized movement, they helped runaway slaves escape to Northern cities and to Canada, and in 1840, women were included in the American delegation that attended the World Anti-Slavery Convention held in London.

Once the Civil War began, the women advocates agreed to abandon their own cause and to support the Union effort. Just as the trade unions' movement agreed not to strike at the onset of World War II, women leaders essentially ceased working for women's goals. The culmination of the abolitionist efforts was the passage of the Thirteenth Amendment to the Constitution, which abolished slavery. With the successful conclusion of the war and the passage of the Thirteenth Amendment in 1865, women activists were ready to return to their original cause, a cause that they had placed on the back burner for more than a quarter of a century. They turned to their allies, the male leaders of the abolitionist movement, but to their surprise did not receive help and support. Once again, the women were told to wait—other problems, other injustices, were more important and more worthy of their attention and their energies.

The leaders of the women's movement watched in shock and disillusionment as the former abolitionists and the Republican leaders of the Congress successfully lobbied for and gained adoption in 1868 of the Fourteenth Amendment and in 1870 of the Fifteenth Amendment to the Constitution, which granted to the new "freedmen" the rights, privileges, and immunities of citizenship, including, under the Fifteenth Amendment, suffrage. None of these rights were granted to women. Before the Civil War, women had been told to wait on their cause, to recognize the abolition of slavery as the major moral priority. They not only acquiesced and waited, they also threw themselves into the struggle against slavery and for freedom.

With the end of hostilities and the end of slavery, the women had every reason to believe that their time had come and their movement would assume center stage as the next major struggle for freedom and equality. The events of 1867 dramatize how wrong they were. In that year leaders of the women's rights movement expected that a referendum would be held in Kansas whereby the citizens of that state would have a chance to vote to remove franchise restrictions on the grounds of sex and race. The suffrage leaders expected the Republicans and the abolitionists to join with them in providing strong support for the referendum. Instead, the Republican leadership, with the support of the abolitionists, decided that "this is the Negro's hour" (the *male* Negro's hour) and that linking race and sex to the referendum could hurt the chances of securing the vote for the Negro. Southern Negro votes were needed to strengthen Republican representation in the Congress. Women were stunned by the rebuff they received. They had lost the only allies they assumed they could count on. The women had no choice but to go it alone.

The lack of support that the women received on that occasion moved Elizabeth Stanton to warn future generations of women:

Woman must lead the way to her own enfranchisement, and work out her own salvation with a hopeful courage and determination. . . . She must not put her trust in man in this transition period, since while regarded as his subject, his inferior, his slave, their interests must be antagonistic.[2]

It turned out to be a long, lonely struggle. Not until August 26, 1920, some fifty-five years after the end of the Civil War and seventy-two years after the first Woman's Rights Convention was held in Seneca Falls in 1848, was the major goal of the women's movement achieved: suffrage. With the adoption of the Nineteenth Amendment, which had been introduced into every session of Congress from 1878 until its passage, women gained the right to vote in all federal, state, and local elections.

In retrospect, we have come to recognize that the event marked both the culmination of the women's movement's greatest victory and its death knell. At the time, the adoption of the suffrage amendment was perceived as an enormous victory because the women's movement assumed that formal and de facto rights were one and the same. The leaders believed that the "right to vote" would empower women and give them the equality they had sought in the political, economic, and social arenas for almost a century. Many women's groups disbanded, not to be revitalized for another forty years.

It is too simplistic to say that nothing was left of the women's movement after the suffrage amendment had been adopted. In the first two decades of the twentieth century, women joined with labor leaders in opposing unlimited immigration and in favoring strict quotas to keep out "unhealthy" types who would never adapt to American society—Jews, Italians, Poles, Greeks, and other non-Protestants from Southern and Eastern Europe. These were people whom organized labor viewed as a threat to their jobs. Women also put forth a socioeconomic agenda that included passage of "protective labor legislation,"—legislation that would, among other things, prohibit employers from making women work the night shift, would provide them with "decent" restroom facilities, and would prevent them from having to lift and heave various pieces of equipment.

With the stock market crash at the end of the decade, which was followed first by the economic depression of the 1930s and then by the United States' entry into World War II, the women's movement all but disappeared. It remained invisible and dormant for some forty years, arising again in the 1960s, initially under the umbrella and within the organizational structure of the civil rights movement, the emergence of a "New Left" Coalition, and the formation of an antiwar movement. More than halfway through the decade, in 1966, women organized and founded an organization that bore their own insignia, the National Organization for Women (NOW).

The events immediately preceding and following the founding of NOW in many ways resembled those women had experienced a century or so earlier in their collaboration with the abolitionists in the years before the Civil War. Once again they experienced disappointment and bitterness because of the behavior of their former allies.

In the early 1960s, women activists made the civil rights movement their cause. They joined in freedom marches, in lunch counter integration activities, in the voting rights campaigns. They believed that the extension of civil rights to blacks would also result in an enhancement of their own status as women. Although there was grumbling early on that the leadership of the civil rights movement was all male, and that more and more women were relegated to coffee making, answering the telephone, getting out the mailings, and similar kinds of services, it was not until Stokely Carmichael, as chairman of the Student Nonviolent Coordinating Committee (SNCC), made his infamous observation in 1964 that "the only position for women in SNCC is prone" that bells began to ring for the women. The memory of how the earlier leaders of women's movements had been treated by friends and allies became a vivid reminder that history might repeat itself.

The men of the New Left also made it clear to their female colleagues that they had no interest in "women's issues" per se or in aiding and abetting an independent women's movement. In the New Left, as in the civil rights movement, women were expected to, and in fact did, perform in traditional sex roles. The men were the leaders, the thinkers, the planners; women served and were available.

Thus, in retrospect, we see that the first women's movement was founded in the 1830s, joined forces with the abolitionists in the 1840s, and stayed with them up to and for the duration of the Civil War. Following the end of the war, the women found themselves with no allies and no supporters from larger political movements or constituencies. They had all gone home. Their work had been accomplished. Women were on their own. It took another fifty-five years before women achieved suffrage. The women activists of the 1960s learned faster. The civil rights movement, worthy and noble as it was, would not work for them. The achievements and rewards of the movement would go to blacks and mostly to black men. The New Left was more concerned with a radical political agenda than it was with changing women's status. As antiwar sentiments loomed larger and larger, women realized that it too would be a movement in which men would act and resist and women would, at best, counsel and serve.

The 1960s served as an important learning experience for women activists. The behavior and rhetoric of the civil rights and New Left movements of the 1960s, coupled with the historic memory of how the women's movement had lost its momentum and its visibility a century earlier, catapulted women into action. They would organize on their own. They would create their own agenda; they would not be persuaded to take a back seat and wait until the goals of other groups and ideologies had been achieved. The movement for women's liberation emerged as an independent entity by the end of the decade and became a voice to contend with in the 1970s.

What was the agenda of this second major (by some counts, third) women's movement? The first had suffrage as its all-encompassing goal. The second (if one counts the movement of the first two decades of the twentieth century) had protective labor legislation and better working conditions as its primary objectives. In its early stages, the third women's movement veered dangerously close to becoming a "one-issue" movement. That issue was the passage of the Equal Rights Amendment (ERA). The women of the 1960s and 1970s saw the ERA as holding the same promise that women of the nineteenth century attributed to the Suffrage Amendment. It took the first movement over seventy years from its Seneca Falls Convention in 1848 to achieve that objective. Would adoption of the ERA take as long? And would the contemporary women's movement focus exclusively on accomplishing that goal? For a while it seemed as if that might be the case. But as the likelihood of passage waxed and waned, at times seeming almost within grasp and at other times seeming to move farther from reality, women added other "issues" to their agenda. Abortion, comparable pay, and day care became "high priority" issues of the 1980s.

Writing today at the beginning of the last decade of the twentieth century, we find an umbrella under which there walks an organized, self-sufficient women's movement that has few alignments with other groups or causes and that has an agenda that says "women's issues" first. Some would say first and exclusively.

ORGANIZATION OF THIS BOOK

This book is divided into three major sections. Each provides a historical perspective and each brings to bear a variety of data that includes legal statutes and judicial decisions, census and demographic information, public opinion polls, biographical excerpts, and narrative accounts of the changes in women's place in American society from the nation's founding to 1990.

Chapter 2 examines the various manifestations of the women's movement within the context of the larger political scene beginning in the 1830s. It traces the battle for suffrage, the formation and dissolution of various women's political organizations from the National Woman Suffrage Association founded in 1869 to the National Organization for Women founded in 1960. It examines the various stages in the battle for the passage of an Equal Rights Amendment beginning in 1937 and continuing until the present.

The second part of the chapter examines how women used their newly gained political power and reports the impact of the "women's" vote on public offices and public policies. It describes men's and women's voting preferences for major political offices from the late 1930s on, and it compares men's and women's responses to national poll items pertaining to domestic and foreign policy. It provides a record of the successes and failures of women as political candidates.

Chapter 3 focuses on women in the labor force. As we did for the political sphere, a brief history is provided of women's experiences in the work place. Part of that history includes women's role in the trade union movement, the role of the Congress and the courts in the passage and interpretation of protective labor legislation, and the movement for equal pay, affirmative action, and, most recently, comparable worth. It provides demographic data on the number and types of women in the labor force, on the types of positions held by women, on provisions working women make for child care, and on the salary differentials between men and women. Changes in the educational levels of women in American society are reported, along with the impact that education has had on their participation in the labor force and among traditionally male-dominated professions such as medicine, law, and engineering. Public opinion data are also included that compare men's and women's attitudes toward women's participation in various types of occupations and the impact that women in the labor force, especially at the professional and managerial levels, have had on the division of labor in the home.

Chapter 4 examines the more personal aspects of women's status and traces political and judicial changes from colonial times to the present in such areas as child custody and the rights of a married woman to enter into contracts, to hold property, and to engage in trade. Divorce reform is traced from the 1830s to the passage of no-fault statutes in the 1970s. The birth control movement and the current bitter struggles on the abortion issue take up major sections of this chapter. As in the political and work place chapters, national poll data are presented that compare men's and women's attitudes on many of the controversies discussed from a historical perspective.

 In sum, this book tells the story of how women's status in American society has changed over a time span of two centuries on such important matters as personal and family life, work and educational experiences, and contributions and visibility in the political and public spheres. We think our examination is a critical one. It shows successes as well as failures. It looks at the bumps and detours that have been part of American women's journey from 1790 to 1990. Where appropriate, it applauds and celebrates events and acts that have enhanced women's status. It does not shy away from indicating where women's movements have failed, on which issues they were divided, and which goals are still being sought.

NOTES

1. Quoted in Nancy Woloch, *Women and the American Experience* (New York: Knopf, 1984), p. 89.

2. Alice S. Rossi, *The Feminist Papers, from Adams to de Beauvoir* (New York: Bantam Books, 1973), p. 412.

Chapter 2

SUFFRAGE, VOTING BEHAVIOR, AND POLITICAL OPINIONS

Unlike slavery and race, which, in the words of James Madison, were "the central problem," women were never mentioned during the debate over ratification of the U.S. Constitution. Indeed, in the document itself no mention is made of the status of women, even though they were treated differently than men in every state on almost every issue that affected the rights of citizens, including suffrage, property, jury service, and education. Historian Robert Goldwin has claimed:

They have always been included in all of the constitutional protections provided to all persons, fully and equally, without any basis in the test for discrimination on the basis of sex.

In the original constitution . . . the words "man" or "male" do not occur, nor does any other noun or adjective denoting sex. By not mentioning women or men, speaking instead only of persons, the Constitution must mean that every right, privilege, and protection afforded to persons in the Constitution is afforded to female persons as well as male persons, equally.[1]

Whatever the intent of the authors may have been on the matter of women, the results of ratification were that women lost rather than gained rights. For example, in states in which women had voted prior to the Constitution, such as Massachusetts from 1691 to 1780 and in New Jersey until 1807, they lost that right.

Women did not appear particularly to want the vote, either. In 1848, the only resolution that was not adopted unanimously at Seneca Falls was the one calling for suffrage. Economic and social rights were considered of paramount importance by women's leaders, who feared that a demand for the franchise would make women look "ridiculous."[2]

It was to be a long and arduous road for the women's movement before suffrage would be welcomed as a popular, acceptable change. Women's suffrage for national offices did not happen until more than a century after women had lost the vote in New Jersey and not before there had been a major rallying cry from every women's movement in the United States.

Leaders of the National Woman Suffrage Association (NWSA) and its off-shoot, the National Woman's Party, argued that with the vote, women would demonstrate their greater (as compared with men) social consciousness and humanitarianism.

Armed with the right to vote, women would also declare their independence from male influence and elect persons who were more competent, more honest, and more caring than those nominated and elected by their husbands, fathers, and brothers. Not only would women demonstrate their independence and greater social consciousness by voting for more qualified candidates, but they would also wield their political power by nominating and supporting other women for public office. Once in office, women governors, representatives, senators, and even presidents would change the character of the nation. Under women's leadership, new, effective, and peaceful means would be found to resolve domestic and foreign disputes. Child care would improve. The elderly and the sick would have greater security. Workers would labor under better conditions and for fewer hours.

As early as 1914, surveys appeared that purportedly demonstrated the truth of the above claims. The *Evening Sun*, a New York City newspaper, sent a questionnaire to its correspondents asking a series of questions dealing with the impact of suffrage in individual states that had given women the vote. Among the laws that had been passed, the study attributed the following to suffrage: labor laws affecting women and children, employers' liability and workmen's compensation laws, factory inspection laws, mothers' pension laws, laws against disorderly women, and laws requiring health certificates before the granting of marriage licenses.[3]

But such "studies" were primarily a prelude, one in a series of events designed to persuade legislators to include suffrage for women in the Constitution. We will show that once the women's movement had won the vote, their predictions—more women entering politics, more "benevolent" legislatures, laws that would more more humane and beneficial to society—did not come to pass.

Not until the 1970s did women's groups even begin to look at ways in which they could promote women as politicians. Recently, however, this relatively new chapter in the women's movement has assumed greater importance among the areas of critical concern to the major women's groups in this country. Several of them are gearing up to play major roles in upcoming elections on both federal and local levels. Similar to the strategies of the suffrage movement in the early 1900s, women's groups are raising money, training their members, and conducting massive outreach programs in an effort to introduce more women into politics. And like the suffrage movement, there has been a radical shift from the extreme, shrill arguments made by the radical movement of the 1960s and early 1970s, to a far more moderate, perhaps conservative, approach that is located squarely within mainstream politics.

In this chapter we first examine the history of the women's movement's fight for enfranchisement. We then look at data concerning the effects of suffrage, including women in public office and patterns of voting behavior. In the final sections, we analyze the recent changes that the women's movement has made in its policies on women in politics and speculate as to the future of those policies.

THE BIRTH OF THE SUFFRAGE MOVEMENT

The first known demand made for suffrage in the United States occurred in 1647 by Margaret Brent of Maryland. She was the heir of Lord Calvert, the brother of Lord Baltimore, and executor of the estates of both men in the colony. As representation in the legislature was based on property, she demanded "place and voyce"—two votes—in that body. Her petition was debated for several hours and finally denied.[4]

Colonial records of Massachusetts show that women voted under the Old Province Charter from 1691 to 1780 for all elective officers. When a constitution was adopted, they were excluded from a vote for governor and legislature but retained it for other officials. Almost one hundred years later, in 1776, the Continental Congress left suffrage to the individual states. New Jersey was the only one to grant women the vote, a right that was rescinded by the legislature in 1807.

In the early nineteenth century, abolition quickly overshadowed the struggle for suffrage. Some historians argue that the role of women in antislavery activities has been ignored and that organized female activity during the years 1836–43 was pivotal in achieving abolition.[5] Beginning with Elizabeth Chandler, an abolitionist writer and reformer, women provided much of the financial support for the abolition movement, wrote and sold literature, and conducted petition campaigns.[6] From the very beginning, women's participation in the abolitionist movement was linked to "the woman question," that women—as well as slaves—were in bondage to white males. In the late 1820s, Chandler wrote at length in a weekly publication, *The Genius of Universal Emancipation*, connecting the cause of slave women to all women.

The introduction of the women's rights struggle into American political life was given a further push by William Lloyd Garrison, perhaps the most prominent abolitionist of his time. One of his goals was to arouse American women to embrace the antislavery cause, and, in so doing, he explicitly tied the plight of slave women to that of all women.

Until the early 1830s, women played an ancillary role in the abolition movement, circulating petitions, organizing new women's groups, and raising funds.

But by 1837, it appears that they desired a more active role, and organized the Anti-Slavery Convention of American Women in May of that year, with about one hundred delegates from ten states attending the three-day meeting. They made petitioning the main object of their activities. Considered to be radical political activity at the time, convention delegates pledged to collect and send petitions calling for the abolition of slavery and the slave trade to each town in their state. In order to do this, the germ of political activity was formed: community organizing, networking, and information dissemination. Sarah and Angelina Grimke lectured extensively in towns where there were female societies, speaking to at least 40,500 people by one account[7] and generating further activity and the formation of new women's societies dedicated to the antislavery cause. Eventually, Angelina Grimke became the first woman ever to speak to an American legislature when in 1838 she brought a women's antislavery petition with 20,000 signatures to the Massachusetts legislature.

While female participation in the antislavery movement eventually decreased, the political momentum gained by a fledgling women's movement did not. Many women remained active in antislavery work during the 1840s, but a few abolitionist women began a different type of feminism, transferring their political concerns to activities that were more directly related to the particular social and economic plight of American women in the middle of the nineteenth century. Women's leaders, such as Lucy Stone, began to spend part of their time on lectures devoted solely to women's rights. Newspapers, such as *Lily*, published by Amelia Bloomer, were established to express women's demands for reform. A state-by-state campaign to gain legal rights for married women began in the 1840s, as did women's participation in the temperance crusade, which underwent a revival during this decade.

The first official expression of this new women's movement came in 1848 at the Seneca Falls Convention. Although that convention failed to pass a resolution in favor of suffrage, the first Women's Rights Convention of Pennsylvania was held in 1852, when there was outspoken support for it.

But the Civil War and its aftermath took precedence for many years both before and after the 1852 convention. In May of 1837, the first Anti-Slavery Convention of American women met in New York City. The convention made petitioning the focus of their activities, although there was considerable debate on the question of whether women should participate in what was considered to be political activity. Within a few years, women had organized in their communities, established a network of petition gatherers, letter writers, agents, and lecturers. Women sent hundreds of petitions to Congress—with a predominance of women among the petition signers.[8]

The vast majority of women, however, did not take a part in political campaigns; indeed, they viewed such activity as tantamount to heresy. One petitioner wrote:

Women have been taught to depend on the man for their opinions. We had occasion to observe this in our efforts to obtain signatures to petitions; my daughter visited almost every house in this town for the purpose and found that it was the men generally, who needed free discussion, for the women would not act contrary to the ideas of the male part of their family.[9]

Such political apathy was reinforced by the economic transformation occurring in the first half of the nineteenth century. As more men entered the burgeoning office and factory labor force, separate "spheres" were created for men and women. Man's sphere was the world of business and politics, while a woman's role was to tend hearth and home for her husband and children. This "cult of domesticity," as it has been referred to, represented a setback to the feminist leaders' demands for greater political, social, and economic equality.[10]

Thus, while women were active in supporting the abolitionist movement prior to and during the Civil War, once that movement shifted from a moral reform movement to a political one, women were often excluded from direct participation.

Finally in 1866, a group of feminists-abolitionists organized the American Equal Rights Association, with Lucretia Mott as president and Susan Anthony and Henry Blackwell as secretaries. The association was to work for the rights of both freedmen and women, but was quickly engulfed in the debate over the Fourteenth Amendment pending in Congress, the wording of which angered feminists by specifically granting the vote to "male citizens" and introducing the word "male" into the Constitution, which had previously not referred to gender and had not explicitly barred female suffrage. The large majority of men and a few of the women at the first convention of the Equal Rights Association, however, were unwilling to jeopardize Negro male suffrage by joining it with women's suffrage.

It was not until 1869 that women's leaders decided that it was necessary to sever their causes from those of the blacks. At the end of an Equal Rights Association meeting in New York, women representatives from nineteen states met at the Woman's Bureau and formed a National Woman Suffrage Association (NWSA), led by Elizabeth Cady Stanton and Susan B. Anthony, whose sole object was to secure a Sixteenth Amendment that would enfranchise women. They targeted both middle- and working-class women, and centered their attention on lobbying efforts in Congress rather than organizing state campaigns.

At this point, there was far from consensus on the desirability of a federal suffrage law. Various women's rights advocates, most notably Lucy Stone and Henry Blackwell, split off from the women's movement to found the more conservative American Women Suffrage Association (AWSA). They promoted a state-by-state approach to women's suffrage—buttressed by well-organized state delegations and strong local affiliates—relying on the belief that abolitionists and Republicans would eventually adopt their cause. It was the NWSA, however, that attracted the lion's share of media and popular attention. The group's reputation quickly became one of radicalism—a reputation that was to dog the women's movement a hundred years later. Anthony's and Stanton's articles in *The Revolution* concerned subjects such as divorce reform and prostitution. The deleterious effect of this emphasis on radical issues was only deepened by Stanton's and Anthony's association with George Francis Train, a radical Democrat whom they had met during an unsuccessful referendum campaign for suffrage in 1867. His extremist policies, which included disfranchising the uneducated while enfranchising women, appeared frequently in *The Revolution*. By 1870, however, Train had literally disappeared from the alliance, leaving Stanton and Anthony in debt. What was worse, he had left the two women's leaders in a position where many NWSA members felt alienated from the movement because they believed suffrage should have remained isolated from other issues. But, instead of launching a concerted effort to mend the rift, Stanton and Anthony allowed further divisions in the women's movement in the person of Victoria Woodhull.

Woodhull, who along with her sister ran the first women's brokerage firm, argued for spiritualism, internationalism, free trade, currency reform, liberalized divorce laws, the licensing of prostitutes, and "a single standard of morality." She attracted a great deal of media attention to NWSA, as well as to herself, especially during her speeches exhorting listeners to accept philosophies of free love. Woodhull also established her own group, the International Workingmen's Association, and in 1872, convinced Stanton that a merger between the Association and NWSA would be beneficial to both leaders.

Anthony, violently opposed to the alliance, took over the meeting at which it was being discussed and barred Woodhull from speaking. Soon after, Woodhull's career and popularity collapsed. But it took years for Stanton and Anthony to unite once again in the name of women's rights. Stanton resigned from NWSA until 1876, when she resumed the leadership and dropped her more radical politics in favor of single-issue politics.

But in the meantime, NWSA's goals suffered a severe setback. Not only were women's rights advocates unable to win voting rights, they were unsuccessful in attracting a large female constituency and lost even the few referenda they were able to convince legislators to hold in various states. While the social and political environment in the late 1800s and early 1900s was considerably different from that of the mid–eighteenth century, when suffrage had been associated with an eccentric, radical position, the vast majority of suffrage campaigns in most states were unsuccessful. The less strident tones and more conservative philosophy led to some early suffrage victories in Colorado (1893), Idaho (1896), Wyoming (1890), and Utah (1896). But no other states enfranchised women until 1910, despite major efforts by suffrage campaigns, which suffered from inadequate organization, too few members, and lack of popular support. (Flexner cites 480 efforts in 33 states, 17 referendum votes, and only two victories from 1897 to 1910.)

Indeed, in 1895, the movement was faced with a demonstration of just how far they had yet to go. When Massachusetts, the center of AWSA activities, allowed women to vote in a state referendum on women suffrage, far more men than women voted in favor of suffrage. This was a phenomenon that was to be repeated in the 1960s when more men than women said they would vote for a woman president.

The string of defeats suffered by the suffrage movement was due in some part to the rise of another women's movement at the same time: the anti-suffragists. While opposition to suffrage was not nearly as well organized as AWSA and NWSA, a number of women, as well as men, urged legislatures to vote against suffrage legislation. Their arguments fell into two broad categories: first, that "women possess far more influence in the state for all moral and unselfish purposes, without the ballot," because they are in the position of acting without any political motive;[11] and second, that women would lose their "womanliness" if given the vote.

In politics woman would "abandon her highest powers"; not merely lose with men influence due to those powers, but lose the power, the quality itself. "In strife," such as politics necessitates, "women become hard, harsh, unlovable, repulsive, as far removed from the gentle creature whom we all love and obey as heaven is removed from the earth."[12]

Other objections to suffrage included the following: most women do not want to vote; there are too many voters; women are represented already; only bad and ignorant women would vote; it would put control of government into the hands of "foreign elements"; it would diminish respect for women; it is contrary to the Bible; women do not have the physical strength to enforce laws and therefore should not help make them; it will cause domestic discord when women vote differently from their husbands.[13]

A NEW STRATEGY AND A MORE CONSERVATIVE PLATFORM

The number of defeats in suffrage campaigns, coupled with widespread opposition to suffrage in the South, persuaded NWSA leaders to adopt a new strategy involving a three-pronged program: a new plan of action, new leadership, and a modified philosophy.

In 1890, following a national trend toward federation, NWSA and AWSA joined to become the National American Woman Suffrage Association (NAWSA), and the shift began toward a narrower political focus. NAWSA agreed to direct all its efforts toward the state level. State campaigns became more numerous and effective, and membership grew. The movement spread to the Western states and to the South, where it capitalized on the already widespread activism of women in club and temperance work. This overlapping pattern of women's groups became prevalent throughout the country as differences between the suffragists and other social reformers became less sharp. NAWSA drew support from leaders in the National Consumers' League (NCL), the Women's Trade Union League, and the settlement movement. Between the two of them, Jane Addams and Florence Kelly held posts in the NCL, WTUL, GFWC (General Federation of Women's Clubs), and NAWSA and in a new Woman's Peace Party.

The suffrage movement's strategy was to develop a sophisticated lobbying effort at every level of state government. At the annual meeting of NAWSA in 1895, a committee on legislative advice was appointed to disseminate information on the best methods of conducting legislative campaigns to secure passage of laws.[14] Women were urged to seek out the probable candidate of each party, months before the legislatures met in order to obtain pledges of support. Once such a promise was obtained, NAWSA members were to form delegations at nominating conventions to urge their candidates' nomination. And finally, NAWSA members were to hold public meetings and distribute documents supporting their chosen candidates.

Carrie Chapman Catt had also devised a plan of action for other legislative sessions. Labeled the "precinct plan,"[15] it was first implemented in the 1896 Idaho and California suffrage campaigns, and reached its most sophisticated form in New York in 1908.[16] The New York suffragists began by appointing a worker for each of the twenty-two senatorial districts.[17] These "chairmen" in turn appointed a chairman for each assembly district, and together they lobbied their respective legislative representatives, both before and after the elections. The membership lists of all the women's clubs in greater New York were classified by district, whose members were then invited, along with all known suffragists in any given district, to attend an assembly district convention.

The district conventions appointed delegates to attend a city convention held in 1909, when 804 suffragist delegates filled Carnegie Hall. The platform issued by that convention called for a referendum on a suffrage amendment to the state constitution, as well as for mandatory appointment of women to the board of education and boards of certain hospitals and other institutions. After the convention, delegates decided to form a Woman Suffrage Party, not to compete against regular parties, but rather to make the district convention a permanent fixture in the women's suffrage movement. From its inception in 1909 to 1910, the Woman Suffrage Party enrolled 20,000 members, held over 500 public meetings, lobbied legislative delegates, published a monthly newspaper, held lectures, and distributed 150,000 leaflets in English, 80,000 in Yiddish, 80,000 in Italian, and 20,000 in Bohemian (Czech).[18]

Similar frameworks for precinct work were undertaken in San Francisco in 1908, Philadelphia in 1910, Baltimore in 1910, and Chicago in 1910. In several urban areas, such as New York, Spokane, Minneapolis, and Baltimore, the Woman Suffrage Party established "political settlements," offices staffed by suffragists whose objective was to disseminate information, mobilize neighborhood interest, and enlist new members in the suffrage movement.

In an effort to attract wider support, especially from women, the leadership of the women's movement changed as well. While Stanton remained in control for the first two years of NAWSA's establishment, Susan B. Anthony replaced her after her retirement in 1892. Carrie Chapman Catt became prominent in the 1890s as a master strategist of state campaigns and served as president from 1900 to 1904 and from 1915 to 1920. Anna Howard Shaw, an ordained minister, physician, and orator, was NAWSA president from 1904 to 1915.

These new leaders spoke in terms that were most compatible to the organization's expanding constituency—language that indicated a radical shift from the ideals of Seneca Falls. Divorce reform, trade unionism, and the legalization of prostitution were dropped from NAWSA's platform. Instead, their philosophy revolved around a woman's traditional role as homemaker. Progressivism and efforts to secure goals such as unadulterated foods, child labor laws, and better government were merely extensions of that role.

NAWSA's narrow issues focus and rationale for seeking the ballot made it radically different from most earlier women's movements. Its members were derived from new spheres like the Women's Christian Temperance Union, the women's clubs, and the South. The tone of the new suffrage movement was firmly based on conservative, traditional values. "The two most strongly marked instincts of woman are those of protection for herself and little ones, and of love and loyalty to her husband and her son. On the other hand, the two strongest instincts that today defend the liquor traffic and drink habit are avarice in the dealer and appetite in the drinker. . . . [M]ay it not be found that in the home, through the reserve power never yet called into government on a large scale, woman's instincts of self-protection and of love are a sufficient offset to appetite and avarice, and will outvote both at the polls?"[19]

Reaffirming woman's place in the home, women's leaders argued that it was precisely *because* of woman's traditional duties that she needed the vote.

If woman would fulfill her traditional responsibility to her own children; if she would educate and protect from danger factory children who must find their recreation on the street; if she would bring the cultural forces to bear upon her materialistic civilization; and if she would do it all with the dignity and directness fitting one who carries on her immemorial duties, then she must bring herself to use the ballot. . . . American women need this implement in order to preserve the home.[20]

The new suffragists capitalized on the prevalent fear in the United States that the newly freed slaves, carpetbaggers, and waves of immigrants all served to corrupt politics. Increasingly, public sentiment turned against "certain segments" of society, especially in the area of politics. "Political capacity" or "educated suffrage" became euphemisms for the notion that only those who had the "ability" to participate should have the right to do so.[21]

NAWSA did not hesitate to play upon these emotions. In 1893, for example, they passed the following resolution: "Resolved, that without expressing any opinion on the proper qualifications for voting, we call attention to the significant facts that in every State there are more white women who can read and write than all Negro voters; more American women who can read and write than all foreign voters; so that the enfranchisement of such women would settle the vexed question of rule by illiteracy, whether of homegrown or foreign-born production."[22] Such politically expedient views continued to be the official policy of NAWSA. As late as 1919, in denying the membership application of a black women's organization, the New England Federation of Women's Clubs, NAWSA justified its refusal by noting its leaders' beliefs that if NAWSA allowed in black women, southern democrats' votes in Congress would be jeopardized.[23]

Such views were simply reflections of middle-class values in the early 1900s. By endorsing these positions and by diluting their original proposals concerning women's employment, the vote, and social policies, the suffrage movement attracted a new and larger constituency, a constituency that was necessary in order to put sufficient pressure on state and national legislators. Focusing on the moral superiority of women and on domestic ideals, suffragists were able to prove their respectability and gain widespread support. In 1917, the *Woman Citizen* (the successor to the NAWSA *Woman's Journal*) boasted that the suffrage movement was "bourgeois, middle class, a great middle-of-the-road movement."[24]

Spearheaded by Alice Paul, NAWSA revived a committee to build support for a constitutional amendment. Nevertheless, most NAWSA members at their 1913 convention rejected the idea of working for a federal amendment. Paul was removed from the chair of the congressional committee, but went on to establish the Congressional Union under NAWSA's auspices, an organization devoted to lobbying for a suffrage bill and campaigning against candidates of the Democratic party for Congress who opposed suffrage.

In 1915, the Congressional Union left NAWSA to join forces with western women voters who formed the National Woman's Party in 1916. Fearing a revival of unpopular extremist tactics (Alice Paul and her supporters had picketed the White House, gone on hunger strikes, and used inflammatory language), NAWSA's leaders were embarrassed by the new party, believing it would alienate their allies, the Democrats, as well as most women. The prevailing sentiment was that the suffrage movement should rise above partisan politics.

NAWSA soon reversed its earlier position against federal lobbying, and its members pressed its leaders to work for a constitutional amendment. Carrie Chapman Catt created a "Winning Plan" to direct all NAWSA's resources and cooperating organizations toward the goal of achieving a woman suffrage amendment by 1922. A key component was national coordination whereby all state association activity would be directed toward one aim.

Associations in suffrage states pressured legislators to request that Congress pass a constitutional amendment. National officers hand picked states for new campaigns where passage of a state amendment was feasible. Efforts were directed toward gaining voting rights for women in party primaries. Carrie Chapman Catt also targeted southern and northern states for intense activity to break the spirit of opponents. And while World War I diverted much attention away from this struggle, Catt insisted that suffrage work continue to come first, and NAWSA continue to follow her plan. Highly sophisticated, detailed strategies were drawn up and implemented by NAWSA, including specific instructions on political, legislative, propaganda, "education for life," and reform activities.[25] Handbooks were distributed by "franchise departments" instructing members how to "convert" editors to the suffrage cause and how to write "short, bright, readable paragraphs and articles" for the newspaper once the editor had been persuaded.[26]

Opposition in the Senate continued, however, until NAWSA leaders launched a campaign to defeat their Senate opponents who stood for reelection in 1918. They succeeded in defeating two such powerful opponents, Senators Weeks of Massachusetts and Saulsbury of Delaware. This show of force, along with the addition of several states to adopt suffrage (South Dakota, Michigan, Oklahoma, Iowa, Minnesota, Missouri, Ohio, Wisconsin, and Maine) guaranteed passage of the Nineteenth Amendment in the next legislative session called by President Wilson. Meeting in a special session in the spring of 1919, the House of Representatives and then the Senate passed the Suffrage Amendment. Ratification by the necessary thirty-six states was completed in 1920, and the first national election in which women could vote occurred in November of that year.

In retrospect, we have come to recognize that the event marked both the culmination of the women's movement of that time and its death knell. The adoption of the Suffrage Amendment was perceived as an enormous victory because the women's movement assumed that formal and de facto rights were one and the same, that the right to vote would empower women and bring political, economic, and social equality in its wake.

Once they won the vote, the composition of NAWSA quickly disintegrated. Though its leaders immediately turned toward passage of an amendment to ban all discrimination based on sex, a majority of suffragists wanted no further changes made in women's status. As a result, NAWSA broke into several factions; some members established the National League of Women Voters in 1919 to educate female voters; others became involved in the growing peace movement. But the efforts of suffragists to secure additional political rights, including jury service, faltered in the mid-1920s.

For a short period, women were able to take advantage of a specific set of factors that promoted a successful social movement. Once NAWSA leaders dropped the more radical demands that had been sought by earlier women's movement leaders, they helped to make suffrage virtually a conservative cause. Their advocacy was based on the vote for women as nonthreatening, indeed as strengthening women's place in society and helping to eradicate "evils" imported by immigrants and minorities. They gained the sympathy and support of politicians in the major parties and passage of the desired legislation, but narrowed their focus to such an extent that further significant gains were stymied for years to come.

In the next section we examine the practical effect of the activism and political accomplishments generated by the women's movement in the nineteenth and twentieth centuries. Using data gathered from various sources, we look at how women have used the right and power of suffrage, both as political candidates and as voters.

WOMEN IN POLITICS, 1945–60

By 1945, the women's movement, such as it was, had divided into three different, though overlapping, groups. The first group, including the National Women's Trade Union League and the National Consumer's League, which had roots going back to the 1890s, pushed for protective legislation for women. Primarily middle-class women had formed organizations to improve conditions for industrial workers (see Chapter 3). During World War I, these organizations persuaded the federal government to create the Women's Bureau within the Department of Labor as a vehicle to protect women who entered defense work. During World War II, a loose coalition of women's groups centering around the Women's Bureau aimed at ensuring safe and adequate workplace conditions for women.[27] After the war, however, they generally concurred with the social consensus of the time that married women should be supported by their husbands.

The second group of feminists, which was smaller and more elite, was led by Alice Paul and centered around the National Woman's Party (NWP). After suffrage was attained, Paul decided to work for a constitutional amendment that would guarantee women complete legal equality with men. While the groups allied with the Women's Bureau feared that such an amendment would destroy the legal foundation for protective legislation, the NWP eventually argued that such legislation was ultimately detrimental to women's causes. Composed mainly of highly educated and wealthy women, the NWP maintained that labor laws should apply to both sexes (see section in Chapter 3 entitled "1900–1940: The Fight for Protective Legislation"). In 1928, the party endorsed the Republican Hoover-Curtis presidential ticket, primarily because Charles Curtis had been a sponsor of the ERA and because many NWP officers were Republicans.

By the 1940s, the National Federation of Business and Professional Women's Clubs, the General Federation of Women's Clubs, the National Association of Women Lawyers, the National Education Association, and various other smaller professional women's organizations had agreed to work on behalf of the ERA. After World War II, the ERA fight continued to be the goal of the single-minded National Woman's Party, despite the fact that its membership had dropped dramatically, from reportedly 10,000 in the 1920s to 4,000 by 1945.[28]

They were also facing strong opposition from the coalition of groups around the Women's Bureau, who continued to fear an erosion of protective legislation from an ERA.

Finally, there existed a group of women who had taken full advantage of suffrage, participating in party politics, the Democratic National Committee, and the Republican National Committee. Their aim was to ensure that women would be appointed to government positions. Some states initially attempted to prevent women from running as political candidates. In Arkansas, female candidates were forced to withdraw from their respective races, and the New Hampshire attorney general issued an opinion stating that women were not made eligible to run for office by the Nineteenth Amendment. That opinion was ignored by women candidates in that state and two were eventually victorious in electoral races.[29] But in most states, the passage of the Nineteenth Amendment was convincing proof that women were allowed to run for office. In the first elections after suffrage was passed, women campaigned for and won public office in twenty-three states.[30]

The battle over the Equal Rights Amendment dominated women's political activities after World War II. Just before the war, in 1937, the National Federation of Business and Professional Women's Clubs, with a membership of 65,000, established the ERA as a legislative priority. The following year, the ERA for the first time reached the floor of the Senate, but was recommitted.

In 1943, the ERA was the first resolution introduced in the House, cosponsored by forty-two members, and it was subsequently approved by the Senate Judiciary Committee. The original amendment read: "Men and women shall have equal rights throughout the United States and in every place subject to its jurisdiction." In order to make the clause correspond more closely to the language of the Nineteenth Amendment, the Judiciary Committee adopted wording provided by Alice Paul: "Equality of rights under the law shall not be denied or abridged by the United States, or by any state, on account of sex."

While the proposed ERA legislation was defeated, the amendment did provide the motivating force for political activity by both women's leaders and women office holders. The NWP created an umbrella organization, the Women's Joint Legislative ERA, with a combined membership of between five and six million. The NWP then conducted an intensive lobbying campaign in Congress and within the political parties.

The Women's Bureau, however, continued its resistance to the amendment. The crux of the debate among women's groups over the ERA was the question of a woman's major responsibility in society. While ERA advocates succeeded in gaining the inclusion of ERA planks at both the 1944 Republican and Democratic National Convention platforms, after the war women were generally expected to step aside from the jobs they had held during the war. As had happened after World War I, emphasis was placed on a return to traditional roles. Not surprisingly, then, liberals—who believed that government had a responsibility to protect women and the family through regulation—were more likely to oppose the ERA. Conservatives, on the other hand, had fewer problems with the ERA in light of their endorsement of free enterprise and individual opportunity.

In 1946, the ERA suffered a decisive blow. The amendment won a majority vote in the Senate, but not the two-thirds majority needed for victory. The *New York Times* commented that "motherhood cannot be amended, and we are glad the Senate didn't try."[31] The battle over the ERA continued over the next decade, but it would take nearly three decades for a revival of public discussion of and significant approval for the ERA.

JURY SERVICE

Jury service was considered to be closely linked to office holding by the suffragist movement. Although state laws concerning both rights frequently referred only to men as eligible to run for office or sit on juries, there was far greater hostility to female jurors than to women officeholders or public officials.[32] Those judges and legislators who viewed jury service as a burden, a forced confrontation with the seamier side of life, felt that women should not be required to leave their children unattended and to risk insult, shock, and embarrassment in the courtroom.

Anthony and Stanton sought a change in the laws prohibiting women from sitting on juries. After the passage of the Fourteenth Amendment, they argued that to allow black men but not women the right to sit on juries violated the protections given citizens by the Constitution. In 1880, the Supreme Court ruled that a black defendant's constitutional rights were violated when blacks were excluded from jury service but confirmed the right of states to confine the selection of jurors to males.[33]

Jury service was never, however, a primary concern of the women's movement, overshadowed as it was by the demand for the vote. Moreover, with the demise of the women's movement after 1920 and the apparent limited power of women as voters, demands for the right to sit on a jury often went unheard by legislators.

In 1957, however, Congress enacted legislation that made all women, regardless of state laws, eligible to sit on federal juries. There were immediate challenges,[34] but many states enacted laws allowing women to serve on state juries on either an "exemption allowed" basis or if women registered willingness to serve. States were allowed to exempt or prohibit women from jury service until 1975. The women's movement continued to concentrate on other rights, until the National Federation of Business and Professional Women submitted an amicus curiae brief in a 1971 case challenging gender-based discrimination in jury service.[35]

But it was not until 1975, in *Taylor v. Louisiana*,[36] that the Supreme Court held that the Sixth Amendment required that a jury be selected from a jury pool representing a cross section of the community. The court declared that when women were systematically excluded from jury panels, as they were in Louisiana, which allowed women to register voluntarily for service, the representative cross section requirement was not fulfilled. Thus, by prohibiting automatic exemptions based on sex, the Court invalidated the laws of almost twenty states. The Court did, however, add that certain types of exemptions, such as for women who cannot make child care arrangements, would be upheld if they did not operate to "unreasonably" exclude large numbers of women.

ELECTION OF WOMEN TO PUBLIC OFFICE, 1960–90

While jury service as a political right was given low priority by the women's movement, access to elective office received considerable attention beginning in the 1960s. As early as June 1963, the President's Commission on the Status of Women asserted that service in a public office should be determined by ability, experience, and effort rather than by a candidate's gender.[37] The commission also recommended in its report, *American Women*, that greater numbers of women be appointed to political positions and that an executive order be issued to ensure that the commission's recommendations be followed through by federal agencies.[38]

Once women felt that they had a voice in the federal government in the form of the commission, the ERA reared its head yet again, reappearing as a fundamental disagreement between women's leaders. The commission ultimately decided that it was not necessary to seek an ERA, but rather that the courts should decide remaining ambiguities concerning the constitutional protection of women's rights.

During the remainder of the 1960s, most of the political activity carried out by women occurred at the state and local levels. The Kennedy Commission had sparked the formation of numerous state commissions on the status of women. But the ERA was not forgotten. The National Organization for Women (NOW) was organized in 1966 to provide a mechanism with which women could pressure the government. Spearheading a national movement to gain passage of the ERA, NOW spent most of the next decade orchestrating an intensive lobbying campaign in favor of ERA. The organization also helped to bridge that long-standing chasm separating the National Women's party and the Women's Bureau. Formulating a new feminist theory, which distinguished childbearing from child rearing, NOW adopted the position that both mothers and fathers were responsible for the care of children.

This distinction was widely adopted by feminist scholars and leaders.[39] They argued that differences between men's and women's roles were culturally based rather than biologically determined, freeing up women to seek special "privileges" not as mothers, but as parents, applicable to both female and male caregivers. In the meantime, NOW singlemindedly assumed the ERA banner, and was the one organization most often associated with the campaign to see an equal rights amendment written into the Constitution.[40]

Despite the logical coherence of the feminist argument resolving the two sides of the ERA debate; despite a widespread, extensive, highly-orchestrated campaign; and despite the energetic sponsorship of Representative Martha Griffiths in the House to achieve passage of the ERA, the amendment's proponents failed to persuade the required number of state legislatures to endorse it. When the extended ratification deadline of June 30, 1982, arrived, only thirty-five of the required thirty-eight state legislatures had ratified the ERA.

ERA was defeated in spite of overwhelming public support—in spite of a campaign that used all the usual political pressure points. . . . We did not win because those in legislative and power positions did not want us to win. Proponents did everything they were told: wear skirts not jeans; involve religious groups; apply pressure from national figures or don't use national figures; rally or don't rally; poll the districts; work in and contribute to campaigns. When all the excuses ran out, legislative sleight-of-hand took over.[41]

The defeat of the ERA is often attributed to legislatures, especially in the South—where no state legislature ratified the amendment. Southern hostility to feminist demands was reflected elsewhere in the country, where ERA opponents took up once again the historical "protectionist" banner, demanding that women, in their positions as wives and mothers, are entitled to protective laws.

The women's movement's reluctance to make any concessions to the more conservative viewpoint stands in marked contrast to the more successful suffrage campaign. While the latter initially presented arguments based on equality, it eventually conceded the importance of appealing to the majority of women who welcomed an emphasis on woman's role as wife and mother. By stressing the relevance of the vote to homemakers, suffragists were able to capture the enthusiastic endorsement of the more moderate members of society.

The campaigns in support of the ERA and suffrage do, however, have something in common: both were followed by a period of relative apathy in the women's movement. While there was a brief effort to revive feminist interest in the ERA in the mid-1980s,[42] women activists began to take interest in issues like child care, parental leave, affirmative action, pay equity, job discrimination, and women in politics.

But there had long been a small, elite corps of women who had turned their attention to more direct and traditional political change. In June 1971, while the ERA was dominating the women's political landscape, Representative Bella Abzug, Gloria Steinem, and Betty Friedan, in cooperation with Representatives Shirley Chisholm and Patsy Mink, held a meeting to propose the formation of a national women's political caucus.

The National Women's Political Caucus (NWPC) was established as an organization where women from the two major political parties, along with independent feminists, would work to persuade both parties to give women and women's issues more attention and significance in the political arena. The caucus's first move was to hold training sessions across the country for women delegates to the 1972 Democratic convention, urging them to take strong positions on women's issues. During the convention itself, NWPC worked with NOW to lobby for planks favoring the ERA and federal funding of child care centers. The NWPC also unsuccessfully introduced a minority plank demanding the right to abortion. And they nominated Frances "Sissy" Farenthold (who was to become president of Wells College in New York) to run as George McGovern's vice-presidential running mate. While Farenthold lost to Thomas Eagleton, party leaders were confronted with an impressive show of force by the women's movement.

Republican women were not as well organized as those in evidence at the 1972 Democratic convention. However, at the urging of Representative Margaret Heckler (Massachusetts), the party platform continued its support of the ERA and added a call for child care provisions.

By 1976, the NWPC had acquired greater sophistication and influence. They questioned presidential candidates on their positions regarding issues important to women, monitored candidates' campaign staffs to determine the number of women in decision-making positions, and led a move for a written guarantee at the presidential nominating convention that women would constitute 50 percent of the delegates at the 1980 convention. While this final proposal failed, Jimmy Carter did meet with women's leaders and agreed to appoint women to high-ranking positions in his administration if he were elected.

NWPC also created, with several other women's organizations, a Coalition for Women's Appointments, which existed during the Nixon and Ford administrations and became particularly influential after Jimmy Carter's election. These groups drew up lists of potential woman appointees, collecting résumés and submitting them to the presidential transition office. Short lists of potential appointees were presented to Cabinet members by women familiar with the work of a particular department, along with a recommended list of actions concerning women's rights and welfare. More women were appointed under the Carter administration than during any previous administration.

Women's groups were also successful in persuading Carter to appoint women to federal judgeships. The Federation of Women Lawyers Screening Panel, NOW, and NWPC drew up lists of qualified women and explained to them how to apply for judicial positions.

In the 1980 presidential elections, much media attention was focused on a supposed "gender gap"—that candidate Ronald Reagan could not attract the same type and numbers of support from women that he could attain from men. As it turned out, the polls demonstrated that this was not true; but the publicity given to this supposed phenomenon engendered both dramatically greater levels of activity by women during the 1984 presidential campaign[43] and increased attention by male politicians on women's issues.[44] The culmination for many women's groups during the 1984 campaign was the nomination of Representative Geraldine Ferraro as the Democratic vice-presidential nominee.

While Ferraro's presence on the Democratic ticket failed to attract the anticipated numbers of women's votes, a record number of women were elected between 1980 and 1984 to Congress and to state and local legislative positions. In part, at least, this newfound electoral success was due to the women's movement's attention to developing education programs for potential women candidates on how to run for public office. NWPC had held training seminars for women candidates and provided financial and volunteer support for them.

In addition to NWPC, the National Women's Education Fund (NWEF) was created in 1973 to use tax-deductible funds and to train women for campaign work and for holding elective or appointive office. The Women's Campaign Fund was established in 1974 to raise money for federal candidates. More recently, EMILY's List was created in 1986 to raise funds and offer training for Democratic women candidates who have a good chance of winning their respective elections.[45]

Thus, the women's movement developed from amateurish participation on the fringes of American political life to sophisticated, highly organized activity at every political level. Nevertheless, for all the strides made by the women's movement in politics, both women politicians and activists complain that it remains far more difficult for a woman to successfully campaign for political office, and once they have entered a political race, women are judged by different and far more stringent standards than are male politicians.[46] In the next section, we look at the reasoning behind such claims and at data to determine their validity.

WOMEN IN PUBLIC OFFICE

Currently, less than 6 percent of the members of the U.S. House of Representatives are women. There has never been a woman president, nor has one ever been nominated by a major political party. At no time have there been more than 3 women senators in any one Senate session; and there have never been more than 23 women in any one session of the House. Of the 114 women who have served in Congress, 33 succeeded a husband or father. Of the 16 women who have served in the Senate, only 4 were elected without filling an unexpired Senate term. Only about 5 percent of elected officials are women. One woman, Geraldine Ferraro, has been nominated for the office of vice-president by the Democratic Party in 1984. In short, while women have served in a variety of appointed positions during the last fifty years, they do not appear to have come a long way in the electoral arena. This impression is further strengthened by a closer look at the facts.

Before women obtained suffrage, only one woman held an appointive position in government—Julia Lathrop, head of the Children's Bureau appointed by President William Howard Taft in 1912. In 1933, President Franklin D. Roosevelt named Frances Perkins as secretary of labor, the first woman to hold a cabinet post. Twenty years later, a second woman was appointed to a cabinet post—Oveta Culp Hobby, designated by President Dwight Eisenhower to head the new Department of Health, Education, and Welfare. And twenty years after that, a third woman, Carla Hills, became secretary of housing and urban development, appointed by President Gerald Ford. Under the Reagan and Bush administrations, Elizabeth Dole served first as secretary of transportation and then as secretary of labor. Ronald Reagan appointed Sandra Day O'Connor to the United States Supreme Court.

Hattie Caraway was the first woman elected to the U.S. Senate after having been appointed to the Arkansas seat in 1931 at the death of her husband. In 1932, with the help of Huey Long, she was elected to the Senate. From 1932 until 1970, there was a total of ten women elected to the Senate; and from 1970 to 1988, eight women served in the Senate.

The dearth of women senators cannot be attributed simply to an absence of women who are willing to run for office. From 1978 to 1988, twenty-three women ran for the Senate in the major parties and three—Paula Hawkins, Nancy Kassebaum, and Barbara Mikulski—were elected.

The story is not much different in the House of Representatives. The first woman elected to the House was Jeannette Rankin, a Republican from Montana who was elected in 1916 from a suffrage state on her own political strength. Between 1920 and 1970, 66 women served in the House; 166 women were elected between 1970 and 1988. In the Hundredth Congress, 23 women served in the House.

As one descends the political hierarchy, the numbers of women serving in office increase marginally. Nellie Taylor Ross was the first woman governor, elected in 1924 to fill the seat of her husband who had died in office. From 1924 to 1980, only five women were elected in gubernatorial races. Ella Grasso was the first woman elected without succeeding her husband. She became governor of Connecticut in January 1975. In 1989, there were three woman governors, Madeleine M. Kunin of Vermont, Kay Orr of Nebraska, and Rose Mofford of Arizona, who succeeded to her position after Governor Edward Meachem had been impeached. There were five women serving as lieutenant governors.

There has been a significant increase during the last decade in the number of women serving in state legislatures. In 1988, women held 15.8 percent of state legislative seats, 228 in the state senates, and 949 in state houses. From 1969 to 1987, the number of women who served in the state legislatures grew from 305 to 1,166, an increase from 3.5 to 15.5 percent.

As of 1985, women made up 14.5 percent of mayors and members of municipal township governing boards; as of 1987, they made up only 8.6 percent of county governing boards. The Center for the American Woman and Politics at Rutgers University has estimated that although there has been a 300 percent increase in the number of women office holders since 1974, at no level of office do women hold more than 15.8 percent of available positions.[47]

Why have there been so few women in public office in the decades following suffrage? Women's leaders claim this is due to three major factors:

1. the perception that women are not tough enough to win political races, or, if they do win, are not strong enough to do the job;

2. the force of precedent (people have been socialized into viewing men, not women, as politicians); and

3. the lack of institutional support for women among the media, among other elected officials, and among powerful political groups. [48]

In the next section, we examine the validity of these claims using data compiled from various sources.

SUPPORT FOR WOMEN CANDIDATES

In 1987, when the Gallup Organization took a poll to ask, "If your party nominated a woman for president, would you vote for her if she were qualified for the job?" 82 percent of the respondents answered yes. Looking back over a fifty-year span, we see that the shift in opinions on this issue by both men and women has been dramatic (see Table 2.1).

Note also that the gap between men's and women's attitudes has closed. In 1937, a third more of the women than the men polled were likely to favor a woman. By the 1970s, there was no difference between male and female opinions. In the 1960s, more men than women said they would vote for a woman.

The support for women seeking other public offices has also increased dramatically and shows practically no difference between male and female preferences (see Tables 2.2 and 2.3).

The problem, say women leaders, is that a question such as that one is contingent on voters who are inclined to view certain women as qualified for the job to begin with, and, they add, such voters are hard to find.

Skepticism continues to haunt women's efforts. Women have to earn voters' trust and confidence. Many candidates and managers are frustrated by the constant pressure to prove themselves over and over again, as if they could never quite resolve the persistent doubts of voters and elites, both male and female. Again, these women [candidates] felt they had to be twice as good as male candidates and prove it at least twice as often. [49]

Indeed, women candidates have even come under criticism by women's groups for reinforcing this stereotype. Organizations such as EMILY's List point out that women candidates often emphasize their commitment to family issues and their concern for people, but unless they include less traditional concerns, such as defense, the economy, and foreign relations, they may be contributing to voters' perception of their weakness.

Table 2.1
Percentages of Women and Men Who Would Vote for a Woman President

Year	National	Women	Men
1937	34	40	27
1945	33	37	29
1949	48	51	45
1955	52	57	47
1958	52	55	51
1963	55	51	58
1967	57	53	61
1969	54	49	58
1971	66	67	65
1975	73	71	75
1976	76	74	78
1978	80	81	80
1983	80	80	80
1984	78	78	78
1987	82	83	81

Source: The Gallup Organization, Princeton, N.J., 1937–87.

Table 2.2
Percentages of Women and Men Who Approve of or Would Vote for a Woman Governor

Year	National	Women	Men
1945	56	60	52
1976	81	80	81
1984	87	86	89

Source: The Gallup Organization, Princeton, N.J., 1945–84.

There is one clear obstacle facing women candidates: incumbency. Ninety-eight percent of House incumbents who seek reelection win.[50] In the 1988 national election, 408 incumbents ran for reelection and 402 were reelected. Of the 6 who lost, 4 were either under indictment or potential indictment.[51] At the present rate of turnover, it would take 410 years to achieve 50 percent representation of women.[52]

Consequently, under the present system, women candidates generally have

Table 2.3
Percentages of Women and Men Who Approve of, Favor, or Would Vote for a Woman for Congress

Year	National	Women	Men
1970	84	84	83
1976	88	89	88
1984	91	91	92

Source: The Gallup Organization, Princeton, N.J., 1970–84.

the greatest chance of election in open seats, of which there were only 27 (out of 435) in the 1988 election. An additional factor is the 1990 Census, which will determine the 1992 redrawing of congressional district lines and create new seats. Women's groups, such as EMILY's List, the Women's Campaign Fund, and the National Women's Political Caucus, are hoping that a large number of representatives will decide to retire as a result of redistricting and are working to prepare potential women candidates to run for those seats.

The highly sophisticated, professional methods used by women's groups to train political candidates marks a distinct change from their methods of the 1960s and 1970s. Until fairly recently, most women entered politics through volunteer work and activism on local issues in organizations such as school boards, utility boards, and church groups. Since the early 1980s, and increasingly so, women's groups have introduced campaign strategy building for their chosen candidates. Of fundamental importance is learning the art of fund raising. The Women's Campaign Fund has been instructing women on how to raise funds for political campaigns for offices from school board to president of the United States.[53] EMILY's List, the organization that raises money from women and uses it to pinpoint Democratic women candidates who have a good chance of winning national office, raised $150,000 for Senator Barbara Mikulski in 1986 and $200,000 for Harriet Woods, who lost her 1986 bid for a Missouri Senate seat.[54] Finally, women's leaders have argued that women politicians have not received the same support that male politicians get from their respective political parties, from the media, and from important organizations.

COMPARING WOMEN'S AND MEN'S VOTING BEHAVIOR

We first look at the question of whether women vote as frequently as do men. For all of the effort to win suffrage, only 26 percent of the eligible women actually voted in the first presidential election in which they were eligible to cast their ballots.[55] In 1940, 49 percent of the eligible women voted, in contrast to 68 percent of the eligible male voters. The gap decreased with 59 percent of the eligible women voting in 1948, as opposed to 69 percent of the men.

By 1952, the voting participation of women approached that of men. From

Table 2.4
Voter Turnout in Presidential Elections (in percentages)

Year	National	Women	Men
1952	62	60	64
1956	59	57	61
1960	63	61	66
1964	69	67	72
1968	68	66	70
1972	63	62	64
1976	59	59	60
1980	59	59	59
1984	60	61	59

Sources: The Gallup Report, March 1976, no. 128: 14 (for 1952–60); U.S. Bureau of the Census (for 1964–84).

Table 2.5
Voter Turnout in Non-Presidential Elections (in percentages)

Year	Women	Men
1966	53.0	58.2
1970	52.7	56.8
1974	43.4	46.2
1978	45.3	46.6
1982	48.4	48.7
1986	46.1	45.8

Source: U.S. Bureau of the Census, *Statistical Abstract of the United States, 1989* (Washington, D.C.: U.S. Government Printing Office), p. 257.

that time forward, the percentage of women voters has matched or, as in the 1984 presidential elections, slightly surpassed that of men. (See Table 2.4.)

The same trend may be seen in nonpresidential elections (see Table 2.5). Between 1966 and 1978, a smaller percentage of eligible women turned out to vote than did men. By 1982, men and women were evenly represented at the polls, and in 1986, a slightly higher percentage of eligible women than of men voted.

Has there been a difference in the candidates women have supported as opposed to men? How important is gender in presidential elections? Going back thirty-five years, we compare male and female voting patterns from 1952 to 1984. Table 2.6 shows the percentage who voted for the elected candidate.

Table 2.6
Percentages of Women and Men Voting for Elected Candidate

Year	National	Women	Men
1952 Eisenhower	55	58	53
1956 Eisenhower	58	61	55
1960 Kennedy	50	49	52
1964 Johnson	61	62	60
1968 Nixon	43	43	43
1972 Nixon	62	62	63
1976 Carter	50	48	53
1980 Reagan	51	49	53
1984 Reagan	59	55	64
1988 Bush	54	52	56

Source: The Gallup Organization, Princeton, N.J., 1952–88.

The most significant observation about the percentages is the overall similarity between men's and women's preferences. The greatest difference between male and female preferences occurred in 1984, at 9 percent. Nor is there any consistent pattern of preferences. When Eisenhower was the Republican candidate, slightly more women than men voted Republican. Women were also somewhat more likely to vote Republican when Nixon lost to John F. Kennedy and when Gerald Ford lost to Jimmy Carter. But women did not support the Republican candidate to the same extent that men did during the Reagan presidential campaigns.

Gender represents far less variance in voting behavior than do other demographic characteristics such as race, education, religion, and occupation. In 1952 (Eisenhower versus Stevenson), for example, when there was only a 5 percent difference between men and women, there was a 36 percent difference between blacks and whites, an 18 percent difference between grade-school and college-educated voters, and a 19 percent difference between Protestants and Catholics.[56] In 1964 (Johnson versus Goldwater), there was a 2 percent difference by sex, but a 35 percent difference by race, a 17 percent difference by occupation, a 14 percent difference by education, and a 21 percent difference by religion.[57] In 1976 (Carter versus Ford), there was a 5 percent difference by sex, but a 39 percent difference by race, a 16 percent difference by education, a 16 percent difference by occupation, and an 11 percent difference by religion. In 1980 (Reagan versus Carter), when there was a 4 percent difference between men and women, there was a 46 percent difference by race, an 11

Table 2.7
Candidates for Whom Women's Votes Meant Victory, 1986

State	Office	Winner	Party	Margin of Victory	Difference in Women's Support
AL	Senate	Shelby	D	2%	+4%
CA	Senate	Cranston	D	2%	+6%
CO	Senate	Wirth	D	2%	+5%
GA	Senate	Fowler	D	2%	+5%
LA	Senate	Breaux	D	6%	+7%
NV	Senate	Reid	D	5%	+9%
NC	Senate	Sanford	D	4%	+5%
ND	Senate	Conrad	D	1%	+9%
WA	Senate	Adam	D	2%	+5%
PA	Governor	Casey	D	3%	+6%
SD	Governor	Michelson	D	4%	+6%
VT	Governor	Kunen	D	9%	+9%

Source: The Gallup Organization, Princeton, N.J., 1986.

percent difference by education, a 9 percent difference by occupation, and a 7 percent difference by religion.[58]

But in the nonpresidential elections in the 1980s, the women's vote was credited with having made the difference between victory and defeat in four senate races in 1984, in nine senate races in 1986, and in three gubernatorial races in 1982, one in 1984, and one in 1986. The candidates for whom the women's vote tipped the balance in 1986 are shown in Table 2.7.

In every case, the women's vote tipped the balance in favor of a Democratic candidate, be it in a gubernatorial or senate race. These data are consistent with the 1980 and 1984 presidential election results, in which women were less likely than men to support the Republican candidate.

MALE AND FEMALE RESPONSES TO MAJOR DOMESTIC AND FOREIGN POLICY ISSUES

Although women's choices for political office do not differ significantly from those of men, women leaders have consistently claimed, from the early suffrage days to the present, that gender influences attitudes toward specific public issues. One way of testing whether women's voting preferences indicate agreement with men's choices is to examine male and female opinions on important national issues during the same period for which we compared the presidential voting preferences.

The issues cover a broad range of domestic matters, including welfare, education, crime, drugs, the environment, health, and some foreign policy matters such as whether the United States ought to be active in world affairs, military involvement, and foreign aid appropriations.

In the period from 1948 to 1952, the major issues of public opinion included revision of the Taft-Hartley Labor Act, understanding how government works, sex education in high schools, U.S. military involvement in Korea, a draft law, interest in political affairs, a welfare state, government spending, a permanent military alliance between the United States and Western Europe, and the first use of atomic bombs. Men and women agreed on all of the above issues, except for the U.S. military involvement in Korea, where 45 percent of the men, as opposed to 33 percent of the women, advocated that the country "do what is necessary even at the risk of starting World War III."

Women also differed on items that asked about their understanding of and interest in government and political affairs. A higher percentage of women consistently indicated that they could not understand what was going on (78 percent of women versus 63 percent of men); that they were not particularly interested in political affairs (69 percent of women versus 55 percent of men), and on the substantive issues, a higher percentage of the women as opposed to the men consistently indicated that they had no opinion about the problem.

A similar pattern prevailed in the early 1960s, when the predominant issues were welfare and relief programs, involvement in Vietnam, government-funded job programs, social security, the death penalty, the stance to be taken regarding the Soviets, money spent on national defense, the costs of sending a person to the moon, attitudes toward having a minority family live next door, preference for living under communism or fighting an all-out nuclear war, and fear about the United States getting involved in another war. Again, most of the substantive issues on which men and women differed involved foreign policy and specifically U.S. involvement in actions that might lead to war. Fifty-five percent of the men as opposed to 42 percent of the women favored greater U.S. involvement in Vietnam. Sixty percent of the men as opposed to 46 percent of the women favored adopting a tougher stance toward the Soviet Union. Men expressed greater willingness to fight an all-out nuclear war rather than live under communism (87 percent versus 75 percent). Forty-two percent of the men were not worried about the United States getting into another war, as opposed to 24 percent of the women. On the death penalty, 64 percent of the men favored it as opposed to 55 percent of women. On the other substantive issues (money spent on a welfare state, the responsibility of the government to find jobs, attitudes toward increasing the social security tax, costs of sending a person to the moon, having a "colored" family move in next door), there were no differences between men and women.

Again, women were more likely to agree that "politics seem so complicated, we cannot understand what is going on" (63 percent as opposed to 52 percent), and women were more likely to have "no opinion" or to say they were "undecided" on every issue than men were.

In the early 1960s, the responses indicated that women were demonstrating a greater concern about U.S. involvement in actions that might lead to war and were less likely to favor the death penalty. Are these attitudes the first manifestations of women's greater compassion, their greater fear and dislike of violence, and their stronger desire for peace, which would become more prominent in later years?

A decade later, in the early 1970s, the issues posed were busing of white and black children to form more integrated schools, allowing young men who fled the United States to avoid the draft to return, beliefs about the poor, permits for hand guns, death penalty for convicted murderers, lesser involvement in world affairs. There were no differences by gender on busing, on attitudes toward the poor, on U.S. involvement in world affairs. Women, however, were more likely to favor allowing men who left the United States to avoid the draft to return without punishment (42 percent versus 32 percent). They were more likely to favor passage of a law that would require a person to obtain a police permit before he or she could buy a gun (82 percent versus 62 percent), and they were less likely to favor the death penalty for convicted murderers (51 percent versus 64 percent).

Do we find more evidence of women's greater compassion and desire for peace in the early 1970s? The answer is a weak and equivocal "yes," as witnessed by their responses to the items cited above. But we note that women did not differ from men in their views about why some people are poor (the American way of life doesn't give all people an equal chance).

It is in the last decade beginning in 1976 that larger and more consistent differences between men's and women's attitudes on public issues emerge. While there were no differences by gender on how much money should be spent on improving the nation's education system, on whether black and white children should be bused from one district to another, and on whether more money should be spent to fight crime, women did differ from men on a range of domestic and foreign policy issues.

On specific items, women were more likely than men to favor greater protection for the environment (51 to 35 percent), oppose the death penalty (77 to 67 percent), favor police permits for use of hand guns (80 to 65 percent), and support programs that would reduce the income gap between rich and poor (73 to 61 percent). On foreign policy, women were more isolationist than men (43 to 31 percent), more favorable toward having the United States stay out of world affairs (39 to 28 percent), less likely to support increased spending for the military (67 to 80 percent), and less likely to favor a return to the draft (39 to 52 percent). In addition to these specific issues, women expressed less confidence in their government and more concern that their country was in "deep and serious trouble" (27 to 39 percent, and 48 to 37 percent).

The trends that emerge in the contemporary period are that women have more compassion for the poor, more concern about protecting the environment, greater antipathy toward violence, and greater desire for the United States to insulate itself from active involvement in world events, especially from those actions that might lead to military intervention. Women are also less optimistic that "all will be well" with their country and are less confident about the future than are men.

NOTES

1. Robert Goldwin, "Why Blacks, Women, and Jews Are Not Mentioned in the Constitution," *Commentary*, May 1987, p. 28.

2. Alice S. Rossi, *The Feminist Papers, from Adams to de Beauvoir* (New York: Bantam Books, 1973), p. 420.

3. "Effect of Vote of Women on Legislation: An Investigation in the Equal Suffrage States Made in December, 1913, by "The Evening Sun" of New York City" (New York: National Woman Suffrage Publishing Company, April 1914), pp. 2–8.

4. Ida Husted Harper, "History of the Movement for Woman Suffrage in the United States" (New York: Interurban Woman Suffrage Council, 1907), p. 2.

5. See, for example, Gerda Lerner, *The Majority Finds Its Past: Placing Women in History* (New York: Oxford University Press, 1979), pp. 112–28; and Blanch G. Hersh, *"The Slavery of Sex": Feminist-Abolitionists in Nineteenth-Century America* (Chicago: University of Illinois Press, 1978), pp. 15–136.

6. For information on these activities, see Jane H. Pease and William H. Pease, *Bound with Them in Chains: A Biographical History of the Antislavery Movement* (Westport, Conn.: Greenwood Press, 1972); Carol Thompson, "Women and the Anti-Slavery Movement," *Current History*, Vol. 23, May 1976, pp. 198–201; Catherine Clinton, *The Other Civil War: American Women in the Nineteenth Century* (New York: Hill & Wang, 1984); and Hersh, *"The Slavery of Sex."*

7. Lerner, *The Majority Finds Its Past*, p. 123.

8. Ibid., pp. 112–29.

9. Ibid., p. 125.

10. For accounts of this period, see James M. McPherson, *Battle Cry of Freedom* (New York: Oxford University Press, 1988); Clinton, *The Other Civil War;* Nancy F. Cott, *The Bonds of Womanhood: "Woman's Sphere" in New England, 1780–1835*, New Haven, Conn.: Yale University Press, 1977; Ellen Carol DuBois, *Feminism and Suffrage: The Emergence of an Independent Women's Movement in America, 1848–1869*, Ithaca, N.Y.: Cornell University Press, 1978.

11. Caroline F. Corbin, *Woman's Rights in America, A Retrospect of Sixty Years*, (Chicago: Illinois Association Opposed to Woman Suffrage, 1908), p. 5.

12. William C. Gannett, "Putting a Smile Into Politics: A Reply to Ex-Senator Root's Objections to Woman Suffrage," The Hanford Collection, 1914, p. 2.

13. Henry B. Blackwell, "Objections to Woman Suffrage Answered," *Woman Suffrage Leaflet*, Boston, March 1896, pp. 1–2.

14. "Legislative Advice," *Woman Suffrage Leaflet*, Boston, May 1895, pp. 1–2.

15. Mary Gray Peck, *The Rise of the Woman Suffrage Party* (Chicago: Myra Strawn Hartshorn, 1911), pp. 1–6.

16. Ibid.

17. H. B. Laidlaw, *Organizing to Win by the Political District Plan, A Handbook for Working Suffragists* (New York: National Woman Suffrage Publishing Co., 1914), p. 3.

18. Ibid., p. 6.

19. Frances E. Willard, "The Ballot for the Home," "Equal Suffrage Leaflet" *The Woman's Journal*, Boston, 1898, p. 1.

20. Jane Addams, "Why Women Should Vote," *Ladies Home Journal* (New York: National American Woman Suffrage Association, 1912), pp. 19–20.

21. One commentator of the time wrote: "It is the influx of foreign ignorance 'en masse' that threatens our country hourly.... There are millions of men in the world for whom despotism is a necessity, and it is this class who immigrate to us everyday. ... If woman Suffrage is to be allowed, we double not only the numerical force of this threatening majority, but its moral—or immoral—influence." Rose Terry Cooke, "Average Woman," *Remonstrance*, 1892, as quoted in Aileen S. Kraditor, *The Ideas of the Woman Suffrage Movement, 1880–1920* (New York: Norton, 1981), p. 20.

22. Ibid., p. 110.

23. Ibid., pp. 168–69.

24. Quoted in Nancy Woloch, *Women and the American Experience* (New York: Knopf, 1984), p. 343.

25. Laidlaw, "Organizing to Win," pp. 8–12.

26. Marie C. Brehm, *Suggestions for Franchise Superintendents* (Chicago: Woman's Christian Temperance Union, Franchise, 1900), p. 5.

27. Groups included the National Women's Trade Union League, the National Consumer's League, the Young Women's Christian Association, the National Council of Jewish Women, the National Council of Catholic Women, the National Council of Negro Women, the League of Women Voters, the American Association of University Women, and various affiliations of the American Federation of Labor and the Congress of Industrial Organizations.

28. Cynthia Harrison, *On Account of Sex, The Politics of Women's Issues, 1945–1968* (Berkeley: University of California Press, 1988), p. 10.

29. J. Stanley Lemons, *The Woman Citizen: Social Feminism in the 1920's* (Urbana, Ill.: University of Illinois Press, 1973), p. 68.

30. Ibid.

31. *New York Times*, July 20, 1946, p. 1.

32. Many state courts followed the reasoning of a New Jersey court ruling that the Nineteenth Amendment, while conferring the right of suffrage, did not make any reference to suffrage. See *State v. James* 114 Atl. 553 (1921). Women were often excluded from jury service by judicial interpretation. In 1921, Justice Oliver Wendell Holmes, then a Massachusetts justice, spoke for the state's highest court and disallowed women from jury service in the absence of specific legislation. (In re *Opinion of the Justices*, 130 N.E. 685 [1921].) Other popular objections were that jury service would unsex a woman or that the overnight sequestration of women jurors would be improper. See Lemons, *The Woman Citizen*, p. 55.

33. *Strauder v. West Virginia*, 100 U.S. 303 (1880).

34. *United States v. Wilson*, 233 F.2d 686, cert. denied, 358 U.S. 865 (1968).

35. *Alexander v. Louisiana*, 405 U.S. 625 (1971).

36. 419 U.S. 522 (1975).

37. As quoted in William H. Chafe, *The American Woman: Her Changing Social,*

Economic, and Political Role, 1920–1970 (New York: Oxford University Press, 1972), p. 52.

38. *American Women*, Report of the President's Commission on the Status of Women (Washington, D.C.: Government Printing Office, 1963).

39. Harrison, *On Account of Sex*.

40. See Marguerite Rawalt, "The Equal Rights Amendment," in Irene Tinker, ed., *Women in Washington: Advocates for Public Policy* (Beverly Hills, Calif.: Sage, 1983), pp. 49–79.

41. Excerpt from the final report of Suone Cotner, executive director of ERAmerica, as quoted in Rawalt, "The Equal Rights Amendment," in Tinker, *Women in Washington*, p. 72.

42. Eleanor Smeal, who successfully ran for the presidency of NOW in 1985, raised the possibility of a new campaign to promote the ERA.

43. Joyce Gelb and Marian L. Palley, *Women and Public Policies* (Princeton, N.J.: Princeton University Press, 1986), pp. 213–15.

44. "Women's Place in the House," *Washington Post*, March 6, 1990, p. C4.

45. EMILY's List (Early Money is Like Yeast, It Makes the Dough Rise) is unique in that its founder, Ellen Malcolm, travels around the country recruiting members who join for $100 and commit themselves to giving at least $100 each election cycle to two or three candidates endorsed by the list. The average member is a working woman who can afford to give $250 to $500 every two years. To be endorsed by EMILY's List, a candidate must support the Equal Rights Amendment and abortion rights, and must be a Democrat who stands a good chance of winning her race.

46. "Women's Place in the House," *Washington Post*, p. C4.

47. "Battle of the Gender Gap," *Ms.*, April 1988, p. 79.

48. See "Campaigning in a Different Voice," Report prepared for the Majority Project, EMILY's List, by Celinda Lake (Washington, D.C.: Greenberg-Lake: Analysis Group, 1988).

49. Ibid., p. 7.

50. Ellen Malcolm, personal interview, Sept. 16, 1989.

51. Ibid.

52. Madeleine M. Kunin, "Politics: Still a Man's World," *Washington Post*, Feb. 3, 1989, p. A25.

53. "Crown and Scepter," *Washington Post*, March 1, 1989, p. D1.

54. Amanda Spake, "Women Can Be Power Brokers, Too," *Washington Post Magazine*, June 5, 1988, p. 32.

55. *Gallup Report*, March 1976.

56. *Public Opinion*, April/May 1984, p. 53.

57. Ibid.

58. Ibid.

Chapter 3

WOMEN IN THE WORK PLACE

Women have always been active participants in the American labor force. *"Femes soles"*—single women—were active in trade and business in the mid–eighteenth century, and were found in every type of occupation, from mortician to blacksmith. But over the past two centuries, a radical transformation of the work force has taken place, with women making up almost half of the labor force. Women are expected to constitute 65 percent of the new entrants into the work force between now and the year 2000.[1] There have been increasing legislation and judicial decisions affecting working women, encompassing a range of issues: equal employment opportunity, sexual harassment, employment discrimination, child care, and equal pay, among others. We examine those areas in this chapter, and we look at data to determine whether women's participation in the work force, child care arrangements, employment discrimination, earnings, and public opinion have kept up with the dramatic changes experienced by working women.

EDUCATION AND THE PROFESSIONS

Long before women were to have any appreciable impact on the work place, they were making their mark in education. As far back as 1642, the Massachusetts Bay Colony passed a comprehensive educational law that specifically referred to "boys and girls." Such laws encouraged education in reading, religion, law, and labor.

Over the years, however, a more conservative attitude toward female education influenced the "common schools"—those schools that were designed to provide elementary education in reading, writing, and arithmetic. For example, Poor Laws enacted in the early and mid–1700s in Massachusetts designated reading, writing, and ciphering as subjects for male instruction; girls were to be taught only reading and writing. While girls were routinely excluded from college preparatory schools and many common schools, they were eligible to attend "dame schools," the quality of which is unknown and appears to have depended on the individual headmistress. These schools were open to boys and girls; their curriculums usually included reading and writing. Among the upper classes, girls were also sent to private boarding schools, where instruction was offered in numbers, foreign languages, arithmetic, navigation, accounting, bookkeeping, writing, drawing, surveying, geography, geometry, trigonometry, astronomy, algebra, ethics, logic, and natural philosophy.[2]

After the Revolution, while there was no "women's movement" as such, new attention was focused on education for girls as well as boys, and brought a marked improvement in general educational standards for girls. For instance, Thomas Jefferson's Bill for the More General Diffusion of Knowledge in Virginia proposed the establishment of a school for each "hundred" to teach reading, writing, arithmetic, and history to all free children, male and female, at public charge for three years and at private expense thereafter. But the bill was never passed. The status of women teachers also rose greatly, as did the number and kind of positions open to them. This new era was marked by the republican philosophy that the country's newfound liberty and independence had to be based on the type of citizenship its children were taught.

After 1776, there were a number of writers, including women, who wrote extensively on education in periodical literature. Judith Sargent Murray was one of the most prominent authors, along with Charles Brockden Brown and Benjamin Rush. Rush's writings were characteristic of the philosophy espoused by more liberal thinkers. He advocated a female ideal "accommodated to the state of society, manners and government" of the United States as distinguished from British models of womanhood, which he and others regarded as solely ornamental.[3]

Murray was perhaps the most forward-thinking of the group of writers who dominated literature on education after the Revolution. While there are no signs that she attempted to create a "movement" per se, she did argue that political independence should be reflected by economically independent women as well as men. Appearing in the *Massachusetts Magazine* between 1792 and 1794, and collected in a series of essays entitled *The Gleaner* in 1798, Murray criticized parents who failed to educate their children and to teach them vocational skills. She was particularly insistent that girls should know a useful skill, should be competent at something in addition to marriage. She also argued for women's right to pursue serious education and intellectual accomplishment, prescribing that women should be able to converse elegantly and correctly, pronounce French, read history (as a substitute for novels), and learn simple geography and astronomy.[4]

No sooner did such writings appear with some frequency on the literary scene than other articles were published that qualified, if not contradicted, such liberal inclinations. For example, the *Lady's Magazine*, which had promised to show that the "females of Philadelphia were by no means deficient in those talents which have immortalized the names of a Montagu, a Craven, a More, and a Seward in their inimitable writings," in 1792 brought out a story about an educated ambitious woman who strives unsuccessfully to write plays and is eventually shunned by both men and women. The moral was:

Such were the effects of an ill-directed study, and such must ever be the consequence of a desertion from nature. This story was intended (at a time when the press overflows with the productions of female pens) to check . . . women, to admonish them, that more amiable accomplishments than reading Greek are attainable by a female mind; and not that because a few have gained applause by studying the dead languages, all womankind should assume their Dictionaries and Lexicons.[5]

Even Judith Sargent Murray repeatedly pointed out that the happiness of the nation depended on the happiness of families and that the "felicity of families" is dependent on the presence of women who were properly educated in economics. Rarely is there any suggestion in the literature that a woman's place might be anywhere but in the home. The overriding purpose of education was simply to make a woman's life happier and more efficient as a wife and mother.

The reason that education for women was given a boost after the Revolution was strictly utilitarian: women who were educated in the right way should be able to run a home more smoothly and, more important, steer their husbands and sons in the direction of sound moral development.[6]

It is on the character and the conduct of the fair sex that man must principally found his hopes of the aggregate of virtue and solid principle that is to be looked for in posterity. It is woman that has the care, almost exclusively, of our younger years; and it is to woman principally that all eminently religious and good characters are primarily indebted for the origin and foundation of their subsequent greatness. . . . By giving *mind* to the fair sex, we shall make them equal to anything that is attainable by rational beings; and by making them acquainted with their own powers, consequence, and influence in the scale of creation, they will gradually become more dignified, and less aspiring; more elevated, and less haughty; more amiable, and less trifling; more useful, and less capricious; more exquisitely fascinating, and less indelicately fashionable.[7]

Despite the limited purpose placed on women's education by the early writers in America, there is no doubt that after 1800 more advanced work was provided for women. This resulted in a growing number of better trained teachers and increasing attention on academic subjects.[8] Female academies became frequent sources of women's education in the late eighteenth century, although they often stressed the more "ornamental" subjects that were designed to enhance a girl's chance at matrimony. Secondary education at coeducational schools became available to girls in the 1780s and 1790s when male teachers, usually ministers, agreed to accept girls as well as boys. Others were administered by women, such as Emma Willard, whose Middlebury Female Seminary opened in 1814, or Catherine Beecher, who established a seminary in Hartford in the 1820s. The goal of these schools was to provide secondary education that went beyond homemaking skills but remained appropriate to a woman's role in society—reflecting the insistence on women's performance as housekeepers and mothers.

By the middle of the nineteenth century, women's institutions for "advanced study" were found throughout the country. One of the major purposes of these schools was to prepare women for jobs as teachers. The expansion of common schooling had created a severe teacher shortage, while men were unwilling to pursue the low-paid, low-status teaching posts. By the 1830s, women had begun to replace men in the winter sessions at common schools, teaching both boys and girls—something that had hitherto been the exclusive realm of male teachers. Women's leaders stressed the fact that women were willing to work for low wages[9] and that women were the "natural" caretakers of children.

Catherine Beecher led a campaign to raise funds for the recruitment and training of teachers and for the establishment of teacher training schools— which she hoped would lead to the creation of a respected profession for women, work that would elevate their professional status above menial labor. Beecher set up the Board of Popular Education and the American Women's Educational Association, and engaged in extensive speaking tours to garner support for teacher enlistment and training.

By the time of the Civil War, one out of four teachers was a woman, earning at most half the salary of a male teacher.[10] After the Civil War, these numbers rose even more sharply, until by 1870, 90 percent of professional women were teachers, and two out of three grammar school teachers were women. By the turn of the century, two out of three professional women were teachers and three out of four teachers were women. Nevertheless, the more elite teaching jobs, located in the secondary schools, were reserved mainly for men. But, all in all, teaching represented unadulterated progress in the eyes of most women's rights activists in the nineteenth century. Both Carrie Chapman Catt and Charlotte Perkins Gilman believed that the advances made in education symbolized a tremendous victory in women's fight for independence.

Coupled with the opening up of teaching jobs for women, there was also an expansion of higher education opportunities for women. Higher education for women was first made available at Oberlin, where girls followed the "ladies course," obtaining special degrees, and participated in men's classes only with special permission. Midwestern land-grant colleges began admitting women during the Civil War, and by 1870, eight state universities admitted women. But such dramatic progress was not the result of any federal or social policy. Rather, it was that after the Civil War, middle-class young men were urged to go into business rather than follow a liberal arts education. Consequently, a large number of higher education spaces opened up, especially with the influx of federal funds and private endowments for private institutions.

Nevertheless, the suffragists of the 1860s and 1870s felt that coeducation had forged major inroads toward social equality. Elizabeth Cady Stanton claimed in 1870 that coeducation would lead to better marriages, a feminist goal at the time. But the public did not support mixed institutions. At Wesleyan, for example, where 8 percent of the students were women, the vast majority of male students opposed coeducation.

Thus, it was the women's colleges that offered superior education for women, providing an arena where women were in control and could be employed without facing discrimination. Vassar, Wellesley, Smith, Bryn Mawr, and Mount Holyoke opened their doors in the late 1800s, with curricula comparable to those at the best men's colleges, taught by female professors and run often by women administrators. These trailblazers had to contend with the continuing bias against women's education, which reasoned that higher education was a terrible threat to women's health and femininity because mental activity drew blood from the nervous system and reproductive organs.[11]

One of the ways in which these institutions combatted such thinking was to include courses in traditionally female subjects such as the arts, music, and domestic science (although Bryn Mawr refused to offer this last subject). The colleges at times emphasized the special nature of their education. Similar to the argument that had been made since colonial times, they claimed that education would enable women to better serve the family and that woman herself would somehow be ennobled through higher education.[12]

The statistics showed, though, that college women did indeed marry later than their noncollege counterparts. In addition, fewer married, and marriage rates were lowest among alumnae of the prestigious, single-sex eastern women's colleges. By 1890, only 25 percent of Bryn Mawr graduates had married; between 1890 and 1908, 45 percent of Bryn Mawr graduates and 57 percent of Wellesley graduates had married.[13] Predictably, then, there was a backlash—some colleges, such as Wesleyan in 1909, ceased to admit women; private colleges formed special women's branches, or "coordinate colleges" to segregate women students; other coeducational colleges, such as the University of Chicago, developed curricula to attract more men.

The "damage" had already been done, however. Significant numbers of women, especially in the East, had completed their higher education. The logical outcome of that participation was their entry into professional work.

Women had entered professional fields—in small numbers—since the colonial era. During the nineteenth century, women had made some gains in medicine; most women professionals were, however, found in teaching, nursing, library work, social work, and academic positions. The first medical school for women, the New England Female Medical College, opened its doors in Boston in 1848. Its aim was to provide the necessary education for women doctors to treat women and children, "the sense of propriety that prevails in every well-regulated mind . . . [dictating] that the presence of a female practitioner is even more desirable than that of a man, however learned or skillful."[14] In other words, women physicians were acceptable because of the common beliefs that they were better suited to take care of the sick and suffering, because mothers were better able to understand how to maintain the health of children, and because women were the "proper" caretakers of their own sex.

By 1875, there were a number of medical schools open to aspiring women physicians, including the Woman's Medical College of Pennsylvania (1850), the Woman's Medical College of the New York Infirmary (1868), the Woman's Medical College of Chicago (1870), and even the University of Michigan Medical School, which opened its doors to women, who received the same instruction as the male students but in separate classes. In a poll published in 1881, out of 430 women respondents who had graduated from some type of medical school, 390 were found to be engaged in active practice, 11 had never practiced, and 29 had practiced but retired due to marriage, ill health, or other work.[15] The study found that the vast majority of respondents were involved in gynecological and obstetrical practices, though 34 percent had been employed as attending or resident physicians in various institutions, particularly in hospitals and dispensaries for women and children.

There was, then, a particular niche that could be filled by women physicians in the late nineteenth century and still conform to prevailing social views. The same did not hold true for other professional fields, such as law and the ministry. The legal profession was a male bastion. The few women who persisted in legal studies were often trained in relatives' offices, and were barred from courtroom practice. Although law schools began to admit women in the 1890s, by 1899, of the 11,874 students enrolled in 96 U.S. law schools, only 167 were women.[16]

In general, women were confined to professions that were associated with their supposedly "natural" inclinations—caring and nurturing for the young, sick, and disabled, as well as educating children and wayward women. Therefore, the vast majority of female college graduates became teachers, librarians, settlement workers (precursors of social workers), and academics. Nurses attended special schools, but did not have to attend college.

While the choice of professions open to women was limited, there was nevertheless a rapid growth in the numbers of professional women. During the 1920s, women professionals increased by 50 percent and the percentage of women workers in professions rose from 11.9 percent to 14.2 percent.[17] But the range of job opportunities remained relatively the same, except that social work had assumed a more professional aspect, including special training and licensing, and women were beginning to enter the communications field as editors, reporters, and journalists. On the other hand, medicine had become a more prestigious and lucrative field since the late 1800s. Foundations had given considerable funding to the better medical schools—which severely limited the numbers of women students, if they admitted them at all—while the lesser-known schools had to close because of insufficient funds. Coupled with the general policy of hospitals to refuse to appoint women interns, this development led to shrinking percentages of women physicians—from 6 percent in 1910 to 5 percent in 1920 to 4.4 percent in 1930.

Education represented perhaps the greatest gain for women professionals in the early 1900s. The proportion of doctorates earned by women rose from 10 percent in 1910 to 15.1 percent in 1920, and the percentage of women on college faculties increased from 18.9 percent in 1910 to 30.1 percent in 1920. By 1920, however, the women's movement was for all intents and purposes shattered, having lost its cohesiveness and much of its motivation after suffrage had been won. Like the generation of college women in the 1980s, feminist zeal had been replaced by confidence that professional positions were indeed open to aspiring career women.

What distinguished women professionals in the 1920s from those who pursued careers in the 1980s was that the former continued to live in a world where men held almost all positions of power. But the work conditions for professional women in these two decades remain remarkably similar. Professional situations were competitive. Women were expected to work toward their own advancement rather than that of a collective body.[18] "Any weakness is likely to be considered feminine," wrote Elizabeth Kemper Adams in a 1921 study of professional women, adding that these women were expected to be more competent than men and were continually being tested for job performance.[19]

It was in the 1920s as well that women called for restructuring society in the interests of opening up the professions to women. Much as combining children and a career dominates women's lives today, accommodating marriage and a career presented the central dilemma in the 1920s. "[The new woman] wants money of her own. She wants work of her own. She wants some means of self-expression, perhaps, some way of satisfying her personal ambition. But she wants a home, husband, and children, too," wrote an editor in 1927.[20] There were even demands made for part-time jobs for women, payments to mothers for child care, and day care centers.[21] In short, although the women's movement was dead for the time being, women—at least professional women— had gained a new sense of individualism and opportunity.

The 1930s brought the Depression, when, from 1932 to 1937, federal law prohibited more than one family member from working in the federal civil service. Women constituted three-quarters of those federal workers forced to resign. More importantly, a strong bias against employing women swept the country—school boards would not hire married women teachers; private businesses discouraged women from competing with men for jobs; and women's colleges asked their graduates not to take paid work. A 1936 Gallup poll asking whether wives should work if their husbands had jobs revealed that 82 percent of the respondents (and 75 percent of female respondents) answered no.

Despite such antagonism toward working women, the proportion of married women in the work force actually rose. This was not, however, the result of persistent efforts by women to remain independent or any of the other guiding forces embraced by the career women of the 1920s. Rather, in most cases, women worked because they had to in order to sustain their families. The Depression, in short, dealt a severe blow to any nascent movement of women professionals, not to mention the public hostility it created toward women's right to work outside the home.[22]

The pendulum swung back again in the following decade, when World War II created an enormous labor shortage as millions of men joined the armed services. While the vast majority of jobs were found in the defense industry and government bureaucracy, there was a dramatic increase of women professionals in, for example, journalism, as male competitors temporarily left the job market.

But, as in the past, the influx of women into the job market, especially into the professions, was temporary. While the proportion of women in the work force plummeted immediately after the war, but then rose by the end of the decade, women were not entering professional occupations. Instead, they were once again working in traditionally "female" jobs, such as office work, sales, and services. Conservative family values pervaded postwar society and, if women worked at all, a wife's job was of minor importance compared with that of her husband. Women were expected to concentrate on domestic roles as opposed to careers. In a throwback to the nineteenth century, articles were written advising women that a career required "a great deal of drive, self-assertion, competition, and aggression"—traits at odds with her biological function of marriage and childrearing, which called for a protective, nurturing, passive temperament. The resulting conflict could cause a mental breakdown.[23] Setting a trend that would be followed until the 1960s, a 1947 best-seller written by psychoanalyst Marynia Farnham and sociologist Ferdinand Lundberg labeled "independent woman" a contradiction in terms and feminism a lethal sickness, exhorting women to find tranquility and happiness in domesticity.[24] Predictably, then, college attendance by women plummeted after the war, dropping from 40 percent of the college population in 1940 to 31 percent by 1950. During the 1950s, however, college enrollment expanded, as did the proportion of women students. Although there was a general emphasis on domestic values for women, colleges continued to offer academic programs to female students. By the early 1960s, there was a new, increasingly liberal, social climate. Nevertheless, quotas for women undergraduates were common, and law and medical schools restricted admissions so that only 10 percent of law school students and 11 percent of medical students were women.[25] Women faculty members earned an average of $3,000 less per year than did their male counterparts, and there were only 100 women out of a total 16,000 school superintendents.[26]

Finally, in the late 1960s, the women's movement turned toward educational equality for women. In 1967, NOW called for passage of federal and state legislation to ensure that women "be educated to their full potential."[27] The Women's Equity Action League, which had been established in 1968, directed its efforts at encouraging girls to adopt higher career aspirations, and at ensuring employment for married women. By the beginning of the 1970s, the women's movement had focused considerable attention on educational opportunity for women, heralding one of the more successful women's rights campaigns of the twentieth century.

These women's groups faced an uphill battle, however, as women in education were not covered by the civil rights laws of the 1960s, including the Equal Pay Act and Title VII of the 1964 Civil Rights Act. In 1970, Representative Edith Green, chair of the House Special Subcommittee on Education, held hearings on sex discrimination, which revealed in its 1,300 pages in published form that there was widespread discrimination against women in education. Soon after, Green introduced a bill that was drafted to eliminate the loopholes in coverage under the Equal Pay Act and Title VII, authorize the Commission on Civil Rights to study discrimination against women, and prohibit sex discrimination in federally assisted programs and in education. She asked that women's groups *not* testify in favor of the bill because chances of its passage would be better if less attention were given to the proposed law's contents. This bill became Title IX of the Education Amendment of 1972, which barred sex discrimination in any education program or activity receiving federal funds.

During 1971–72, a group of women, including Bernice Sandler from the Association of American Colleges; Shirley McCune from the National Education Association; Arvonne Fraser from the Women's Equity Action League (WEAL); Arlene Horowitz, a secretary to the House Education and Labor Committee; and Olya Margolin of the National Council of Jewish Women, among others, drafted a bill to authorize funds for education programs designed to counter sex-role stereotyping found in textbooks. Representatives from women's and education groups from around the country testified in favor of the bill, which was eventually passed in 1974 as the Women's Educational Equity Act.

In 1974, the Department of Health, Education, and Welfare (HEW) released for public comment the proposed administrative regulations for Title IX, governing the implementation of laws regarding education. That year, women's groups organized the Education Task Force, soon to become the National Coalition for Women and Girls in Education, which was to monitor Title IX enforcement and to lobby on behalf of sex equity in education. At the same time, Marcia Greenberger of the Women's Rights Project at the Center for Law and Social Policy, along with members of NOW and WEAL, began to file suit against the Department of Health, Education and Welfare and the Department of Labor for the nonenforcement of Title IX and Executive Order 11246, which prohibited discrimination by federal contractors.

The Title IX regulation was submitted to Congress in 1975 after HEW had transmitted it to President Gerald Ford, who approved it. Women's groups decided to support the legislation and launched a cohesive, forceful lobbying effort in support of the legislation. In order to convey a united, indivisible presence, the National Coalition for Women and Girls in Education, along with forty-five education, women's rights, and civil rights groups, established a coalition of organizations. After having received training by the League of Women Voters and the American Association of University Women, representatives from these groups descended on the House Education and Labor Committee. The campaign was successful, and the Title IX regulation went into effect in 1975.

By 1975, the coalition consisted of thirty to thirty-five organizations involved with women's education. In addition, various professional associations and civil rights groups had organized a women's rights project of women's offices, resulting in the creation of a substantial Washington, D.C., presence for women's education advocates. Their accomplishments included a regulation in 1977 to address sex bias in vocational training programs aimed at encouraging states and local communities to end discrimination against women in job-oriented education programs, and reauthorization in 1978 of the Women's Educational Equity Act, which provided funding to assist school districts and institutions in achieving educational equity and to ensure compliance with Title IX at the local level.

The 1980 election dramatically changed the composition of Congress and introduced new obstacles for the women's movement, including its work on women's education. In 1981, the Reagan administration sent a budget reconciliation bill to Congress that proposed, among other things, consolidating forty education grant programs (including the Women's Educational Equity Act [WEEA] and Title IV) into a single block grant. Enlisting the sponsorship of Representative Margaret Heckler, the Coalition for Women and Girls in Education, along with the Women's Equity Action League and other networks, began to coordinate campaigns to convince Republican senators to remove WEEA from the budget bill. Flooded by telegrams, letters, and telephone calls, Senator Orrin Hatch, who led the refusal by Senate Republicans to omit WEEA from the budget bill, changed his mind and his vote and saved WEEA.

That same year, Senator Hatch made an attempt to restrict Title IX's coverage when he introduced an amendment that would limit protection to the specific activities supported by federal funds. The coalition once more called on its constituent members to organize a "Title IX watch," and ultimately a resolution not to repeal or alter Title IX gained more than one hundred House cosponsors, while Hatch withdrew his own support for his bill in 1982.

In 1990, it is generally taken for granted that women have equal access to university educations and professional degrees. The data provided in Tables 3.1 and 3.2 describe how far women have come in higher education since the middle of the century and reveal in which professional fields big differences between men and women still exist.

In 1950, 24 percent of all degree earners were women. Late in the decade

Table 3.1
Earned Degrees Conferred upon Women (in percentages)

Year	Total		Bachelor's[a]		Master's		Doctorate	
	Total Number	% Women	Total Number	% Women	Total Number	% Women	Total Number	% Women
1950	497	24.4	432	23.8	58	29.3	7	14.2
1960	477	34.2	392	35.2	75	32.0	10	10.0
1965	664	38.5	502	12.4	118	33.8	17	11.7
1970	1065	40.4	792	43.0	209	39.7	30	13.3
1975	1305	43.2	923	45.2	293	44.7	34	20.5
1976	1334	43.8	926	45.4	312	46.4	34	23.5
1977	1334	44.6	920	46.1	317	46.9	33	24.2
1978	1332	45.7	921	47.1	311	48.2	32	25.0
1979	1324	46.7	921	48.2	301	49.2	33	27.2
1980[b]	1330	47.4	930	49.0	298	49.3	33	30.3
1981[b]	1336	48.2	935	49.7	296	50.3	33	30.3
1982[b]	1353	48.8	953	50.3	296	50.7	32	31.3
1983[b]	1365	48.9	969	50.5	290	50.0	33	33.3
1984[b]	1366	48.8	974	50.5	285	49.5	33	33.3
1985[b]	1374	49.3	980	50.3	286	50.0	33	33.3
1986[b]	1384	50.6	988	50.8	289	50.1	34	35.3
1987[b]	1388	49.8	991	51.4	289	51.2	34	35.3

Numbers are in thousands. Except as noted, data include Puerto Rico. Beginning in 1960, data include Alaska and Hawaii.

[a]Includes first professional degrees.

[b]Data for 50 states and D.C.

Source: Adapted from U.S. Bureau of the Census, *Statistical Abstract of the United States, 1990* (Washington, D.C.: U.S. Government Printing Office), table 274, p. 161.

the gap narrowed: women constituted just over a third of the degree earners between 1955 and 1960. This direction continued, so that by 1970, 40 percent of earned degrees were conferred on women. By the 1980s, the gap in the higher education of men and women was virtually eliminated at the undergraduate and master's degree levels. It is only at the Ph.D. level that women still lag behind men, earning only 34 percent of doctoral degrees in 1985.

The data in Table 3.2 attest to the significant increases in the percentage of women who have been awarded professional degrees in traditionally male-dominated, high-status professions.

Women have been most successful in permeating the legal profession, receiving 39 percent of the law degrees awarded in 1985, as compared with 2.5 percent awarded to them in 1960. In medicine, 30 percent of the degrees awarded in 1985 went to women, compared with 5 percent in 1960. Women still lag far behind men in dentistry and especially in engineering, in which they received only 12 percent of the degrees in 1985.

Table 3.2
Professional Degrees Conferred upon Women (in percentages)

Year	Medicine (M.D.)		Dentistry (DDS or DMD)		Law (LLB or JD)		Engineering	
	Total Number	% Women	Total Number	% Women	Total Number	% Women	Total Number	% Women
1960	7032	5.5	3247	0.8	9240	2.5	45624	0.4
1970	8314	8.4	3718	0.9	14916	5.4	63753	0.8
1975	12447	13.1	4773	3.1	29296	15.1	65308	2.2
1978	14279	21.5	5189	10.9	34401	26.0	74492	6.2
1979	14786	23.0	5434	11.8	35206	28.5	80376	7.7
1980	14902	23.4	5258	13.3	35647	30.2	87643	8.7
1981	15505	24.7	5460	14.4	36331	32.4	94270	9.7
1982	15814	25.0	5282	15.4	35991	33.4	100580	10.8
1983	15484	26.7	5585	17.1	36853	36.4	111451	11.6
1984	15813	28.2	5353	19.6	37012	36.8	118086	12.2
1985	16041	30.4	5339	20.7	37491	38.5	120892	12.5
1987	15620	32.4	4741	24.0	36172	40.2	93074	13.7

Source: U.S. Bureau of the Census, *Statistical Abstract of the United States, 1988 and 1990*
(Washington, D.C.: U.S. Government Printing Office), tables 256 and 276, pp. 151, 163.

EARLY ATTEMPTS AT ORGANIZING WORKING WOMEN

The first attempts to organize working women were the result of efforts to change laws that applied equally to men and women. As early as 1828, there are reports of women striking unsuccessfully against a wage cut and for a ten-hour work day law in a Dover, New Hampshire, cotton mill.[28] Another strike of eight hundred women in Dover five years later was more organized, though not much more successful. Adopting a resolution terming their treatment by employers and "unfriendly newspapers" as "insulting to the daughters of free men," they voted to raise a fund to pay the expenses of those women who did not have the means to return to their homes. By 1834, when women in Lowell, Massachusetts, went on strike, they had already formed a union, the Factory Girls' Association. It had twenty-five hundred members and was led by one of the Dover women who had gone to work in a Lowell factory.

In 1869, the first national women's trade union was founded in Massachusetts after a strike of male and female shoemakers. The Daughters of St. Crispin, as the union was called, consisted of members from six states (including California) and was closely affiliated with male counterparts, the Knights of St.

Crispin. There are even reports that the Knights in Syracuse and Baltimore went on strike in sympathy with the women union members who had been discharged because of their union membership.

In 1845, a newly organized Lowell Female Labor Reform Association began to petition the state legislative committee for special treatment—a ten-hour work day for women.[29] The union also appointed a committee to investigate and expose false statements published in newspapers concerning factory workers. Finally, in 1847, the New Hampshire legislature passed a ten-hour law, followed in 1848 by Pennsylvania and in 1851 by New Jersey. There was a significant proviso, however, that in effect nullified the very law itself: a clause permitted employers to hire for more than ten hours by "special contract." Three days before the law went into effect in New Hampshire, employers submitted "special contracts" to their employees, giving them the option of working more than ten hours or not working at all.

From 1840 to 1900, young, primarily single, women left homes in increasing numbers to seek employment in the textile industry. Union organizers often excluded women, fearing that female employees threatened men's own job security.[30] Independent efforts to unionize women were hampered by the absence of skilled female organizers.

In the late 1860s, however, leaders of the women's rights movement sought to organize working women as a new source of potential supporters. In 1868, Susan B. Anthony announced in the *Revolution* a meeting to organize working women. That meeting was presided over by Anthony and Augusta Lewis Troup, a *Revolution* typesetter who later became a prominent union organizer. It resulted in the formation of the New York Working Women's Association in 1868.

That association only lasted a few months. Troup, believing the women's rights movement to be one of "short hair, bloomers and other vagaries,"[31] founded the Women's Typographical Association (WTA), which focused almost entirely on union issues. When Troup, as president of the WTA, protested the low wages Anthony paid typesetters, she was fired. Troup then led the successful fight to prevent both Anthony and Stanton from being designated as delegates from the Working Women's Association at the 1869 National Labor Union convention.[32] Anthony and Stanton, on the other hand, sought to attract the new middle-class working women, such as writers, teachers, and a few other professionals. By 1869, the association's active membership was entirely middle class.[33]

In short, with one exception, there was a split between working-class and middle-class women from the very beginning of women's movements in America. That schism has been evident, in varying degrees, throughout women's movements in the last two centuries. In the early days of organizing for women, union organizers focused on wages and hours, while women's leaders, such as Anthony and Stanton, focused on issues such as property rights, suffrage, and education—privileges that most working women had not even considered.

By 1900, the composition of the female labor force began to change with the influx of immigrant women into the labor force and the growth of white-collar jobs for single, middle-class women. The latter, preoccupied with suffrage, were far less concerned with eliminating legal, social, and economic barriers for working women. Moreover, suffragists wanted little to do with immigrant and poor women who worked in factories at the turn of the century. Instead, they began to focus on protective legislation, the drive for which was generally based on the same arguments that they used for the vote—the view that a woman's proper place in life was in the home, as a devoted wife and mother. Even those suffragists concerned with working-class women, such as the National American Woman Suffrage Association (NAWSA), ultimately adopted goals of protective legislation.[34]

Thus, in the space of fifty years, a far less radical feminism had arisen from that expressed at Seneca Falls. The early women's rights leaders had adopted radical positions, advocating the inherent equality of men and women; the current feminists seemed at best untroubled by notions of inequality. Radical feminists simply had failed to capture a mass following due to a combination of factors: lack of organization, elitist tendencies, and the assimilation of their ideas and goals into those of a more submissive movement. The radical feminists had by and large concentrated on middle- and upper-class women, who turned out to be more interested in gaining the vote than in establishing fundamental reform. Consequently, the broad goal of seeking equality was replaced by the more specific goal of enfranchisement.

The narrowness of purpose eventually embraced by the predominant women's movement in the late 1800s and early 1900s was no doubt due in part to the fact that the majority of its leaders were middle and upper middle class. Many of them were wealthy and did not have to seek the menial, service-oriented, teaching or clerical jobs generally open to women who needed an income. Moreover, the women who did choose to attempt to enter the male-dominated professions were generally not active in the women's movement—"the overwhelming majority of these first women lawyers were individualists ... who were content to earn their law degrees and then to disappear from public life. Rarely do we find these first women lawyers speaking out publicly for women's issues, demanding the vote or greater rights for women, or seeking legislation to further woman's cause."[35]

Thus, women's leaders remained primarily interested in preserving the woman's place in the family.

Medical testimony showed the physical differences between men and women; the lesser power of women to endure long hours of standing. . . . The testimony of factory inspectors . . . revealed the bad effect of long hours on women's safety . . . [and] the good effect on the individual health, home life, and general welfare of short hours of labor.[36]

Accordingly, the women's movement focused on ways of protecting women in the work place rather than improving their chances of promotion once they got there.

1900–1940: THE FIGHT FOR PROTECTIVE LEGISLATION

Protective legislation became the dominant goal of both the mainstream women's movement and the National Consumers' League (NCL), formed in 1899 by the merger of several city leagues working for the improvement of working conditions in retail shops and factories. NCL adopted as its major concern the eradication of substandard conditions in U.S. factories and retail establishments. Eventually, these efforts resulted in the passage of maximum-hour legislation for women in several states, laws that were to come under attack in several of the most prominent legal cases of the twentieth century.

Another women's group, the Women's Trade Union League (WTUL), was founded in 1903 by a coalition of upper-class reformers and women unionists. Its goal was "largely educational" because most of its members were not employed and were therefore unable to form unions themselves. They viewed the WTUL as a bridge between the working and leisure classes. The group devoted itself to training women wage earners to organize and fight for better pay, shorter work days, and better treatment in the work place, and to demand that more goods bear the union label.[37]

While the WTUL did succeed in organizing women workers in a variety of trades (bookbinding, tobacco manufacture, laundries, and some textile mills), it encountered several insurmountable problems indicative of the obstacles facing the entire women's movement in the early part of the twentieth century. First, working women—the vast majority of whom were young and single— did not view themselves as pursuing a career; most of them expected to marry and leave their jobs. Moreover, the prevailing public sentiment was that women belonged in the house, not in the union hall—which was often located in the back of saloons or questionable districts where young working women refused to go.[38] Second, union men were great supporters of the domestic ideal: "Woman was created to be man's companion, to be the presiding deity of the home circle . . . to guide the tottering footsteps of the tender infancy," according to one National Labor Union official in the 1860s.[39] The American Federation of Labor (AFL), which had over four million members by the 1920s, advocated equal pay for women, but at the same time denied the need of women to work, viewing them as a threat to working men because they accepted less pay for the same work.[40] Because of the obstacles placed in the path of the WTUL and other women's groups, the League consigned itself to an educational and lobbying role. It was the latter that helped to bring about the protective laws that were the trademark of the women's movement in the first half of the twentieth century.

Protective laws were intended to ensure the welfare of working women by limiting their hours, increasing their wages, and establishing better work conditions. They were viewed as a substitute for unionization, providing the benefits they would otherwise receive from unions. They also conformed to the AFL's goals: by limiting work hours for women and insisting on a minimum wage, the laws would remove the incentives for employers to hire women.

By 1914, twenty-seven states were regulating women's working hours, and by the 1920s, fifteen states had minimum wage laws. Between 1908 and World War I, numerous states enacted protective laws, and others made earlier measures more rigorous. These new regulations included restricting women from working at night, carrying heavy weights, and working in dangerous places or in "morally hazardous" places such as bars. This legislation gave rise in turn to a spate of precedent-setting legal cases.

Perhaps the most famous of the cases concerning protective legislation in the first decade of the century was *Muller v. Oregon*,[41] which upheld the constitutionality of an Oregon statute prohibiting women from working more than eight hours a day. The NCL, represented by Louis Brandeis in the famous "Brandeis brief," basically argued the ideology of the suffrage movement: that statistics show the deleterious effects of long hours of work on a woman's health and her reproductive capacity, and that, in short, women have unique characteristics and are therefore in need of special protective labor legislation.

The Supreme Court agreed, establishing the principle that women could legally be treated differently from men. The NCL leaders regarded this decision as a milestone in the struggle to help working women; but in fact many employers used this decision to justify treating women unfairly or not hiring women.[42]

In 1923, however, NCL suffered a major defeat in *Adkins v. Children's Hospital*.[43] A District of Columbia statute had created a wage board empowered to set minimum wages so as to allow women workers to maintain their good health and protect their morals.[44] During oral arguments, lawyers for the hospital pointed out that the National Women's Party supported total equality of the sexes and viewed protective legislation as inherently unequal treatment of women that would prevent full sexual equality.[45]

With overruling *Muller*, the Supreme Court struck down the D.C. law, declaring, "[W]e cannot accept the doctrine that women of mature age, *sui juris*, require or may be subjected to restrictions upon their liberty of contract which could not lawfully be imposed in the case of men under similar circumstances."[46]

The National Woman's Party (NWP) was the only major women's group that advocated full equality in the work place. Its objections to protective legislation were, however, eventually overruled when its leaders failed to attract the very women it sought to represent. Working women, those who were directly affected by protective legislation, were often too busy working and tending their families to have the time or energy to devote to fighting its passage. And neither the NWP or any other women's group made any successful drive to mobilize working or trade union women.

The break in the ranks of the women's movement, reinforced by *Adkins*, forced the NCL to keep a low profile, recognizing that public opinion in the United States was not receptive to the idea of protective legislation. The group avoided litigation for several years, going so far as to actively discourage the enactment of new protective legislation, fearing that additional challenges from powerful, well-financed employers would give the Supreme Court the opportunity to overrule *Muller*.

During this same period (1900–30), there was a shift in the kinds of work women did. By 1930, 30 percent of the employed women in the country were found in nonmanual occupations, usually as clerical workers. From 1890–1920, the percentage of women in white-collar clerical and sales jobs rose from 5.3 to 25.6.[47] Moreover, the Depression severely curtailed job opportunities for women. Employers had specific policies prohibiting the hiring of married women, and twenty-six states passed laws specifically barring the employment of married women in some occupations.[48] Even the federal government passed a law barring the employment of more than one family member per household. Again, there was a split among women's groups concerning such legislation. While the National Federation of Business and Professional Women's Clubs lobbied against state laws prohibiting the employment of more than two persons from one household, the NCL—in the spirit of upholding a woman's place in the home—opposed any effort or legislation to further employment opportunities for married women.[49]

In 1933, the NCL tried again to have minimum wage laws enacted. While the group worked in New York, the state of Washington passed legislation creating a Minimum Wage Board to determine the adequacy of wages for women to ensure "the decent maintenance of women" and to protect their "health and morals." Alleging a violation of that law, a woman sued her employer for back pay. The Supreme Court upheld the constitutionality of the Washington law, overruling *Adkins*. Justice Hughes wrote, "The Legislature of the state was clearly entitled to consider the situation of women in employment, the fact that they are in the class receiving the least pay, that their bargaining power is relatively weak and that they are the ready victims of those who would take advantage of their necessitous circumstances."[50]

Thus, the NCL and its allies were ultimately successful in ensuring that working women would be granted certain special rights, distinguishing them from their male counterparts in the work force. NCL's opponents, particularly the National Woman's Party, were defeated in their struggle to promote equality between men and women. And the working women who would be most directly affected by protective legislation were often too busy working and raising families to participate in any political or social struggle, let alone to organize themselves into a coalition or group. The vast majority of women's leaders were established, well-connected women, belonging to a social and intellectual elite—precisely the kinds of people who viewed a woman's role in life as requiring special attention and safeguards from perceived outside "threats" in the work place.

There are striking parallels between the situation of the women's movement from 1920 to 1945 and that of the movement since the early 1980s. Both periods followed a long-term and widespread campaign for women's rights, and both can be viewed in terms of specific legislative successes. The 1920s and the 1980s witnessed a dramatic increase in the education opportunities opened up to women and in the rise of female professionals. But both periods have also been subject to criticism for ignoring the needs of minority and working women—including access to education, health care, and child care, among others. It took a social upheaval in the 1960s to finally end a period of general apathy in the women's movement. It remains to be seen whether current issues, such as abortion and child care, will bring about a surge of activism in the name of women's rights.

WORLD WAR II AND ITS AFTERMATH

For almost fifty years following acceptance of the Nineteenth Amendment in 1919, women voted and worked solidly within the narrow social, legal, and economic parameters characterized by protective legislation and strictly circumscribed professions. The U.S. Women's Bureau had been established in 1920, supposedly marking the recognition of women in the work force and electorate. But the Bureau repeatedly produced voluminous, scarcely noticed statistics that were rarely acted upon. Its reports covered the same issues each year: the narrow band of women's occupations, the intermittence of their employment, the necessity for incomes for women, dual employment as wives and mothers and wage earners, unemployment, pay differentials, and the effect of labor legislation on women's welfare.

The Bureau was a carry-over from the progressive era, but it had no enforcement power and failed to convince those who did—the politicians—of the inequities of the work place. Their powerlessness is exemplified by the equal pay bill introduced in Congress in 1945. Based on the concept of comparable worth, it stated that pay differentials based on sex constituted an unfair labor practice. It prohibited wage differentials for "work of a comparable character, the performance of which requires comparable skills."[51] The bill failed to pass, and was reintroduced and failed again to pass in every subsequent Congress for eighteen years.

The Bureau, however, did set a foundation for what followed in the 1960s and 1970s. After a hiatus of several decades, women's groups began once again to forge networks, to practice coalitional politics in order to introduce at least the idea of change.[52] In 1952, the Bureau encouraged the establishment of a nongovernmental lobbying organization, the National Committee for Equal

Pay, a coalition of twenty large national organizations, to push for the passage of an equal pay act.

The legal and social climate of the 1930s—with its emphasis on the "special" role of women and the absence of significant numbers of women in the work force—was dramatically reversed with the onset of World War II. Women workers were necessary to produce armaments and to run factories. The government campaigned actively to recruit women into the labor force, scrapping the discriminatory hiring practices of the Depression. But it remained legal for employers to refuse to hire older or married women, nor were there any legal prohibitions against refusals to employ women at all. Consequently, many job classifications remained male or were temporarily staffed by women until a more "appropriate" person could be found.

More "appropriate" persons were quickly found when the war ended. Within two months, almost 800,000 women had lost their jobs in the aircraft industry alone.[53] Many corporations reestablished prewar prohibitions against the employment of women, and protective legislation was reinstituted in many states. Nevertheless, within a few years women were reentering the work force in large numbers, but were taking traditional jobs at far lower pay than they had during the war.[54]

There was a heavy demand in the 1950s and 1960s for women workers. Traditional "women's jobs," generally those in the service sector, were one of the fastest-growing areas of the economy. Yet, as a result of the Depression, when there was a decline in the birthrate, there were fewer people reaching adulthood in the 1950s and 1960s. Coupled with a trend toward earlier marriage, this decline resulted in a shortage of women workers. The increased need for additional income by many families, combined with these other factors, served to increase job opportunities for large numbers of working mothers during the two decades after the war. Women remained relegated to "female" jobs, however, with a few professions, such as nursing and teaching, almost totally dominated by women.

This state of affairs—significant numbers of women working in comparatively low-level, low-paying jobs—gave rise in the 1960s to a reemergence of an organized women's movement after a lull during the country's preoccupation with World War II and its aftermath.

THE 1960s

In the early 1960s, yet another national commission was designated to study the status of women. But this time there was a difference: the new Women's Bureau director, Esther Peterson, had special access to President John F. Kennedy. The President's Commission on the Status of Women (PCSW) and the state commissions that followed are often credited with creating the conditions that marked the resurgence of the feminist movement in the 1960s. Although the term "women's rights" was not used within the government until

1969, when President Nixon set up the President's Task Force on Women's Rights and Responsibilities, the PCSW "changed discussions of women's roles and status from ridiculous to respectable."[55] More important, the 1960s heralded a new era in the creation and enforcement of women's rights legislation.

Eleanor Roosevelt was appointed chair of the PCSW, and its 265 members included representatives of both houses of Congress, the secretaries of Labor, Commerce, and Health, Education and Welfare, the attorney general, the chairman of the Civil Service Commission, and prominent representatives of industry, labor, education, and women's organizations.

By February 1967, commissions had been set up in all fifty states and the District of Columbia. The state commissions played a major role in promoting reforms in national, state, and local legislation and in promoting reforms in national, state, and local legislation and in providing leadership for a national women's movement. While congressional hearings on equal pay legislation had been conducted in the years immediately following World War II, no legislation was enacted, and interest waned until 1962. In that year, hearings were resumed and the Equal Pay Act (EPA) was passed in the following year with the support of the Kennedy administration.

There were a number of forces at work during the early 1960s that heralded a pervasive change in laws concerning working women, of which the EPA was only the precursor. By then women comprised one-third of the total labor force and were an increasingly important part of the nation's work force.[56] In 1963, Betty Friedan's book *The Feminine Mystique* was published, calling for drastic changes in societal roles for women. The development and popularity of the birth control pill also contributed to demographic and cultural changes. Increasing numbers of women were attending colleges and universities and entering the labor force, while the exodus of young men from the labor force to fight in Vietnam increased job opportunities for women. By the end of the decade, the women's movement had been reborn. Both national organizations, which appealed generally to middle-class professional women (for example, the National Organization for Women, the National Women's Political Caucus, and the Women's Equity Action League), and small, local, less organized groups, which catered to more radical women, flourished.

At first, it was the EEOC's nonenforcement of Title VII that provided the catalyst for the formation of women's groups devoted to ensuring women's legislative rights. EEOC officials consistently neglected to investigate complaints of sex discrimination, prompting Representative Griffiths to attack the agency's inaction from the House of Representatives floor. In 1966, Betty Friedan and twenty-eight delegates to the Third National Conference of Commissions on the Status of Women formed the National Organization for Women when they became frustrated by the conference's failure to ratify a resolution urging the EEOC to treat sex discrimination with the same seriousness as race discrimination.

NOW was created to influence national legislation and to build a mass-based national organization. Its tactics involved staging media events, picket lines, and protests, along with lobbying campaigns.[57] They first put pressure on the EEOC to hold hearings so that it could issue regulations to implement the sex-discrimination prohibition of Title VII. NOW members also sought to influence employers through pickets and protests. For example, in 1967, they picketed the *New York Times* offices to protest its maintenance of sex-segregated help-wanted advertisements. In December of that year, they held what one writer calls "perhaps the first contemporary feminist demonstration,"[58] when NOW members, along with other representatives from women's rights groups, picketed EEOC offices around the country to draw attention to EEOC inaction.

At NOW's national conference in 1967, it adopted a "bill of rights," calling for passage of the ERA, enforcement of employment rights law, establishment of child care centers, equal education, and acknowledgment of the "right of women to control their reproductive lives."[59] As had happened several times in the preceding two centuries, this was too radical a platform for a number of more moderate professional women. Both the ERA and the abortion section triggered considerable controversy. While members of the National Woman's Party joined NOW to vote for the ERA, union members opposed it. A number of these dissatisfied feminists formed the Women's Equity Action League in 1968 as an alternative to NOW. They adopted plans to intervene in political systems through lobbying and litigation unimpeded by NOW's more radical image. Its members believed that abortion was too divisive an issue, Friedan too controversial, and NOW's mission too diffuse to command the respect of lawmakers.[60] In the years to come, the various women's groups, while splintered by differences of opinion on abortion and ERA, were bound by several common threads, most of which concerned employment rights. It was in the legal arena that these rights were forged.

LEGAL AND LEGISLATIVE CHANGE

The EPA was the beginning of a surge of measures affecting a broad spectrum of civil and political rights. While the EPA was a symbolic victory for women's commissions, it contained no viable enforcement mechanisms; moreover, it excluded from its purview executive, administrative, and professional employees. In the following year, however, a far more potent mechanism was created to set the scene for a number of important legal battles against employment discrimination: the Civil Rights Act of 1964.

Title VII of the Civil Rights Act prohibits discrimination based on sex in all terms, conditions, or privileges of employment.[61] Title VII was originally drafted to deal with discrimination based on race, national origin, and religion; the ban on sex discrimination was inserted one day before its passage with little accompanying discussion to clarify legislative intent. The courts and the Equal Employment Opportunity Commission, which was created to enforce the act, have struggled with a wide variety of issues involving sex discrimination. Some cases have involved specific interpretations of EEOC guidelines, such as sexual harassment. Others have concerned legal theories, such as the doctrine of comparable worth. Questions, such as those regarding maternity leave and benefits, contributions to pension plans, veteran preference, newspaper advertising, stereotyping in hiring and assignments, marital status, breast-feeding at work, and grooming standards have all been litigated as a result of Title VII.

Unlike the large number of women's groups that had testified in favor of the Equal Pay Act, no organized women's group spoke on behalf of Title VII. However, soon after the Act's passage, women's groups began to take an active part in litigation, lobbying, and mobilization efforts. As each issue arose in the courts, the women's movement—often split by differing factions—played a prominent role in the ensuing legal battle.

In addition to women's groups, unions began to take a more active part in promoting and opposing legislation that would affect women's rights. Unions were longtime supporters of protective legislation, but female union members argued that Title VII superseded state protective laws. Their male colleagues, however, were slow to accept this. Many union leaders, as well as the rank and file, fought to retain protective legislation—not surprising, considering the lack of women's representatives in the union leadership.[62] But during the late 1960s, there was a widespread drive among women union members to push for equal rights and opportunities within the unions themselves. This culminated in 1974 with the formation of the Coalition of Labor Union Women (CLUW). The founding of CLUW facilitated contact between labor union women and other women's groups; labor leaders took the lead in forming coalitions around such issues as pregnancy disability benefits, comparable worth, and occupational health and safety.

The composition of CLUW—while organized under the umbrella of the trade union movement—ultimately resembled that of other women's movements of the 1960s and 1970s, and was strongly reminiscent of the Women's Trade Union League of the early 1900s. That is, public-sector employees were the predominant contingent within CLUW; government and white-collar workers made up more than 60 percent of the group's membership.[63] In 1974, CLUW's founders outmaneuvered the more radical members who wanted the organization to take stands on support for United Farm Workers and other controversial issues. Instead, CLUW adopted a program consisting of organizing women, bringing affirmative action to the work place, and seeking change through political action and legislation. In 1979, CLUW passed resolutions favoring comparable worth and increased female representation on the executive boards of unions.

Years before CLUW was formed, however, women's rights groups recognized that they would need to litigate to obtain employment rights. Although the EEOC had been empowered to bring lawsuits against private employers, it was unable to keep up with the number of complaints.[64] NOW formed a legal arm to litigate violations of both the Civil Rights and the Equal Pay Acts. While other women's groups disagreed with the more controversial NOW positions, they also took steps to establish legal funds to litigate sex-discrimination complaints.

NOW brought suit against the EEOC for failing to enforce Title VII, and in Pittsburgh, in response to a complaint filed by NOW, the Commission on Human Relations brought suit against the Pittsburgh Press Company, claiming it violated Title VII by publishing sex-segregated advertisements.[65] Finally, in 1972, the EEOC acquired the power to sue discriminating employers in federal court.

In the mid–1960s, one of the first actions taken by NOW was an effort to limit the scope of the bona fide occupational qualification (bfoq) exception of Title VII, which allows an employer to take sex into account when it is a bfoq for a particular position. Examples include hiring only females as wet nurses or hiring only male actors to play Batman. Interpretation of the provision, however, led to controversy among women's groups, because an expansive interpretation of the bfoq provision would allow most protective legislation to remain on the law books, while a narrow one would have invalidated such laws.

Several reform women's and labor groups wrote to the EEOC director urging him to construe Title VII to allow "differential legislation" for women, noting that it had beneficial effects on their health and well-being.[66] On the other hand, representatives from the National Woman's Party spoke in favor of a narrow construction, which would deny the need for protective legislation. Marguerite Rawalt, legal counsel for NOW, testified that NOW opposed state maximum-hour laws and laws setting weight-lifting maximums or limiting night work. NOW's position was that protective legislation often only protected women from obtaining or retaining higher-paid jobs.

The EEOC in 1968 submitted an amicus brief in a case originally sponsored by NOW stating that Title VII invalidated California's laws prohibiting women from lifting weights or working overtime. The federal district court agreed with the EEOC's position and in *Rosenfeld v. Southern Pacific Co.*[67] ruled that the California law, cited by the railway company as its reason for not hiring women as agent-telegraphers, was a violation of Title VII.

In 1971, the Supreme Court let stand a Fifth Circuit Court of Appeals ruling that the bfoq exception allowed only for business necessity and not convenience exceptions. Thus, Pan American Airline's refusal to hire male attendants because of alleged "customer preference" was judged to be illegal.[68]

The courts generally have narrowly construed the bfoq exception, particularly where the question involves the ability to perform the job. Ironically, this brought to an end—at least for a few years—the long struggle for protective legislation, which was regarded as an impediment to job equality.

Trends within the legal profession during the 1970s also created certain pressures upon the courts. By 1971, a number of law school journals had published articles or symposia on women's rights questions. In May 1971, the

California Supreme Court—one year earlier than the U.S. Supreme Court—declared that sex classifications were "suspect" and required, therefore, "compelling justification."[69]

An additional possible influence on the Supreme Court may have been the passage of the Equal Rights Amendment in the House of Representatives in August 1970, by a margin of greater than ten to one. In the next session of Congress, the House, after voting in favor of equal rights legislation for twenty-three years, again overwhelmingly endorsed the ERA. Spearheaded by Representative Martha Griffiths (D-Michigan), women's organizations began to inundate congressional offices with letters supporting an Equal Rights Amendment. While some prominent women's organizations—the National Council of Jewish Women, the National Council of Catholic Women, and the National Council of Negro Women, among others—opposed the amendment, the voices that were heard on Capitol Hill were those belonging to the "Women's Liberation Movement":

Until recently, the Congressional concept of "militant women" was shaped by such things as the annual gathering of ex-suffragettes around the statue of Susan B. Anthony in the basement of the Capitol on that gallant lady's birthday. Otherwise, the almost quiescent feminist movement came to the legislator's attention only through small delegations from polite women's organizations . . . lobbying for more rights and being received like Puerto Ricans who want independence. . . . Then came the Lib movement . . . [which] absolutely ignited the old Establishment outfits like Business and Professional Women, and they in turn began to put the heat on Congress as never before. Suddenly it was difficult to find a member of either house of Congress who didn't think that NOW meant him and right now.[70]

In November 1970, the landmark *Reed v. Reed* was handed down—and the Supreme Court showed that it was following in the same general trend as the Congress and the president, who was issuing executive orders barring sex discrimination by employers under federal contract or subcontract. In *Reed*, the Supreme Court ruled that a legislative preference for men over women as estate administrators was "arbitrary" and therefore not reasonable.

Two years later, the ERA won the needed two-thirds majority in each house, and the Supreme Court decided *Sharron and Joseph Frontiero v. Elliot Richardson, Secretary of Defense.*[71] While there was only a plurality decision in that case, four justices did admit that the *Reed* result would have been different if the Supreme Court had followed the reasonableness test it was espousing in *Frontiero*. This case indicated that sex classifications were being examined with something more than the traditional minimal scrutiny. In short, the Court would not apply the "compelling" reason test to sex discrimination, but there nevertheless had to be "a pretty good reason" before it would hold that such discrimination is justified.[72]

PREGNANCY DISCRIMINATION

One of the first issues to be reviewed by the Supreme Court regarding the reasonableness of discrimination was the role played by pregnancy in employers' decisions to discriminate in certain areas. These included forced leave, loss of seniority, lack of medical coverage, and outright dismissal. Women's rights groups challenged these policies from the very beginning.[73]

Again, however, pregnancy issues were too controversial for some women's rights advocates, such as those in WEAL. The first split occurred when the Women's Law Fund was set up by some WEAL leaders who disagreed over WEAL's involvement in *Cleveland Board of Education v. LaFleur* (1974),[74] a case challenging the automatic dismissal of pregnant school teachers in their fourth month. Nevertheless, both NOW and the Women's Rights Project of the ACLU filed amicus briefs to support the arguments of the Women's Law Fund, which sponsored the case. The Supreme Court eventually ruled that the school board's policy violated the due process clause of the Fourteenth Amendment. The Court concluded that the mandatory cutoff dates bore "no rational relationship to the state's interest in preserving the continuity of instruction."

While *Cleveland* represented a victory for women's rights groups, the Court failed to address the question of whether employers should categorize pregnancy along with other medical conditions rather than as a condition unique to women. Numerous women's rights groups in the 1970s embraced the former interpretation, arguing that treatment of pregnancy as a "special" condition would provide ammunition for employers seeking grounds to treat women employees differently from men. Feminist lawyers turned to Title VII for possible relief against job pregnancy discrimination after the Supreme Court ruled in *Geduldig v. Aiello* that California's refusal to pay disability benefits to women workers was constitutional because there was "no evidence in the record that the selection of the risks insured by the program worked to discriminate against any identifiable group or class in terms of the aggregate risk protection."[75] Women's rights groups suffered another defeat a few years later when the Court ruled in *General Electric Co. v. Gilbert* that pregnancy "is not a disease at all and is often a voluntarily undertaken desired condition," and therefore a private employer did not violate Title VII by excluding pregnancy from its disability coverage.

Immediately after *Gilbert*, women's rights groups began to lobby Congress for legislation that would prohibit discrimination against pregnant women. In 1978, Congress passed the Pregnancy Discrimination Act, which barred the disparate treatment of pregnant women for all employment-related purposes.[76]

More recently, however, there has been a subtle shift in the views of women's rights advocates, a return to a more protective stance (although it is not described as such). Rather than concentrating on actual cases of discrimination, women's groups are pushing for what appears to be a return to special treatment of pregnancy. NOW, the National Women's Political Caucus, the American Association of University Women, and numerous other groups have been concentrating on ensuring special job protection to employees who are physically unable to work because of pregnancy. In 1976, 1977, and 1978, legislation was introduced that would require employers to grant up to eighteen weeks of unpaid leave to workers to take care of newborn or seriously ill children.

On the other hand, the National Association of Women Business Owners, the largest U.S. women's business group, who have pushed for worker perrequisites such as job sharing, flexible benefits, and office day-care centers, are fighting against mandatory parental leave. At a 1986 White House Conference on Small Business, the association called for an end to all government-mandated workplace benefits.

In 1987, in a case widely hailed by women's groups as a resounding success, the Supreme Court ruled in *California Federal Savings & Loan Association v. Guerra* that states may require employers to grant special job protection to employees who are physically unable to work because of pregnancy. The Court upheld a California law requiring employers to grant up to four months of unpaid leave to women disabled by pregnancy and childbirth, even if similar leaves are not granted for other disabilities. The law is only applicable to cases with special medical problems and does not provide leave to care for newborn children.

Justice Thurgood Marshall, writing for the majority, distinguished the California pregnancy leave law from "the protective legislation prevalent earlier in this century" by noting that the former covered only "actual physical disability," rather than being based on "stereotypical notions" that pregnant workers suffered from an inherent handicap. But neither the federal law nor the California law provides a definition of disability or specifies any part of the pregnancy for which disability is presumed.

The decision was applauded by feminist groups, even those that have historically argued against the kind of preferential treatment for pregnant employees that the Court found lawful in *Guerra*. The case deepened the split among feminist groups over whether to support such treatment, with NOW in opposition because of the fear that it might reinforce sexist stereotypes and make employers reluctant to hire women of child-bearing age. NOW argued that the Court should instead require California employers to extend the same benefits to all disabled employees. But after the ruling, the president of NOW, Eleanor Smeal, called the decision a "solid victory,"[77] though she acknowledged that some groups, including NOW, were concerned that the court might endorse laws that would lead down a "slippery slope" to the inhibiting laws of the past.

Employer groups and the Reagan administration agreed with NOW that the 1978 Federal Pregnancy Discrimination Act barred preferential treatment of pregnant women compared with other temporarily disabled employees, but argued that the remedy was simply to strike down the California law, leaving employers free to deny disability leave to all employees.

In general, however, this case underscored the way in which women's groups had turned their attention to the establishment of special legal provisions, albeit ones that enabled a greater number of women to work—but special nonetheless. Perhaps the difference between the era of protective legislation and the current time is that women today are arguing that such legislation is *worth* it. Similar to the situation in the 1950s, the population is shrinking, and so is the pool of talented workers. A recent article in *Harvard Business Review* opens with the statement that the cost of employing women in management is greater than the cost of employing men, and goes on to admit that women are more likely to leave their jobs, taking the company's investment with them, and more likely to drop off the fast track. The reason, suggests the author, is that it becomes too difficult for the vast majority of women who want to balance a high-powered career and motherhood. To protect their investments, she argues, companies should make it easier for women, should deal with maternity more openly and flexibly, and should "take an active role in providing family supports and child care and alternative work schedules."[78]

SEXUAL HARASSMENT

Public awareness of sexual harassment has evolved only during the last decade. It was not until 1977 that a federal Court of Appeals found that sexual harassment constituted sex discrimination prohibited by Title VII.[79] In 1979, another appeals court concluded that an employer could be held liable under Title VII for a supervisor's harassment of female employees.[80] And in 1980, the EEOC, at the urging of several women's rights groups, adopted regulations making sexual harassment an impermissible form of sex discrimination prohibited by Title VII.

In the women's movement, numerous groups spoke out against this form of discrimination. One of the most vocal feminists on this subject is Catherine MacKinnon, who published a book in 1979 entitled *Sexual Harassment of Working Women.*[81] She stated that until the late 1970s, the concept of sexual harassment had been "legally unthinkable."[82] That is, the laws at that time did not include the idea of sexual harassment of women on the job or in educational institutions as "discrimination on the basis of sex."

Six years later, the prohibition of sexual harassment was considered by the Supreme Court, who unanimously decided that "when a supervisor sexually harasses a subordinate because of a subordinate's sex, that supervisor discriminates on the basis of sex"[83]—the first time the Supreme Court ruled on the viability of a legal cause of action for sexual harassment claims under Title VII. One of the key phrases in that decision was "hostile environment"—that sexual harassment, to be actionable, must be "sufficiently severe or pervasive" to change the conditions of employment and create "an abusive working environment."

Since *Meritor Savings Bank,* a number of sexual harassment cases have been filed,[84] but a milestone was reached in 1987 when Catherine A. Broderick, an attorney at the Securities and Exchange Commission, filed suit against the SEC charging that the atmosphere of the office was so polluted that she was unable to obtain promotions.[85] The case was the first instance of a "work environment on trial," setting a precedent when the U.S. District Court ruled that Broderick's supervisors had created a "hostile and offensive work place" by granting promotions, bonuses, and other job benefits to women who submitted or consented to their sexual advances. In addition, Broderick's complaint was not that she herself was sexually harassed by her supervisors; rather, the court found that Broderick's supervisors retaliated against her for complaining about the office atmosphere. In short, *Broderick* served to delineate how pervasive an atmosphere of sexual harassment must be in order to be actionable.

RETIREMENT BENEFITS

Long before the rise of the current women's movement, the National Federation of Business and Professional Women had attempted to secure passage of legislation to remedy inequities in the Social Security system. The 1963 report of the President's Commission on the Status of Women noted the pervasive discrimination against women in the system. Women's groups made three basic charges against the Social Security Insurance (SSI) program: its assumption of traditional roles, with the husband seen as the sole salaried wage earner and the wife assumed to be at home and rearing her children; the program's lack of recognition of the unsalaried woman's contribution to the economic unit; and the lower benefits for working married women.[86]

The SSI program's assumption of traditional roles was attacked by the ACLU's Women's Rights Project in *Weinberger v. Wiesenfeld*[87] in 1975. The Supreme Court ruled that the "gender-based discrimination [of the Act] was entirely irrational," and therefore unconstitutional.

Government pension plans and the treatment of unsalaried married women have also been the target of women's groups, particularly after the Supreme Court rendered its decision in *McCarty v. McCarty* that federal law precluded a state court from dividing military nondisability retirement pay pursuant to state community property laws. Shortly after *McCarty,* women's groups began to lobby Congress for legislation to invalidate the Court's decision. In 1982, an amendment to the 1983 defense appropriation bill required that military personnel retirement pay must be given the same status by divorce courts as any other pension in the consideration of the division of marital assets.

Since 1982, women's groups have continued an active lobbying campaign for pension reform, though one of their major reform proposals—recognition of a housewife's contribution in the form of a credit for a portion of the salary earned by her spouse—has not been seriously considered by Congress.

In addition to government retirement programs, working women have historically been treated differently from men in private retirement plans as well. Often these plans either required women to pay more into a plan to get a pension equal to their male coworkers, or the plan paid women less if they paid in equally to men. In 1977, women's rights groups submitted an amicus brief in *Los Angeles Department of Water and Power v. Manhart*,[88] urging that a pension plan that required female employees to make larger monthly pension fund contributions than male employees constituted illegal sex discrimination. A large group of the department's female employees, joined by their union, the International Brotherhood of Electrical Workers, launched a class action suit on behalf of all women working or formerly employed at the department. Both parties in *Manhart* accepted the actuarial tables that established that women, as a class, live longer than men. Women's groups contended, though, that under Title VII, women must be treated as individuals. Therefore, they argued, women employees' larger contributions to the pension plan equaled employer discrimination. The Supreme Court agreed that Title VII prohibited this kind of sex-based distinction in assessment of pension contributions.

In the wake of this decision, women around the country began to challenge the legality of their pension plans.[89] But, although NOW and several other women's groups participated in some of these cases, they were also lobbying Congress to pass legislation that would prohibit the use of gender in establishing insurance rates or payout levels. NOW, NWPC, the Women's Legal Defense Fund, WEAL, BPW, and the American Association of University Women have directed considerable efforts toward passage of a sweeping package of reforms included in what is called the Women's Economic Equity Act. Pension reform, both in terms of equalizing benefits and expanding coverage for women workers, remains an important—though not a highly visible—goal of women's groups.

COMPARABLE WORTH

Often called the civil rights issue of the 1980s,[90] comparable worth is a theory for proving sex discrimination in wages that would allow employees to compare their wages to those of other workers performing different jobs with equivalent skills, responsibility, work conditions, and effort in order to establish Title VII pay violations. According to the theory, whole classes of jobs are undervalued because traditionally they have been segregated by sex. In order to break this cycle of sex segregation and underevaluations, which distorts compensation for the intrinsic worth of jobs, the theory holds, Title VII pay-discrimination cases must be permitted to be brought without being limited by the standard established in the Equal Pay Act, that jobs must be found to be substantially equal before differing pay rates can be considered discriminatory.

The doctrine of comparable worth is a high-priority issue on the agenda of many women's groups, as women full-time workers earn roughly 60 percent of what males earn, and that gap is often attributed to the fact that jobs held largely by women tend to have lower wages than jobs held largely by men.[91] But, according to a May 1987 report by the U.S. Chamber of Commerce, corporate women at the vice-presidential level and higher earn 42 percent less than their male counterparts.

The push to establish comparable worth as a recognized doctrine began long before the notion came up before the courts. Early in the 1970s, Irene Tinker and representatives of the Organization for Professional Women met with Barbara Newell, the recently appointed president of Wellesley College, and established the Center for Research on Women in Higher Education and the Professions to study, among other things, ways in which comparable worth could be introduced into mainstream legal and legislative thought. In late 1978, Winn Newman, counsel to the International Union of Electrical Workers and later counsel for AFSCME, helped to establish the subject of comparable worth as a conference topic at the Antioch School of Law. From that conference, the Committee on Pay Equity was begun, a national coalition of labor, women's, public interest, legal, government, and educational organizations. The Committee on Pay Equity (later renamed the National Committee on Pay Equity) was responsible for much of the early formulation of the doctrine of comparable worth and for organizing a widespread and sophisticated campaign to influence legislators in favor of the doctrine.

Courts have only very recently begun to decide the limits of Title VII suits alleging sex-based wage discrimination and whether the Title VII claims of sex discrimination in wages can be pursued under the comparable worth theory without restriction by the equal work standard of the Equal Pay Act. In 1981, the Supreme Court decided *County of Washington v. Gunther* on very narrow grounds.[92] The Court ruled that intentional sex-based wage discrimination is indeed the subject of Title VII challenges, not bound by the equal work standard of the Equal Pay Act. But the majority took pains to deny that it was endorsing "the controversial theory of 'comparable worth,' "[93] and the dissenters made the same point. All that the Court decided was that the "equal work" limitation of the Equal Pay Act had not been incorporated into Title VII.

Women's rights advocates generally regard this decision, despite its narrowly drawn ruling, as encouraging. They hope to be able to convince the courts of the weakness of employer's claim that paying lower wages for women-dominated jobs is simply a response to market forces. That, argue employers, fits into the "factor other than sex" defense for differentials in pay.

On the state level, a number of legislatures have moved to implement comparable worth pay programs for state employees, sometimes dubbing these "pay equity" programs in order to avoid the connotation of controversy surrounding comparable worth.[94] On the other hand, in a landmark post-*Gunther* decision, the Ninth Circuit held that the state of Washington lawfully paid employees in predominantly male job classifications more than it paid employees in predominantly female job classifications even though a state-commissioned study concluded that the male- and female-dominated classifications were comparable in worth.[95] According to the decision, the state "may" have discretion to enact a comparable worth plan, but "Title VII does not obligate it to eliminate an economic inequality which it did not create." The EEOC and state and federal courts have taken positions similar to that of the Ninth Circuit.[96] Comparable worth is therefore far from attaining the status of either constitutional right or legal right.

THE 1980s: "THE MOMMY TRACK"

One trend has been apparent since the beginning of the contemporary women's movement: Feminists have urged women to enter the work place on male terms, that is, to accept and compete on the same terms as men. The National Organization for Women, among others, promised that women could and would function exactly as men did in the office. That position has come under some fire by those who believe that feminists have ignored families and women who desire them and have consequently failed to focus attention on the problems of working mothers.

Some of these critics have claimed that the vast majority of women, if not all of them, want to have children. Those who also want to work should be able to combine a career and parenthood. But, given the fact that few fathers put in equal time, they argue, women should be provided with paid maternity leaves, subsidized child care, and flexible work schedules to allow for household chores. In other words, women need *more* than equal treatment.[97] Other commentators go even further, maintaining that the women's movement oversold the joys and benefits of careers, and underestimated the importance of motherhood.[98] Some go so far as to contend that younger women are beginning to realize that being a good parent cannot be combined with demanding work, that women still put their households and husbands first, and have no wish to enter the job market.[99] Friedan, in her 1981 book *The Second Stage*, called on feminists to go beyond "sexual politics" that portrayed men as the enemy. Rather than exhorting women to enter a man's world on a man's terms, she urged the women's movement to seek ways to balance women's new roles in the work place with their more traditional roles as mothers and wives.

Not surprisingly, Friedan's book and the similar sentiments expressed by critics of the radical feminism of the 1960s have become buzz words in the 1980s. Recently, one poll found that its participants rated "helping women balance work and family" as the number one goal of the women's movement today.[100] "In the second stage, we will not enter the work force as imitators of men. We will not deny the fact that we have children and, yes, think about them during the day. Nor will we deny that we, as society's caretakers, have responsibility for elderly parents. We bring those values with us."[101]

Indeed, one of the prevailing explanations for why the women's movement lost the ERA was that while most women told pollsters they were in favor of ERA, in fact many had misgivings that were passed on to legislators. Virtually all the anti-ERA mail came from housewives, whose concern was not so much the actual amendment as their feeling that they would lose any remaining social respect they had once had as homemakers.[102]

Most recently, Felice N. Schwartz, founder and president of Catalyst, a New York–based research organization that promotes women as successful business persons, proposed a new alternative for women who desire to combine career and motherhood. She also unleashed a barrage of criticism and controversy with her proposal, which appeared in the *Harvard Business Review*.[103] She asserts that there are two tracks for women in business: a fast one for those who are childless and a slower one for mothers who will pause or stay in middle management. In other words, Schwartz advocates that women should be treated differently because they cost more to employ in management, and business should distinguish those who will follow the fast track from those who will spend time with their families.

Schwartz claims that "the demographic realities and the training women have received means they don't have to try to be just like men."[104] That, in turn, means that women have a choice of options in the business world: "career primary" women are those who are geared to reach the top, and "career and family" women are those who accept lower pay and less responsibility in exchange for greater flexibility and more family time. Given this situation, Schwartz advises companies to provide flexible work schedules and to offer supports such as child care.

The question raised by critics of a "mommy track" is whether corporations will use Schwartz's advice as an excuse to penalize women and to push them into dead-end middle management jobs. Moreover, feminists charge that the "mommy track" approach firmly places child rearing in the woman's field of responsibility. "Now, pregnancy, childbirth, and nursing do qualify as biological processes. But slipping childrearing into the list, as if changing diapers and picking up socks were hormonally programmed activities, is an old masculinist trick. Child-raising is a *social* undertaking, which may involve nannies, aunts, grandparents, day-care workers, or, of course, *fathers*."[105]

While Schwartz herself denies that she believes in a "mommy track,"[106] there has undoubtedly been a change across the country: female managers and professionals with young families are leaving the "fast track" for some other kind of arrangement. Employers—concerned about losing top performers and attracting new talent—have adopted a number of measures designed to stem the tide of women who want to leave the work place so that they can spend more time with their children. For example, in accounting, law, and consulting, part-time options and slower tracks to partnerships are becoming options. There is also extended leave available in some companies—IBM, for instance, allows employees to take up to three years off, with benefits and the guarantee of a comparable job on return, as long as leave-takers are on call for part-time work during two of the three years. Other businesses have instituted options like flexible scheduling, flex time, job sharing, and telecommuting.

Women's leaders all agree that child care and job arrangements for working mothers will be at the top of the list of priorities for the women's movement in the 1990s. As greater numbers of women enter middle- and top-management jobs, and at the same time decide to have children, increasing emphasis will be placed on issues such as day care, flexible work situations, and participation by fathers in childrearing.

A question raised by some women's leaders is to what extent the solutions to work place–related problems lie in legislative reform.[107] Legislation on both parental leave and child care has appeared before Congress several times, but was never passed. Seven states have already adopted comprehensive parental leave laws, and ten others have passed maternity leave policy for parents and tax breaks for low-income families who require child care. But few of the dilemmas faced by middle-class working women lend themselves to the same kind of legislative approaches on such issues as pay equity and equal employment opportunity. Legislation cannot force businesses to hire and promote women with children into better positions. Legislation cannot make it easier for women to spend more time with their families once their maternity or parental leave is over. And legislation cannot persuade firms that part-time associates or those who take parental leave should be equally eligible for partnership or high-level status as full-time employees.

The women's movement has yet to develop solutions to the problems of working mothers. One suggestion is that the sheer force of numbers of women in the work place—more than half of new mothers remain in the job market[108]—will cause a change "from the bottom up." In the next section, we examine, among other things, just how far the women's movement has to go in terms of changing public attitudes.

WORK-FORCE PARTICIPATION AND PUBLIC PERCEPTIONS

From *Muller* to *Broderick,* courts and legislatures have grappled with the distinctions between sex-neutral language and language that preserves equal opportunity, between protecting women's rights in the work place and their rights to raise a family. A complex body of laws has developed around those issues, while women's movements have often been divided over how far such laws should be applied, or whether they should be applied at all.

What has not been in dispute is that large numbers of women are entering and remaining in the work force. After that fact is acknowledged, however, disputes arise as to whether there should be a "mommy track," whether there is a "glass ceiling" in the executive job market that women can overcome only if they work harder and sacrifice more than their male counterparts. In the following section, we look at some data that will help to resolve these disputes.

WOMEN'S PARTICIPATION IN THE WORK FORCE

Before the Civil Rights Act of 1964 was enacted, an employer could fashion his personnel policies on the basis of assumptions about the differences between men and women, whether or not the assumptions were valid.

It is now well recognized that employment decisions cannot be predicated on mere "stereotyped" impressions about the characteristics of males or females. Myths and purely habitual assumptions about a woman's inability to perform certain kinds of work are no longer acceptable reasons for refusing to employ qualified individuals, or for paying them less.

Justice John Paul Stevens[109]

It is now a firmly entrenched principle, both legislatively and judicially, that employers cannot discriminate on the basis of sex. Some statistics seem to indicate that employers have taken that principle to heart: currently, women constitute 40 percent of all managers and administrators, 39 percent of graduating lawyers, and 31 percent of graduating M.B.A.'s.[110] And during this century, the percentage of the labor force made up by women has increased from 18.1 percent to 45 percent (see Table 3.3).

Instead of only one in five women being in the labor force, as they were in 1900, more than half of the adult women in the United States were in the labor force by 1987. In addition, as shown in Table 3.4, the gap between the percentage of men and women who work full time year round has narrowed from 28.6 in 1950 to 17.6 in 1987.

Education seems to play a large part in women's participation in the work force. The more schooling a woman has, the more likely she is to be in the labor force and on a year-round, full-time basis. The figures in Table 3.5 show that women who do not complete high school are less likely to be working, a pattern that has remained unchanged since at least 1960. Over 30 percent of the women with some college education worked full time, and over 70 percent of the women with some college education were in the labor force in 1980, compared with less than 50 percent of high-school dropouts.

In contrast to the early part of this century, the most dramatic increase in female labor force participation has occurred among married women. While many early feminists tempered their arguments with reaffirmations that a woman's true place was in the home, the years following World War II have seen a jump from 25 percent of married women constituting the labor force in 1950, to 41.4 percent in 1970, to over 50 percent in 1980. By 1987, 56 percent of all married women in the United States were in the labor force (see Table 3.6).

Table 3.3
Women in the Labor Force

Year	Number (1,000)	Percentage of Total Labor Force	Percentage of All Women
1900	4,999	18.1	20.0
1910	8,076	21.2	23.4
1920	8,220	20.4	22.7
1930	10,396	21.9	23.6
1940	13,007	24.6	25.8
1950	18,389	29.6	33.9
1955	20,548	31.6	35.7
1960	23,240	33.4	37.7
1965	26,200	35.2	39.3
1970	31,543	38.1	43.3
1975	37,475	40.0	46.3
1980	45,487	42.5	51.5
1983	48,503	43.5	52.9
1984	49,709	43.8	53.2
1985	51,050	44.2	54.5
1986	52,413	44.5	54.7
1987	53,658	45.0	55.4
1988	54,742	44.9	56.6

Note: 1900–30 data are for employed workers aged 10 and over; 1940 data are for employed workers aged 14 and over; 1950–83 data are for employed civilian workers aged 16 and over and are based on annual averages derived from the Current Population Survey; 1900–40 data are based on the decennial census.

Sources: S. M. Bianchi and D. Spain, *American Women in Transition* (New York: Russell Sage Foundation, 1986), table 5.2, p. 141; U.S. Department of Labor, Bureau of Labor Statistics, *Women in the Labor Force: Some New Data Series*, report 575 (October 1979), table 1; *Handbook of Labor Statistics* (Washington, D.C.: U.S. Government Printing Office, 1983), tables 1 and 2; *Employment and Earnings*, vol. 31 (January 1984), table 1; and U.S. Bureau of the Census, *Historical Statistics of the United States* (Washington, D.C.: U.S. Government Printing Office, 1976), series D11–25 and D29–41.

Table 3.4
Workers Employed Full Time, Year Round (in percentages)

Year	Women	Men	Diff. (M-W)
1950	36.8	65.4	28.6
1955	37.9	67.5	29.6
1960	36.9	63.9	27.0
1965	38.8	67.3	28.5
1970	40.7	66.1	25.4
1975	41.4	63.8	22.4
1980	44.7	65.2	20.5
1983	47.7	64.2	16.5
1987	50.7	68.3	17.6

Source: S. M. Bianchi and D. Spain, *American Women in Transition* (New York: Russell Sage Foundation, 1986), table 5.6, p. 157; U.S. Department of Labor, Bureau of Labor Statistics (Washington, D.C.: U.S. Government Printing Office, 1983), table 45; and press release, June 26, 1984 (1983 data).

This trend does not change when one focuses on women with children: there has been a more than fivefold increase between 1948 and 1987 in the number of working women who have children under six years of age (see Table 3.7).

Today, more than one out of every two mothers of infants go to work—the fastest-growing sector of the paid labor force.[111] In addition, in 1987, 50.8 percent of new mothers remained in the job market, marking the first time a majority of women reported they were working or seeking employment within a year of giving birth.[112] It is estimated that by 1995, 75 percent of mothers of preschoolers will be employed outside the home.[113]

With so many working mothers, it is not surprising that child care has become one of the predominant concerns of the contemporary women's movement. In earlier times, working women could leave their children with relatives and family members who lived nearby. But with the growing mobility of the American family, many working mothers have been forced to choose other child care arrangements. Now most working mothers take their children to someone else's house and leave them in the care of a nonrelative. As of 1982, more women opted for another home (43.8 percent) than for either their own home (25.7 percent) or a group care center (18.8 percent), as shown in Table 3.8.

Given that women now make up more than half of the work force, women's groups charge employers with a more subtle form of discrimination than simply refusing to hire women. Rather, the problem is that women are promoted only up to a certain point; once they have reached that level, it is nearly impossible to climb further unless a woman is willing to sacrifice much of her personal

Table 3.5
Labor Force Participation of Women, by Educational Attainment
(in percentages)

Age and Yrs. of School	In Labor Force			Worked Preceding Year			Worked Full-Time, Year-round		
	1960	1970	1980	1960	1970	1980	1960	1970	1980
>/=25 yrs	35.3	40.8	48.4	41.0	46.9	52.5	14.9	17.3	22.3
Not High School Grad	30.8	33.3	30.8	36.1	38.5	33.5	12.0	13.1	12.4
High School, 4 years	39.1	46.7	53.6	45.1	52.9	57.9	19.5	21.9	26.6
College,									
1-3 yrs.	40.9	44.8	58.8	47.5	51.9	64.0	18.0	20.4	29.6
4 yrs.	47.7	50.0	62.3	53.9	58.4	68.0	15.8	15.4	27.0
>/=5 yrs.	66.6	66.0	72.7	71.8	73.0	77.9	19.7	21.7	26.5
25-34 yrs.	34.8	44.9	64.5	43.7	54.5	70.8	13.6	16.6	29.2
Not High School Grad	33.2	29.3	48.6	41.6	47.3	53.2	10.7	12.5	16.8
High School, 4 yrs.	34.3	44.4	61.7	42.9	54.0	68.0	15.7	18.2	28.9
College,									
1-3 yrs.	35.5	46.4	69.5	46.2	57.5	76.3	14.6	20.4	34.6
4 yrs.	41.6	53.4	74.8	52.5	66.2	81.3	14.6	14.9	35.0
>/=5 yrs	58.6	70.6	79.6	67.4	79.0	86.7	17.6	21.9	30.3

Source: S. M. Bianchi and D. Spain, *American Women In Transition* (New York: Russell Sage Foundation, 1986), table 4.9, p. 136; U.S. Bureau of the Census, 1960, 1970, and 1980 Census, 1/1,000, Public Use Microdata Sample.

life. Moreover, according to women's groups such as NOW and the Women's Legal Defense Fund, there is massive pay discrimination. In the next section, we look at the data surrounding these claims.

EMPLOYMENT AND PAY DISCRIMINATION

Much of the debate surrounding the "mommy track" discussion centers around the question of whether women are automatically limited in their career choices if they intend to have children. What this translates into is fewer career choices for women, as well as fewer opportunities for advancement. Looking at the data, it seems that, in fact, women do continue to work primarily in "support" positions—clerical, secretarial, and administrative work—that often allow time and energy to be directed to the home as well as the office.

The majority of women in the work force hold some type of clerical or administrative work. In 1985, for example, 80 percent of all "administrative

Table 3.6
Women in the Labor Force as Percentages of All Women,
by Marital Status

Year	Total	Single	Married	Widowed/ Divorced
1940	27.4	48.1	16.7	32.0
1944	35.0	58.6	25.6	35.7
1947	29.3	51.2	21.4	34.6
1950	31.4	50.5	24.8	36.0
1955	33.5	46.4	29.4	36.0
1956	34.2	46.4	30.2	36.9
1957	34.8	46.8	30.8	37.9
1958	35.0	45.4	31.4	37.9
1959	35.2	43.4	32.3	38.0
1960	34.8	44.1	31.7	37.1
1961	36.8	44.4	34.0	39.0
1962	35.7	41.7	33.7	36.6
1963	36.1	41.0	34.6	35.8
1964	36.5	40.9	34.4	36.1
1965	36.7	40.5	35.7	35.7
1966	37.3	40.8	35.4	36.4
1967	39.7	50.7	37.8	35.9
1968	40.7	51.3	38.3	35.8
1969	41.6	51.2	39.6	35.8
1970	42.6	53.0	41.4	36.2
1971	42.5	52.8	41.4	35.7
1972	43.7	55.0	42.2	37.2
1973	44.2	55.9	42.8	36.7
1974	45.3	57.4	43.8	37.8
1975	46.0	57.0	45.1	37.7
1976	46.8	59.2	45.8	37.3
1977	48.0	59.2	47.2	39.0
1978	49.2	60.7	48.1	39.9
1979	50.8	62.9	49.9	40.0
1980	51.1	61.5	50.7	41.0
1981	52.0	62.3	51.7	41.9
1982	52.1	62.2	51.8	42.1
1983	52.3	62.6	52.3	41.2
1984	53.2	63.1	53.3	42.1
1985	54.5	65.2	54.7	42.8
1986	54.7	65.3	55.0	43.1
1987	55.4	65.1	56.1	42.9
1988	55.9	65.2	56.8	43.4

Source: U.S. Bureau of Census, *Statistical Abstract of the United States, 1990* (Washington, D.C.: U.S. Government Printing Office), table 274, p. 161.

Table 3.7
Labor Force Participation of Married Women with Children
(in percentages)

Year	Total	Children under 18	Children 6-17 (none under 6)	Children under 6
1948	22.0	28.4	26.0	10.8
1949	22.5	28.7	27.3	11.0
1950	23.8	30.3	28.3	11.9
1951	25.2	31.0	30.3	14.0
1952	25.3	30.9	31.1	13.9
1953	26.3	31.2	32.2	15.5
1954	26.6	31.6	33.2	14.9
1955	27.7	32.7	34.7	16.2
1956	29.0	35.3	36.4	15.9
1957	29.6	35.6	36.6	17.0
1958	30.2	35.4	37.6	18.2
1959	30.9	35.2	39.8	18.7
1960*	30.5	34.7	39.0	18.6
1961	32.7	37.3	41.7	20.0
1962	32.7	36.1	41.8	21.3
1963	33.7	37.3	41.5	22.5
1964	34.4	37.8	43.0	22.7
1965	34.7	38.3	42.7	23.3
1966	35.4	38.4	43.7	24.2
1967	36.8	38.9	45.0	26.5
1968	38.3	40.1	46.9	27.6
1969	39.6	41.0	48.6	28.5
1970	40.8	42.2	49.2	30.3
1980	50.1	46.0	61.7	45.1
1982	51.2	46.2	63.2	48.7
1983	51.8	46.6	63.8	49.9
1984	52.8	47.2	65.4	51.8
1985	54.2	48.2	67.8	53.4
1986	54.6	48.2	68.4	53.8
1987	55.8	48.4	70.6	56.9

Note: Data indicate married women in the labor force as a percentage of married women in the population.

*First year for which figures include Alaska and Hawaii.

Sources: U.S. Bureau of the Census, *Historical Statistics, Colonial Times to 1970,* series D 63–84 (Washington, D.C.: U.S. Government Printing Office, 1975), table D 63–74, and *Statistical Abstracts of the United States, 1988,* table 624, p. 374.

Table 3.8
Labor Force Participation of Women, by Type of Child-Care Arrangement
(in percentages)

Type of Child Care Arrangement	Worked Full-Time			Worked Part-Time		
	1965	1977	1982	1965	1977	1982
Total	100.0	100.0	100.0	100.0	100.0	100.0
Care in Child's Home	47.2	28.6	25.7	47.0	42.7	39.3
By Father	10.3	10.6	10.3	22.9	23.1	20.3
By Other Relative	18.4	11.4	10.3	15.6	11.2	12.7
By Nonrelative	18.5	6.6	5.1	8.6	8.4	6.3
Care in Another Home	37.3	47.4	43.8	17.0	28.8	34.0
By Relative	17.6	20.8	19.7	9.1	13.2	15.6
By Nonrelative	19.6	26.6	24.1	7.9	15.6	18.4
Group Care Center	8.2	14.6	18.8	2.7	9.1	7.5
Child Cares for Self	0.3	0.3	----	0.9	0.5	----
Mother Cares for Child While Working	6.7	8.2	6.2	32.3	18.5	14.4
All Other Arrangements	0.4	0.8	0.3	----	0.4	0.1
DK/No Answer	----	----	5.3	----	----	4.7

Note: Data are for children under age 6 of ever-married women, 1965; for youngest two children under age 5 of ever-married women in 1977; for youngest child under age 5 of all women in 1982.

Sources: S. M. Bianchi and D. Spain, *American Women in Transition* (New York: Russell Sage Foundation, 1986), table 8.1, p. 227; Marjorie Lueck, Ann C. Orr, and Martin O'Connell, *Trends in Child Care Arrangements of Working Mothers*, Current Population Reports, series P-23, no. 117, U.S. Bureau of the Census (Washington, D.C.: U.S. Government Printing Office, 1982), table A; and Martin O'Connell and Carolyn C. Rogers, *Child Care Arrangements of Working Mothers: June 1982*, Current Population Report, series P-23, no. 129, U.S. Bureau of the Census (Washington, D.C.: U.S. Government Printing Office, 1982), table A.

support" types of positions were held by women: 53.4 percent in supervisory capacities, 98.4 percent as secretaries, and 95.6 percent as clerks (see Table 3.9).

But, there has been a shift in women's occupations from 1970 to 1980 (see Table 3.10), with the largest differences apparent in the managerial, administrative areas: in 1970, 18.5 percent of those jobs were held by women; in 1980, 30.5 percent were held by women.

Just as education is positively related to whether a woman enters the labor force, so is the type of job she holds connected to the years of schooling she has had (see Table 3.11). As of 1980, almost half of the female high-school

Table 3.9
Women in Major Occupational Groups, 1985

Major Occupational Group	Total Employed (1,000)	Percent Women
Executives, Managers	12,221	35.6
Professional Specialty	13,630	49.1
Technicians	3,255	47.2
Sales	12,667	48.1
Administrative Support, Including Clerical	17,309	80.2
Private Household	1,006	96.2
Protective Service	1,718	13.2
Other Service	11,718	64.4
Farming, Forestry, Fishing	3,470	15.9
Precision Production, Including Craft	13,340	8.4
Machine Operators	7,840	40.3
Transportation Workers	4,535	8.3
Handlers, Laborers	4,441	16.7

Source: U.S. Bureau of the Census, *Statistical Abstracts of the United States, 1985*, table 657.

graduates were employed in the "administrative support" field. By contrast, women with five years or more of college were far more likely to be employed as "professionals" and "executives" (59 and 16 percent).

Women are entering the work force in greater numbers today than during any other period in history. This increase has brought about shifts in child care arrangements, with the ensuing arguments over the question of how much a woman should or can sacrifice for her career. Complicating that debate is the issue of the "glass ceiling"—whether a woman is inherently barred from rising above a certain point on the career ladder. Our data indicate that, while women are occupying a higher percentage of the professional, technical, and managerial positions than they did two decades, or even one decade, ago, their professional progress is not comparable to their advancements in areas such as legislative change. Only about 2 percent of corporate officers at major public companies are women—and, perhaps more telling, about 60 percent of top female executives do not have children, while 95 percent of the men do.[114] To make matters worse, women's salaries show an even greater lack of progress.

Table 3.10
Women in Major Occupational Groups, 1970 and 1980 (in percentages)

Major Occupational Group	1970	1980	1970–1980 Net Growth
Executives, Managers	18.5	30.5	46.9
Professional Specialty	44.3	49.1	61.2
Technicians	34.4	43.8	57.5
Sales	41.3	48.7	75.4
Administrative Support, Including Clerical	73.2	77.1	89.2
Private Household	96.3	95.3	
Protective Service	6.6	11.8	23.2
Other Service	61.2	63.3	67.5
Farming, Forestry, Fishing	9.1	14.9	
Precision Production, Including Craft	7.3	7.8	10.2
Machine Operators	39.7	40.7	48.5
Transportation Workers	4.1	7.8	23.9
Handlers, Laborers	17.4	19.8	38.8
Total	38.0	42.5	57.5

Note: Percentage shown in column 3 is calculated in the following way: The number of women in the occupational group in 1970 is subtracted from the number in 1980 to form the numerator of the fraction. The denominator is the total civilian labor force in the occupational group in 1980 minus the total in 1970; this fraction is multiplied by 100. Percentage female is not calculated for occupational groups that declined in size between 1970 and 1980.

Source: U.S. Bureau of the Census, "Detailed Occupation of the Experienced Civilian Labor Force by Sex for the United States and Regions: 1980 and 1970," *Census of Population, 1980,* Supplementary Report, PC80-S1–15 (Washington, D.C.: U.S. Government Printing Office, 1984).

PAY EQUITY

When it comes to the issue of pay equity, the data in Table 3.12 show even more glaring discrepancies and may well qualify as the area in which women have made the fewest gains. From 1955 to 1987, the ratio of women's earnings to those of men, among full-time workers, has never been higher than .65.

When age and education are controlled for, the figures are only slightly better. The ratio improves from .64 to .75 for young, college-educated work-

Table 3.11

Distribution of Full-Time, Year-Round Workers Aged 25 and Over, 1980 (in percentages)

Major Occupational Group	High School 4 years		College 1 to 3 years		College 4 years		College 5 years or more	
	Women	Men	Women	Men	Women	Men	Women	Men
Total	100.0	100.0	100.0	100.0	100.0	100.0	100.0	100.0
Executives, Managers	10.4	10.8	15.1	20.5	20.7	34.3	16.2	26.7
Professional Specialty	3.3	3.1	14.7	8.3	38.0	21.4	59.5	51.3
Technicians	3.3	2.8	5.6	6.5	4.5	4.5	4.7	3.3
Sales	8.4	8.9	7.6	13.3	7.0	16.2	3.9	7.0
Administrative Support, Including Clerical	46.8	8.3	43.9	9.0	24.2	8.0	10.7	4.0
Private Household	0.3	0.0	0.2	0.0	0.3	0.0	0.0	0.0
Protective Service	0.4	3.0	0.5	4.4	0.4	2.1	0.4	1.1
Other Service	10.1	4.6	5.7	2.9	1.9	1.0	2.0	0.7
Farming, Forestry, Fishing	0.9	4.0	0.6	2.3	0.8	2.2	0.5	0.8
Precision Production, Including Craft	6.7	32.1	3.0	21.8	1.0	7.2	1.3	3.7
Machine Operators	7.3	15.0	2.2	7.6	0.8	2.0	0.6	0.9
Transportation Workers	0.2	3.1	0.1	1.1	0.1	0.5	0.0	0.2
Handlers, Laborers	1.9	4.3	0.8	2.3	0.3	0.6	0.2	0.3

Source: S. M. Bianchi and D. Spain, *American Women in Transition* (New York: Russell Sage Foundation, 1986), table 4.8, p. 134; U.S. Bureau of the Census, 1980 Census, 1/1000, Public Use Microdata Sample, table 657, pp. 384–85.

ers. Between 1967 and 1982, 25-to-34-year-old college-educated women earned between two-thirds and three-quarters of the salaries made by their male counterparts. Young women without a college education earned between 62 and 72 percent of men's salaries (see Table 3.13).

As shown in Table 3.14, when age is not taken into account, the ratio between the salaries of men and women who are in college or are college-graduated, .59 and .61, is even greater than that for high school graduates, .63.

On the other hand, college-educated women who are under 40 fare better in relation to male workers than do women who have had less education.

Taking race and gender into account, white males have historically been, and continue to be, the standard by which the other race/gender categories are ordered. In 1982, black males ranked second after white males, earning 75 percent of the white male annual median income, followed by white females,

Table 3.12
Ratios of Women's Earnings to Men's among Full-Time, Year-Round Workers

Year	Median Annual Earnings		
	Women	Men	Ratio (W/M)
1955	2,719	4,252	0.64
1956	2,827	4,466	0.63
1957	3,008	4,713	0.64
1958	3,012	4,927	0.63
1959	3,103	5,209	0.61
1960	3,257	5,368	0.61
1961	3,315	5,595	0.59
1962	3,412	5,754	0.59
1963	3,525	5,980	0.59
1964	3,669	6,203	0.59
1965	3,828	6,388	0.60
1966	3,946	6,856	0.58
1967	4,150	7,182	0.58
1968	4,457	7,664	0.58
1969	4,977	8,227	0.60
1970	5,323	8,966	0.59
1971	5,593	9,399	0.60
1972	5,903	10,202	0.58
1973	6,335	11,186	0.57
1974	6,772	11,835	0.57
1975	7,504	12,758	0.59
1976	8,099	13,455	0.60
1977	8,618	14,626	0.59
1978	9,350	15,730	0.59
1979	10,169	17,045	0.60
1980	11,197	18,612	0.60
1981	12,001	20,260	0.59
1982	13,014	21,077	0.62
1983	13,915	21,881	0.64
1984	15,006	23,816	0.63
1985	15,728	24,839	0.63
1986	16,336	25,676	0.64
1987	17,047	26,312	0.65

Note: Annual earnings collected in March CPS; weekly earnings collected on wage/salary workers in May CPS for years 1967 and 1969–78; beginning in the second half of 1979, figures represent average of quarterly averages (weekly earnings collected monthly).

Sources: Adapted from S. M. Bianchi and D. Spain, *American Women in Transition* (New York: Russell Sage Foundation, 1986), table 5.b, p. 157. Data from U.S. Bureau of the Census, *Money Income of Households, Families, and Persons in the United States*, Current Population Reports, series P-60, nos. 37, 39, 41, 43, 47, 51, 53, 60, 66, 75, 80, 85, 90, 97, 101, 105, 114, 118, 129, 132, 137, 142, and 146 (Washington, D.C.: U.S. Government Printing Office, 1960–85), data on work experience by total money earnings; U.S. Department of Labor, Bureau of Labor Statistics, *Labor Statistics Derived from the Current Population Survey: A Databook*, bulletin 2096 (September 1982), table C-19; U.S. Department of Labor, Bureau of Labor Statistics, *Perspectives on Working Women: A Databook*, bulletin 2080 (October 1980), table 52; U.S. Department of Labor, Bureau of Labor Statistics, *Handbook of Labor Statistics*, bulletin 2217 (June 1985), table 41.

Table 3.13
Ratios of Women's Earnings to Men's among Full-Time, Year-Round
Workers Aged 25–34

Year	All Workers Median Annual Income	College-Education Workers Median Annual Income
1955	0.66	
1956	0.68	
1957	0.67	
1958	0.63	
1959	0.64	
1960	0.65	
1961	0.64	
1962	0.63	
1963	0.62	
1964	0.62	
1965	0.62	
1966	0.60	
1967	0.62	0.67
1968	0.63	0.67
1969	0.62	0.65
1970	0.65	0.68
1971	0.65	0.68
1972	0.65	0.67
1973	0.63	0.68
1974	0.63	0.69
1975	0.66	0.71
1976	0.68	0.71
1977	0.68	0.71
1978	0.66	0.70
1979	0.66	0.71
1980	0.69	0.74
1981	0.70	0.73
1982	0.72	0.75

Source: Adapted from S. M. Bianchi and D. Spain, *American Women in Transition* (New York: Russell Sage Foundation, 1986), table 6.1, p. 170. Data from U.S. Bureau of the Census, *Money Income of Households, Families, and Persons in the United States*, Current Population Reports, series P-60, nos. 23, 27, 30, 33, 35, 37, 39, 41, 43, 51, 53, 60, 66, 75, 80, 85, 90, 97, 101, 105, 114, 118, 129, 132, 137, 142, and 146 (Washington, D.C.: U.S. Government Printing Office, 1955–84), data on educational attainment by total money income and earnings.

who made 62 percent, and black females, who made 57 percent of the white male standard, (see Table 3.15). This same trend of income ranking has persisted since the 1960s, when black males began out-earning white females.

While gender has always interacted with race in determining the nature of income differentials in U.S. society, the 1960s and 1970s began to bring a qualitative change in the nature of this interaction. Most significant, in the 1970s, the income gap between black and white women began to close, and race began to be a less salient factor among women than among men. In other words, the incomes of black women and white women became more similar

Table 3.14
Age-Earnings Profiles of Women and Men, 1982 (mean earnings)

Age	All Educational Levels			High School Graduate		
	Women	Men	Ratio	Women	Men	Ratio
Total 18 yrs. and Over	14,331	23,653	0.61	12,993	20,480	0.63
18-24 years	10,903	13,225	0.82	10,235	13,088	0.78
25-29 years	14,276	19,501	0.73	12,634	17,556	0.72
30-34 years	15,536	22,993	0.68	13,507	20,171	0.67
35-39 years	15,803	26,326	0.60	14,287	22,857	0.63
40-44 years	14,751	27,409	0.54	13,069	24,188	0.54
45-49 years	14,843	27,401	0.54	13,791	23,451	0.59
50-54 years	14,824	27,194	0.55	13,816	22,744	0.61
55-59 years	14,771	26,805	0.55	14,312	23,800	0.60
60-64 years	14,319	25,265	0.57	14,084	23,379	0.60
65 years +	12,653	20,712	0.61	12,812	19,123	0.67

Age	College Graduate			Graduate/Professional Training		
	Women	Men	Ratio	Women	Men	Ratio
Total 18 yrs. and Over	17,331	29,547	0.59	21,871	36,079	0.61
18-24 years	14,436	17,984	0.80	---	---	---
25-29 years	16,232	21,975	0.74	19,702	23,953	0.82
30-34 years	18,063	25,988	0.70	21,458	30,337	0.71
35-39 years	19,608	29,232	0.67	22,452	36,059	0.62
40-44 years	19,244	32,775	0.59	21,612	40,036	0.54
45-49 years	17,561	37,246	0.47	24,050	41,315	0.58
50-54 years	18,521	37,265	0.50	23,867	42,489	0.56
55-59 years	17,217	39,849	0.43	23,578	43,645	0.54
60-64 years	17,040	34,546	0.49	---	40,770	---
65 years +	---	28,281	---	---	34,095	---

Note: Data indicate mean earnings of full-time, year-round workers; "All Educational Levels" includes those with less than a high school education.

Source: S. M. Bianchi and D. Spain, *American Women in Transition* (New York: Russell Sage Foundation, 1986), table 6.3, p. 175. Data from U.S. Bureau of the Census, *Money Income of Households, Families and Persons in the United States, 1982*, Current Population Reports, series P-60, no. 142 (Washington, D.C.: U.S. Government Printing Office, 1984), table 48.

to one another than they were to those of black men, and more similar to one another than were the incomes of black men and white men. While the increased earnings of both black men and black women, coupled with the stagnation of white women's earnings compared with those of white males, has made race a less important factor than gender in comparing annual incomes, it has by no means rendered it unimportant. The importance of race is underscored by the declining trend from 1975 to 1982 of black women's gains compared with those of white women.[115]

Thus, the data show relatively minor changes in the income ratio between

Table 3.15
Ratios of Median Annual Income of Black and White Women and Men

Year	BF/WM	BF/BM	BF/WF	WF/WM	WF/BM	BM/WM
1955	0.34	0.35	0.51	0.65	1.07	0.61
1956	0.35	0.59	0.56	0.63	1.06	0.60
1957	0.37	0.61	0.58	0.64	1.04	0.61
1958	0.39	0.58	0.59	0.63	1.00	0.63
1959	0.41	0.67	0.64	0.61	1.05	0.58
1960	0.41	0.62	0.68	0.61	0.92	0.66
1961	0.39	0.61	0.66	0.59	0.93	0.63
1962	0.36	0.61	0.61	0.60	1.00	0.60
1963	0.37	0.57	0.62	0.59	0.92	0.64
1964	0.41	0.63	0.69	0.59	0.91	0.66
1965	0.39	0.63	0.68	0.58	0.92	0.63
1966	0.41	0.65	0.71	0.58	0.92	0.63
1967	0.43	0.65	0.75	0.57	0.86	0.67
1968	0.43	0.63	0.74	0.58	0.85	0.69
1969	0.47	0.70	0.82	0.58	0.85	0.68
1970	0.49	0.70	0.84	0.59	0.83	0.70
1971	0.52	0.74	0.90	0.58	0.82	0.71
1972	0.49	0.70	0.87	0.57	0.81	0.69
1973	0.49	0.69	0.87	0.56	0.80	0.70
1974	0.55	0.73	0.94	0.58	0.78	0.75
1975	0.57	0.75	0.98	0.58	0.76	0.77
1976	0.55	0.75	0.94	0.59	0.80	0.73
1977	0.55	0.77	0.95	0.58	0.80	0.72
1978	0.56	0.70	0.94	0.59	0.75	0.79
1979	0.55	0.73	0.93	0.59	0.78	0.75
1980	0.56	0.74	0.94	0.59	0.79	0.75
1981	0.55	0.74	0.92	0.60	0.80	0.74
1982	0.57	0.75	0.91	0.62	0.83	0.75
1983	0.56	0.80	0.90	0.62	0.88	0.71
1984	0.56	0.82	0.91	0.61	0.91	0.68
1985	0.57	0.83	0.91	0.62	0.91	0.68
1986	0.56	0.82	0.89	0.63	0.91	0.69
1987	0.59	0.83	0.93	0.63	0.90	0.71

Note: Data are for full-time, year-round workers; BF = black and other race females; WF = white females; BM = black and other race males; WM = white males.

Source: Adapted from S. M. Bianchi and D. Spain, *American Women in Transition* (New York: Russell Sage Foundation, 1986), table 6.5, p. 179. Data from U.S. Bureau of the Census, *Money Income of Households, Families, and Persons in the United States, 1982,* Current Population Reports, series P-60, no. 142 (Washington, D.C.: U.S. Government Printing Office, 1984), table 40.

men and women. While younger, college-educated women earn more than their older or less-educated sisters, taken as a whole, women still earn two-thirds of what men do. Moreover, unlike the steady gains shown by data regarding labor force participation and education, that ratio has not changed since 1955.

PUBLIC OPINION

With all their legislative successes, has the women's movement influenced public opinion in marshaling support for its goals and objectives concerning women in the labor force? The following data address questions about the way men and women have reacted to issues such as jobs, incomes, career aspirations, children, women's status within the family, and support of the equal rights amendment.

Working Women, Equal Pay, and Employment Discrimination

During the depression years of 1936 and 1938, only 25 percent or less of males and females favored married women working outside their homes. But in the postwar era and during the early period of the women's liberation movement, there was a jump in both men's and women's approval. As the women's movement gained momentum, support for married women who worked increased so that by the mid–1970s a majority of both men and women indicated approval (see Table 3.16). Indeed, from 1977 on there have been years in which men's support for married women working outside their homes has been greater than that of women.

We see in Table 3.17 that as far back as 1942, there has been widespread support for equal pay among men and women and since 1962, the differences between men's and women's views have almost disappeared despite the continuing differences, in fact, between men's and women's salaries.

When asked in general about perceptions of employment discrimination, we see that in 1987, a higher percentage of women perceived discrimination than did in 1975. Among men, the trend was weaker and reversed: 50 percent felt that women were discriminated against in 1975; in 1987, only 46 percent believed women did not have equal job opportunities (see Table 3.18).

In summary, the data show that there is public approval of working women and support for pay parity. Growing numbers of women, however, have viewed themselves as not having the same job opportunities as men. That has been reflected in the contemporary women's movement, which has pursued both legislative and social remedies for employment discrimination. As mentioned above, however, the late 1980s have introduced a new element: an apparent incompatibility between motherhood and working at the highest professional levels. We look at data concerning public opinion about that dilemma.

Table 3.16
Percentages of Women and Men Approving of Married Women Working Outside the Home

Year	Women	Men
1936	18	12
1938	25	19
1946	42	34
1967	47	40
1972	66	62
1974	71	65
1975	71	69
1977	64	67
1978	74	71
1982	75	73
1983	75	75
1985	84	85
1986	76	78

Sources: The Roper Organization for *Fortune* as cited in Hazel Erskine, "The Polls: Women's Role," *Public Opinion Quarterly*, 1977, p. 35 (for 1936 and 1946); The Gallup Organization (for 1938, and 1972–86; The Roper Organization for *Saturday Evening Post*, 1977 (for 1967).

Table 3.17
Percentages of Women and Men Approving of the Same Salary to Women and Men Doing the Same Work

Year	Women	Men and Women	Men
1942	85		71
1945		76	
1954		87	
1962	92		88
1973	96		94
1977		94	

Sources: Surveys by American Institute of Public Opinion (Gallup), 1942 and 1962; Daniel Starch and Staff, Inc., 1973; NBC News, Nov. 29–30, 1977, as cited in *Public Opinion*, Jan./Feb. 1979, p. 36; and 1945 and 1954 Gallup Poll, as cited in Erskine, "The Polls," 1977, p. 287.

Women Executives: The "Mommy Track"

Although only a small minority of top executives are women, in 1987, 46 percent of women and 50 percent of men polled believed that a woman has

Table 3.18
Percentages of Women and Men Believing That Women Have Equal Job Opportunities with Men

	Women		Men	
Year	Yes	No	Yes	No
1975	49	46	46	50
1982	41	54	46	50
1987	35	56	48	46

Source: The Gallup Organization, Princeton, N.J., 1975–87.

Table 3.19
Percentages of Women and Men Believing Women Have as Good a Chance as Men to Become Executives

	Women			Men		
	Yes	No	No Opinion	Yes	No	No Opinion
1970	39	54	7	39	56	5
1975	37	59	4	43	54	3
1982	40	56	4	45	49	6
1987	46	50	4	50	42	8

Source: The Gallup Organization, Princeton, N.J., 1987.

the same chance as a man to become a corporate executive (see Table 3.19).

Polls restricted to *working women* show them to be more optimistic than their male colleagues about their chances for promotion and advancement (see Table 3.20).

But note that a smaller percentage of both men and working women agreed that women had an equal chance of becoming an executive than agreed in the areas of salary, responsibility, and promotion. Referring back to the poll that included working and nonworking women, a higher percentage of women as a whole believed that women had as good a chance as men to become executives. It is noteworthy, though, that working women seemed to be more cautious about expressing their opinions, given the higher percentage who responded "don't know."

The pessimism evident in the answers given by women regarding their chances of working their way up to executive positions may be related to their views on whether women *should* be in such positions, given their other tra-

Table 3.20

Percentages of Women and Men Believing Women Stand an Equal Chance with Male Coworkers

	Working Women			Men		
	Equal Chance	Not Equal	Don't Know	Equal Chance	Not Equal	Don't Know
	Percent believe women stand an equal chance with men they work with					
Salary						
1970	54	33	13	45	49	6
1980	55	32	13	54	40	6
1985	57	33	10	48	46	6
Responsibility						
1970	67	21	12	56	39	5
1980	68	20	12	62	32	6
1985	73	18	9	61	33	6
Promotion						
1970	51	32	17	43	50	7
1980	52	33	15	49	42	9
1985	53	35	12	45	49	7
Becoming Executive						
1970	33	46	21	32	58	10
1980	34	47	20	42	48	10
1985	38	45	17	37	54	9

Source: For 1970, Lou Harris; for 1979 and 1985, the Roper Organization for Virginia Slims: 1979, as cited in *Public Opinion*, Aug./Sept. 1981, p. 32; 1985, as cited in Shirley Wilkins and Thomas A. W. Miller, "Working Women: How It's Working Out," *Public Opinion*, Oct./ Nov. 1985, p. 46.

ditional responsibilities such as family and children. Women who work outside the home predictably feel differently about this than do housewives. In 1984, about twice as many of the former believed they should have an equal role with men. But over a twelve-year span, more than half of the women employed outside their home and at least 70 percent of the women who were housewives did not support full equality with men in the running of business, industry, and governmental affairs (see Table 3.21).

Again, this may tie in with the "mommy track" debate: because of the work involved in childrearing and housekeeping, both working women and housewives may agree that women cannot, or should not, be subject to the additional stress of the work place.

Table 3.21
Women's Positions on Egalitarian versus Traditional Roles (in percentages)

	(Egalitarian=1;		Traditional=7)				
Categories of Women	1972	1974	1976	1978	1980	1982	1984
Employed							
1. Egalitarian	38	40	37	49	40	47	43
2., 3.	16	19	26	19	29	23	26
4. Neutral	25	21	19	16	16	17	20
5., 6.	9	12	12	9	9	9	9
7. Traditional	13	8	6	7	5	5	3
Housewives							
1. Egalitarian	25	21	24	26	27	29	22
2., 3.	14	19	13	15	27	18	16
4. Neutral	21	23	25	24	17	19	30
5., 6.	11	17	16	17	18	14	18
7. Traditional	29	20	23	18	12	19	14

Source: University of Michigan election surveys, as cited in Harmon Aiegler and Keith Pole, "Political Woman: Gender Indifference," *Public Opinion*, Aug./Sept. 1985, p. 55.

Another factor in the different responses by working women and housewives could be the level of professional achievement reached by the various poll respondents. Predictably, education plays an important role in influencing women's responses. In 1984, 63 percent of the women who were employed outside their homes and who graduated from college placed themselves in the fully egalitarian position, as opposed to 33 percent of the working women who were high school graduates. Among the housewives, 33 percent of the college graduates favored equality compared with 19 percent of the high school graduates.[116] This points to another important problem that will have to be addressed by the women's movement in the coming decade: educating both housewives and women who work in blue-collar jobs, service industries, and other nonprofessional jobs that it is in their interests, as well as in the interests of their professional sisters, to fight for equality. Moreover, these women must be convinced that working women *are* able to be a success both in raising a family and in the work place.

The data show that for over a decade, most women have expressed a desire for the whole package—marriage, children, and a career. In 1974, 38 percent and in 1985, only 26 percent opted for the traditional role of a stay-at-home wife and mother (see Table 3.22).

Especially young women (18 to 29 years) and college graduates in 1985

Table 3.22
Women's Choices for Most Satisfying Life

Choices	1974	1985
	(Percent)	
Combining marriage, career, children	52	63
Marriage, children, no career	38	26
Career, marriage, no children	4	4
Career, no marriage, no children	2	3
Marriage, no career, no children	1	1
Don't know	3	2

Source: The Roper Organization for Virginia Slims, as cited in Shirley Wilkins and Thomas A. W. Miller, "Working Women: How It's Working Out," *Public Opinion,* Oct./Nov. 1985, p. 45.

wanted the whole package. In both categories, 70 percent chose to combine marriage, children, and careers. Clearly, women do not want careers instead of marriage or in place of childless marriages. And, in fact, mothers of newborns are actually less likely to be back at work than they were earlier—50.8 percent of women with children under one year old were in the labor force in 1988, compared with 51.9 percent a year earlier.[117] It is this determination to spend time with their children that has led large numbers of women to exert pressure in the work place for ways to accommodate their child-rearing responsibilities.

Thus, traditional values—family, children, marriage—remain a predominant force in American life and, more specifically, in the contemporary women's movement.

In conclusion, the good news is that there are growing convergences and shared perspectives on the part of men and women toward strengthening women's status in U.S. society. On none of the polled issues were there big differences in the opinions and preferences of women and men. Responses to items about women in the work force belie the image of women as victims of discrimination and arbitrary treatment. While not optimistic about their chances of becoming an executive, the majority of women believe that they have as good a chance as men to increase their salaries, enhance their responsibilities, and gain promotion (and men agree). In addition, men are as supportive of the issues for which the women's movement has struggled as are women.

The bad news for the women's movement is that much of this changes when it comes to women working in the higher echelons of corporate and professional power. The first hurdle is to overcome the often incompatible pressures imposed by the fast track and motherhood. This is at the top of the agenda for many current women's groups, as it already is for some corporations and many women executives.

In short, the women's movement has not radicalized the American woman (or man). Unless she is one of the fraction of women working as top-level executives, she is still prepared to put marriage and children ahead of career and to allow her husband's status to determine the family's position in society. Contemporary women's advocates have some firmly entrenched beliefs to overcome before they will make any headway in their professed struggle for equal opportunity in the work place.

NOTES

1. Elizabeth Ehrlich, "The Mommy Track," *Business Week*, March 20, 1989, p. 127.

2. Huey B. Long, "The Education of Girls and Women in Colonial America," *Journal of Research and Development in Education* 8, no. 4 (1975), pp. 80–81.

3. Benjamin Rush, "Thoughts upon Female Education," *New England Quarterly Magazine*, April-June 1802, p. 146. Rush made these comments in a speech to the Board of Visitors of the Young Ladies' Academy of Philadelphia, which claimed to be the first female academy chartered in the United States.

4. Judith Sargent Murray, *The Gleaner* 1 (Boston, 1798), pp. 70–71.

5. *Lady's Magazine* 2 (December 1792), p. 69.

6. See Linda K. Kerber, "Daughters of Columbia: Educating Women for the Republic, 1787–1805," in Jean E. Friedman and William G. Shade, eds., *Our American Sisters: Women in American Life and Thought* (Boston: Allyn and Bacon, 1976), pp. 176–92.

7. "Present Mode of Female Education Considered," *The Lady's Weekly Miscellany* 3, no. 7 (June 11, 1808), pp. 100–104.

8. Elizabeth Anthony Dexter, *Career Women of America, 1776–1840* (Boston: Houghton Mifflin, 1950), p. 6.

9. When Catherine Beecher appealed to Congress in the 1850s for appropriations for women's teacher training, she stressed that "women can afford to teach for one-half, or even less, the salary which men would ask, because the female teacher has only to sustain herself." Quoted in Nancy Woloch, *Women and the American Experience* (New York: Knopf, 1984), p. 129.

10. Ibid., pp. 246–47.

11. See Edward Clarke, *Sex in Education; or, a Fair Chance for the Girls*, reprint of 1873 edition (Salem, N.H.: Ayer, 1972).

12. See Joyce Anter, "After College, What? New Graduates and the Family Claim," *American Quarterly* 32 (Fall 1980), pp. 409–35; Patricia Palmieri, "Patterns of Achievement of Single Academic Women at Wellesley College, 1880–1920," *Frontiers* 5 (Spring 1980), pp. 63–67; Roberta Wein, "Women's Colleges and Domesticity, 1875–1918," *History of Education Quarterly* 14 (Spring 1974), pp. 31–47; and Adele Simmons, "Education and Ideology in Nineteenth-Century America: The Response of Educational Institutions to the Changing Role of Women," in Berenice Carroll, ed., *Liberating Women's History* (Urbana, Ill.: University of Illinois Press, 1976), pp. 115–26.

13. Quoted in Woloch, *Women and the American Experience*, p. 282.

14. Samuel Gregory, M.D., *Circular* (Boston: New England Female Medical College, 1853).

15. Emily Pope, M.D., "The Practice of Medicine by Women in the United States," paper read before the American Social Science Association, Boston, 1881.

16. W. T. Harris, "Why Many Women Should Study Law," *The Ohio Educational Monthly*, July 1901, p. 1.

17. Woloch, *Women and the American Experience*, p. 391.

18. See, for example, Dorothy Dunbar Bromley, "Feminist—New Style," *Harper's* 155 (Oct. 1927), pp. 552–60; Elizabeth Kemper Adams, *Women Professional Workers* (New York, 1921), as quoted in Woloch, *Women and the American Experience*, p. 394; Charlotte Perkins Gilman, "The New Generation of Women," *Current History* 18 (Aug. 1923), pp. 735–36.

19. Adams, *Women Professional Workers*, as quoted in Woloch, *Women and the American Experience*, p. 394.

20. *The Nation*, 1926–27, reprinted in Elaine Showalter, ed., *These Modern Women: Autobiographical Essays from the 1920's* (Old Westbury, N.Y.: Feminist Press, 1978), p. 68.

21. See Alice Beal Parsons, *Women's Dilemma* (1926; reprint, Salem, N.H.: Ayer, 1974).

22. See Lois Scharf, *To Work or to Wed: Female Employment, Feminism, and the Great Depression* (Westport, Conn.: Greenwood Press, 1980).

23. Marynia Farnham, "Women's Opportunities and Responsibilities," *Annals of the American Academy of Political and Social Science*, May 1947, p. 251.

24. Ferdinand Lundberg and Marynia Farnham, *Modern Woman: The Lost Sex* (1947; reprint, Philadelphia: West, 1977), p. 36.

25. Mary Ann Millsap, "Sex Equity in Education," in Irene Tinker, ed., *Women in Washington: Advocates for Public Policy* (Beverly Hills, Calif.: Sage, 1983), pp. 91–119.

26. Ibid., p. 91.

27. "NOW Demands," in Judith Papachristou, *Women Together: A History in Documents of the Women's Movement in the United States* (New York: Knopf, 1976), p. 126.

28. Ruth Delzell, *The Early History of Women Trade Unionists of America* (Chicago: National Women's Trade Union League of America, 1914), p. 2.

29. An example of working conditions can be found in the cotton mills of Pittsburgh, where employees worked from 5:00 A.M. until 7:15 P.M., getting off at 4:00 P.M. on Saturday. When these hours were increased by one hour each day without extra pay, the women workers rebelled. Ibid., pp. 4–8.

30. W. Elliot Brownlee and Mary M. Brownlee, *Women in the American Economy: A Documentary History, 1675 to 1929* (New Haven, Conn.: Yale University Press, 1976), p. 16.

31. Eleanor Flexner, *Century of Struggle: The Woman's Rights Movement in the United States* (New York: Atheneum, 1974), p. 134.

32. Edward T. James, *Notable American Women, 1607–1950: A Biographical Dictionary*, vol. 2 (Cambridge, Mass.: Belknap Press, 1971). See also Israel Kugler, "The Trade Union Career of Susan B. Anthony," *Labor History* 2 (Winter 1961), pp. 90–100.

33. Ellen Carol DuBois, *Feminism and Suffrage: The Emergence of an Independent Women's Movement in America, 1848–1869* (Ithaca, N.Y.: Cornell University Press, 1978), pp. 112–15.

34. Originally, middle-class women from the settlement house movement and

women from the trade union movement combined to form the National Women's Trade Union League in 1903. They adopted a six-point platform: equal pay for equal work, full citizenship for women, the organization of all workers into trade unions, the eight-hour day, a minimum wage scale, and the principles embodied in the economic program of the American Federation of Labor. Although there were some early successes, after 1909 the League became increasingly devoted to securing protective legislation for women.

35. D. Kelly Weisberg, "Barred from the Bar: Women and Legal Education in the United States, 1870–1890," *Journal of Legal Education*, 1977, p. 485.

36. Rheta Childe Dorr, *Women's Demand for Humane Treatment of Women Workers in Shop and Factory* (New York: The Consumer's League of the City of New York, 1909), p. 6.

37. Florence Kelley, "Women in Trade Unions," *The Outlook*, New York, 1906, pp. 1–7.

38. Woloch, *Women and the American Experience*, p. 204.

39. Ibid., p. 241.

40. See Carol Groneman and Mary B. Norton, eds., *To Toil the Livelong Day: America's Women at Work, 1780–1980* (Ithaca, N.Y.: Cornell University Press, 1987); Susan H. Van Horn, *Women, Work, and Fertility, 1900–1987* (New York: New York University Press, 1987); Edward T. James, ed., *Papers of the Women's Trade Union League and Its Principal Leaders* (Woodbridge, Conn.: Research Publications, 1981).

41. 208 U.S. 421 (1908).

42. For example, in New York City, hundreds of women typesetters lost their jobs at several local newspapers in the aftermath of *Muller* because their employers claimed they would be in violation of the law if they forced women to work long hours on the night shift; these were, ironically, high-paying positions.

43. 261 U.S. 525 (1923).

44. Ibid.

45. Barbara Babcock, *Sex Discrimination and the Law* (Boston: Little Brown, 1975), p. 48–49.

46. *Adkins v. Children's Hospital*, at 525.

47. Scharf, *To Work and To Wed*, p. 110.

48. Carol Hymowitz and Michaele Weissman, *A History of Women in America* (New York: Bantam Books, 1978), p. 308.

49. Lois Scharf, *To Work and To Wed*, p. 10.

50. *West Coast Hotel v. Parrish*, 300 U.S. 379 (1937).

51. Philip S. Foner, *Women and the American Labor Market: From World War I to the Present* (New York: Free Press, 1980), p. 398.

52. For example, in 1937, five national women's organizations, led by the Bureau, produced reports on women's economic situation for the International Labor Organization. By 1948, the number of national women's civic, professional, and labor groups participating in bureau conferences had risen to over ninety. See Women's Bureau, *Women's Bureau Conference* (Washington, D.C., February 1948).

53. Carol Hymowitz and Michaele Weissman, *A History of Women in America* (New York: Bantam, 1984), p. 312.

54. Barbara J. Harris, *Beyond Her Sphere: Women and the Professions in American History* (Westport, Conn.: Greenwood Press, 1978), pp. 154–55.

55. Catherine East, "Newer Commissions," in Irene Tinker, ed., *Women in Washington: Advocates for Public Policy* (Beverly Hills, Calif.: Sage, 1983), p. 35.

56. Walter Fogel, *The Equal Pay Act: Implications for Comparable Worth* (New York: Praeger, 1984), p. 15.

57. For an example of the rhetoric and tactics used by the women's movement during the 1960s, see Robin Morgan, ed., *Sisterhood Is Powerful* (New York: Vintage Books, 1970).

58. Ibid., pp. 67–180.

59. Marguerite Rawalt, "The Equal Rights Amendment," in Tinker, ed., *Women in Washington*, p. 60.

60. A. Daniels, "Feminism and Unions," in Bernice Cummings and Victoria Schuck, eds., *Women Organizing: An Anthology* (Metuchen, N.J.: Scarecrow Press, 1979), pp. 133–34.

61. The inclusion of sex as a protected category was accomplished by amendment very late in Congress's consideration of Title VII. It has been suggested that sex was included in an effort to defeat the bill, it being felt that certain legislators would drop their support if it also covered sex discrimination. Martha Griffiths (D-Mich.) intended to sponsor the addition, but upon hearing of a Southern representative's decision to include sex in the bill, she deferred, believing that his sponsorship would bring one hundred additional votes. In any case, there is sparse legislative history on this section of Title VII—possibly indicating that Congress had no idea that sex discrimination would eventually take on the prominence that it did. See Robert B. Barnhouse and Donald F. Burke, *EEO—Preventive Action* (Baltimore: Maryland Institute for Continuing Professional Education of Lawyers, 1980).

62. In 1972, 142 of 177 unions had no women officials; from 1950 to 1970, there had been only two woman presidents of national unions.

63. Elaine Johansen, *Comparable Worth: The Myth and the Movement* (Boulder, Colo.: Westview Press, 1984), p. 41.

64. For example, in 1977, approximately 130,000 complaints had not been investigated. It was not uncommon for an aggrieved party to wait as long as three years before the EEOC attempted to resolve her suit. See Norma K. Raffel, "Federal Laws and Regulations Prohibiting Sex Discrimination," in Eloise C. Snyder, ed., *The Study of Women: Enlarging Perspectives of Social Reality* (New York: Harper and Row, 1979), p. 107.

65. *Pittsburgh Press Co. v. Pittsburgh Commission on Human Relations*, 413 U.S. 376 (1973). NOW became a party to the suit at the Supreme Court level, and amicus curiae briefs were also filed by the Women's Equity Action League, the Women's Law Fund, and the Women's Rights Project of the ACLU. Although the EEOC had announced regulations prohibiting male and female help-wanted ads, the Supreme Court upheld the agencies' construction of Title VII by a one-vote majority.

66. These groups included the Young Women's Christian Association, the American Association of University Women, the NCL, the ACLU, and the International Union of Electrical, Radio and Machinists Union.

67. 444 F.2d 1219 (9th Cir. 1971).

68. *Diaz v. Pan American Airlines*, 442 F.2d 385 (5th Cir. 1971), *cert. denied*, 404 U.S. 950 (1971).

69. *Sail'er Inn. v. Kirby*, 485 P.2d 529 (1971).

70. Robert Sherrill, "That Equal-Rights Amendment—What, Exactly, Does It Mean?" *New York Times Magazine*, Sept. 20, 1970, pp. 98–99.

71. 411 U.S. 677 (1973).

72. Leslie Friedman Goldstein, *The Constitutional Rights of Women* (Madison: University of Wisconsin Press, 1988), p. 127.

73. NOW included paid maternity leaves, laws to allow women to return to their jobs with no loss of seniority, and child care centers in its demands made at its first conference.

74. 414 U.S. 632 (1974).

75. 417 U.S. 484 (1974).

76. The law does the following: It prohibits termination of or refusal to hire or promote a woman solely because she is pregnant; bars mandatory leave for pregnant women; protects reinstatement rights of women on leave for pregnancy-related reasons; and requires employers to treat pregnancy and childbirth in the same way they treat other causes of disability under fringe benefit plans.

77. *Washington Post*, Jan. 14, 1987, p. A8.

78. Felice Schwartz, *Harvard Business Review*, January 1989, as quoted in Ellen Goodman, "Employing Women: A Price Worth Paying," *Washington Post*, January 24, 1989, p. A23.

79. *Bundy v. Jackson*, 561 F.2d 983 (D.C. Cir. 1977).

80. *Miller v. Bank of America*, 600 F.2d 211 (9th Cir. 1979).

81. Catherine A. MacKinnon, *Sexual Harassment of Working Women: A Case of Sex Discrimination* (New Haven, Conn.: Yale University Press, 1979).

82. Ibid., p. 8.

83. *Meritor Savings Bank v. United States*, 106 S.Ct. 2399, (1986) at 2404.

84. See, for example, *Starrett v. Wadley*, 876 F.2d 808 (10th Cir. 1989) (sexual harassment constitutes sex discrimination under the equal protection clause where public employees are involved); *Sparks v. Pilot Freight Carriers*, 830 F.2d 1554 (11th Cir. 1987) (an employer may be liable even where an agent acts outside of the scope of his agency, if the harassing employer has the authority to alter the plaintiff's employment conditions); *Lipsett v. University of Puerto Rico*, 664 F.2d 881 (1st Cir. 1988) (sexual harassment also violates Title IX of the Education Amendments); and *Hicks v. Gates Rubber Co.*, 883 F.2d 1406 (10th Cir. 1987) (when there is objectionable conduct aimed at a person because of her gender, even if not directed at sexual activity, Title VII is violated).

85. *Broderick v. Ruder*, 685 F. Supp. 1269 (D.D.C. 1988).

86. Grace Ganz Blumberg, "Federal Income Tax and Social Security Law," in Anne Foot Cahn, ed., *Women in the U.S. Labor Force* (New York: Praeger, 1979), pp. 237–48.

87. 420 U.S. 636 (1975).

88. 435 U.S. 702 (1978).

89. See, for example, *Arizona Governing Committee for Tax Deferred Annuity & Deferred Compensation Plans v. Norris*, 463 U.S. 1073 (1983); *Bazemore v. Friday*, 478 U.S. 385 (1986); and *Florida v. Long*, 101 L.Ed.2d 206 (1988).

90. See Goldstein, *Constitutional Rights of Women*, p. 537.

91. Ibid.

92. *Washington County v. Gunther*, 452 U.S. 161 (1981).

93. Ibid., at 166.

94. See Goldstein, *Constitutional Rights of Women*, p. 538.

95. *AFSCME v. State of Washington*, 770 F.2d 1401 (9th Cir. 1985).

96. See *American Nurses Association v. State of Illinois*, 783 F.2d 716 (1985); and *Spaulding v. University of Washington*, 740 F.2d 686 (9th Cir. 1984).

97. For an example of this argument, see Sylvia Ann Hewlett, *A Lesser Life: The Myth of Women's Liberation in America* (New York: Morrow, 1986).

98. See, for example, Betty Friedan, *The Second Stage* (New York: Summit Books, 1982); and Germaine Greer, *Sex and Destiny: The Politics of Human Fertility* (New York: Harper and Row, 1984).

99. See Hewlett, *A Lesser Life*; and Deborah Fallows, *A Mother's Work* (Boston: Houghton Mifflin, 1985).

100. A Time/CNN poll by Yankelovich Clancy Shulman, cited in Claudia Wallis, "Onward, Women!" *Time*, December 4, 1989, p. 86.

101. Ibid.

102. Jane Mansbridge, *Why We Lost the ERA* (Chicago: University of Chicago Press, 1986), pp. 102–13.

103. "Management Women and the New Facts of Life," *Harvard Business Review*, January-February 1989, pp. 65–76.

104. " 'Mommy Track' Author Answers Her Many Critics," *Washington Post*, March 19, 1989, p. A1.

105. Barbara Ehrenreich and Deirdre English, "Blowing the Whistle on the 'Mommy Track,' " *Ms.*, August 1989, p. 56.

106. " 'Mommy Track' Author Answers Her Many Critics," *Washington Post*.

107. Interview with Ellen Malcolm, Sept. 16, 1989.

108. "Working Mother Is Now Norm, Study Shows," *New York Times*, June 16, 1988, p. A19.

109. *Los Angeles Department of Water and Power v. Manhart*, 435 U.S. 702 (1978).

110. Ehrlich, "The Mommy Track," p. 134.

111. Kim Triedman, "A Mother's Dilemma," *Ms.*, August 1989, p. 62.

112. "Working Mother Is Now Norm, Study Shows," *New York Times*.

113. Kim Triedman, "A Mother's Dilemma."

114. Ehrlich, "The Mommy Track," p. 132.

115. See Augustin Kwasi Fosu, "Trends in Relative Earnings Gains by Black Women: Implications for the Future," *Review of Black Political Economy* 17, no. 1 (Summer 1988), pp. 31–45.

116. Harmon Aiegler and Keith Pole, "Political Woman: Gender in Difference," *Public Opinion*, Aug.-Sept. 1985, p. 55.

117. Census Bureau Report, 1988, as quoted in "Are Working Mothers a Trend That's Peaked?" *Wall Street Journal*, Nov. 2, 1988, p. B1.

Chapter 4

PERSONAL STATUS: MARRIAGE, FAMILY, DIVORCE

From colonial times onward, women's movements in the United States have fought, lobbied, and argued more vehemently for rights associated with marriage and the family than for almost any other causes they have embraced. And it is arguably in this area that they have been most successful in achieving their goals. Since the late 1960s, women's rights advocates have rallied around the banner of abortion rights. After several years of relative quiet in the 1970s, a new generation of activists have begun to organize a campaign in the wake of several blows dealt to certain privacy rights by the Supreme Court and some state legislatures. Indeed, some women's leaders of the 1960s now see the fight for abortion rights as an opportunity for the rebirth of the women's movement after several decades of complacence.[1]

Abortion rights, however, represent only the latest of a long series of struggles led by women's leaders who sought to raise the social, economic, and legal status of women to a footing more equal to that of men. Much of that effort took place in the courts, and legal cases are full of dramatic examples of the inequities that have existed for women in their personal lives. But even a superficial glance at women's history of the last two hundred years reveals that the women's movement has made profound changes in the way women and men view marriage, divorce, sexuality, children, and family.

In this chapter we look at women's movements in terms of the "personal" issues they have embraced: marriage, divorce, birth control, and custody, among others. In addition, we present data that demonstrate just how great an impact the changes achieved by women's movements have had on U.S. life, including the way Americans view marriage, children, divorce, and abortion.

HISTORY

One of the first battles undertaken by women's rights advocates was the blatant discrimination embodied in the property laws confronting married women in colonial times.[2] Under English common law, widely adopted by the first American colonies, a husband and wife were one person. Colonial jurists looked to the works by Sir William Gladstone (1723–80) concerning English laws for their definitions of a married woman's legal status. His is the classic expression of that theory:

By marriage, the husband and wife are one person in law, that is, the very being or legal existence of the woman is suspended during the marriage, or at least is incorporated and consolidated into that of the husband: under whose wing, protection, and *cover*, she performs everything; and is therefore called in our law-French a *feme-covert*. . . . Upon this principle, of a union of person in husband and wife, depend almost all of the legal rights, duties, and disabilities, that either of them acquire by the marriage.[3]

Once a woman married, she became a *"feme covert,"* that is, her personal property automatically came into her husband's possession, her real property came under his management, her wages belonged to him, and even her movement could be restricted by her husband. Prior to marriage, on the other hand, men and women held virtually equal positions before the law: women could own property, enter into contracts, bequeath their possessions, and buy and sell real property. A married woman, by contrast, could not create a binding contract, could not devise property unless she possessed it under a trust estate, and could only own property separate from that of her husband if he consented. She had a veto power over the sale of family real estate, but could not initiate any financial agreement.

While some American lawyers, such as Thomas Jefferson, criticized lawyers' subservience to Blackstone's theories,[4] they remained the standard reference for American jurists. But arrangements developed outside of the common law system enabling married women to own and control property. Equity courts, which in the colonial years governed trusts and marriage settlements, were able to mitigate some of the hardships imposed by the law on women. If a husband and wife had entered into a marriage settlement, a married woman could control her own estate, operate a business, sue and be sued, and could make her own decisions regarding her real property.

There were also vast differences among the colonies regarding the laws governing married women, and historians differ concerning the extent to which the seventeenth-century colonies adopted English common law.[5] For example, Connecticut and Massachusetts, unlike Maryland, Virginia, and South Carolina, departed from English law on conveyancing, dower, and marriage settlements in order to impede the creation of separate marital estates.[6] Strongly influenced by the rigid Puritan ethic that stressed a strong family unit as a vehicle for social control, these state legislatures increased men's power to control their wives' estates, eliminating or changing procedures designed to protect women from coercion. They also improved the ability of husbands to control their own property and discouraged the use of separate estates.

In the South, by contrast, courts tended to follow English rules on property. These included private examinations whereby a judge assured himself during a private discussion with a woman that she understood the terms of any deed she signed, and significant dower rights, entitling a woman to shares of personal as well as real property.[7] South Carolina enacted statutes for governing the activities of *feme-sole* traders and recognized the rights of women to manage businesses through the tacit consent of their spouses. Maryland also granted widows extensive dower privileges, refusing to follow the English law denying women dower in personal property. Indeed, unlike any other colony, Maryland allowed widows who owned slaves to devise them to their children.

After the Revolution, the diversity of American law remained, but commercial interests required new legal policies on land conveyances and dower estates.[8] The courts realized that many women found it difficult to support themselves from the proceeds of a business or of small sections of land. Furthermore, creditors' interests were damaged by the encumbrance of a life estate. Consequently, the state courts adapted English law to the new American social and economic conditions.[9]

While a husband still could exercise almost total control over his wife's personal estate[10] and a married woman's legal status remained that defined by English common law, the law of spousal unity no longer completely governed real estate. A *feme covert* could not retain ownership of her real property, and a husband could not by himself convey her interest in those lands (although he could manage and collect the profits for his own use).[11]

This growing commercial emphasis required passage of dower laws to promote easy land transfers and strong credit systems. The rights of widows often acted as encumbrances on land transfers. Therefore, while nine of the original states provided that a widow would receive one-third of the real estate her husband owned at any time during the marriage, the other four granted her only one-third of the lands that her husband held at the time of his death.[12] Thus, a wife might be deprived of her dower if the husband disposed of land during the marriage.

A further consideration in the passage of married women's property acts in the late 1830s and the 1840s was a gradual shift in the distribution of wealth among various family members. Women in some families were increasingly granted more important roles as custodians of property and assumed greater authority in family financial matters.[13] The reason for this was an exodus by children leaving their families to pursue work in more urban areas. Agriculture no longer offered all family members employment, particularly in New England.

Consequently, wives, rather than eldest sons, became more responsible for educating the children and maintaining the home, and when a husband died, for assuming the reins of control over an estate.

The expanding importance of commercial interests and the gradual changes in the early nineteenth-century family eventually led to the passage of married women's property acts during the middle of the nineteenth century. But the first married women's property acts had little to do with feminist efforts or even concern for female equality. Mississippi led the way of reform in 1839 when its legislature passed a law specifying that slaves owned by a wife at the time of marriage or later acquired by inheritance could no longer be considered a husband's "property" when paying his debts.[14] Mississippi's law, and others like it that were soon to follow, simply prevented a man's creditors from seizing his wife's property, but left him with management and control of that same property.

A bill similar to that of Mississippi's had been introduced in 1836 in Albany, New York, where a women's pressure group was formed. Under the leadership of Ernestine Rose, a twenty-six-year-old Polish woman who had immigrated to New York, six women petitioned and lobbied for an end to the most egregious inequities of *feme covert* status. By 1840, Rose was joined by other feminists such as Pauline Wright Davis and Elizabeth Cady Stanton. While Rose's efforts still garnered more ridicule and indifference than support, her work constitutes one of the earliest examples of concerted feminist action.[15] Three months after the New York legislature passed its married women's property act in 1848, women's leaders met in Seneca Falls, New York, to discuss women's legal and social plight in the United States. The Declaration of Sentiments issued by that convention condemned, among other things, the common law for its economic and domestic exploitation of women:

> He had made her, if married, in the eye of the law, civilly dead.
> He has taken from her all right in property, even to the wages she earns.
> In the covenant of marriage, she is compelled to promise obedience to her husband, he becoming, to all intents and purposes, her master—the law giving him power to deprive her of liberty, and to administer chastisement.
> He has framed the laws of divorce, as to what shall be the proper causes, and in case of separation, to whom the guardianship of the children shall be given, as to be wholly regardless of the happiness of women—the law, in all cases, going upon the false supposition of the supremacy of man, and giving all power into his hands.[16]

While the Seneca Falls rhetoric was perhaps more strident than was warranted by the actual conditions for women in the nineteenth century,[17] that meeting gave impetus to leaders such as Susan B. Anthony, Elizabeth Cady Stanton, and others who thereafter led lobbying campaigns supporting women's rights. Anthony gave lectures throughout New York during which she declared that a wife had a right to her wages and an equal role in appointing guardians for her children. In 1854, she led a lobbying effort to convince the New York

State legislature that public sentiment was in favor of allowing wives to keep the wages that they earned rather than placing them under the legal supervision of a husband. The bill was defeated, but the struggle continued. Finally, in 1860, the New York legislature passed the Married Women's Earning Act and gave wives equal authority with their husbands in guardianship matters.[18]

Women's leaders in other states led similar campaigns. For instance, Mary Upton Ferrin of Salem, Massachusetts, carried out a petition drive supporting property rights for wives, leading in 1854 to a Massachusetts married women's property act that gave wives title to their property and enabled them to enter into contracts and make wills.[19] In Ohio, feminists successfully lobbied for a broader married women's property act in 1861.[20] By the end of the Civil War, twenty-nine states had similar statutes on the books.

Historians, lawyers, feminists, and other scholars have analyzed married women's property acts in detail, examining both their origins and their ramifications for women. Elizabeth Cady Stanton, along with some contemporary historians, argues that the statutes were a response to feminist demands for women's equality.[21] Other scholars view the acts as a part of the nineteenth-century drive for codification of U.S. law and the attempt to regulate debtor-creditor relations.[22]

Viewing the state legislatures' enactments within the context of the rest of U.S. jurisprudence at the time, it seems more plausible that the married women's property acts were primarily a result of commercial factors, especially the rising wealth in urban centers and the desire of men to protect that wealth. The urge to break away from English common law, the drive for codification, the desire by men to retain control over their property (in cases where a wealthy father might bequeath or give property to his daughter before or after her marriage), and the influence of equity law (which had always done more than the common law to address inequities regarding women's rights) were the driving forces behind advances in women's rights prior to the Civil War.[23] It is difficult to asses the influence of the few women's rights activists during this time. While one can argue, as do some historians,[24] that the women's rights movement had some connection with the most liberal legislation in the North, it is virtually impossible to be more specific because of the scarcity of specific and consistent records and data from that period.

The legislation did not herald a new age for women, nor did it significantly open the way for economic independence. The bills passed by various state legislatures are marked more by their embodiment of the status quo than by a revolution in women's legal status. What these laws did provide was a springboard for women's leaders who were beginning to address the wider issues involved in female legal and economic equality.

MARRIAGE/DIVORCE/THE FAMILY

Similar to the establishment of property laws, most divorce provisions in colonial America can be traced to English law. While some colonial assemblies refused to grant any divorces, equity courts gave relief in cases of abuse and abandonment by ordering separate maintenances out of the husband's property. Technical divorces, however, were rare. When a couple did succeed in obtaining a divorce, it was either *a vinculo matrimonii*—absolute divorce with the right to remarry—or *a mensa et thoro*—separation from bed and board. The former was granted in very few cases, the latter, while rare, was more prevalent.

While there are significant differences among the colonies concerning divorce laws, colonial policy on separations was generally rooted in paternalism. Courts reasoned that because the law gave men so much power over women, they had an obligation to protect fragile and helpless wives when husbands abused that power. Under English law, if a wife left her husband because of ill treatment, he was obligated to provide maintenance. Six states—New Hampshire, Rhode Island, Connecticut, Pennsylvania, New Jersey, and North Carolina—went further, stipulating that any wife who had been deserted without provisions for her support was entitled to a divorce or legal separation.

In addition to divorces, many jurisdictions in colonial and early national America instituted the option of a binding separation agreement between husbands and wives. Under the rules of contract law, as it had been enforced in equity, couples could draw up private contracts to live apart and divide property in the form of postnuptial trusts. Until the late eighteenth century, most courts supported these agreements as long as they were made in the form of trusts, that is, as contracts made through third parties rather than directly between a husband and wife.

There were considerable differences in the divorce law practiced in the country's jurisdictions after the Revolution. In Massachusetts, for example, a 1786 law enabled courts to grant divorces on grounds that would have been unrecognized in England.[25] The Massachusetts General Court granted divorce to men for their wives' adultery, and to women for neglect or abuse in addition to adultery. Moreover, the statute mandated that property that women had brought to the marriage would be restored to them after divorce, and it provided procedures to discover husbands' dispositions of real and personal property brought to the marriage.[26] In Connecticut, there was no division of the types of divorce granted—all divorces were absolute and gave the right to remarry. Other colonies followed English divorce law, but their courts of chancery also granted legal separations on grounds of desertion and cruelty, and sometimes for sexual offenses such as adultery, homosexuality, or bigamy.

Generally, there was, however, a gradual liberalization of divorce laws between the end of the Revolution and the 1850s. While courts and legislatures continued to uphold the supposed sanctity of marriage and to disapprove of easy divorces, there was a shift in views concerning what type of behavior should be tolerated in a marriage.[27] Grounds such as cruelty and desertion, as well as adultery and criminal conviction, were increasingly accepted in divorce proceedings, especially in those initiated by women.

For example, Pennsylvania passed a divorce statute in 1785 that allowed men and women to choose which kind of divorce they wanted—*a vinculo matrimonii* or *a mensa et thoro*—for most grounds. Both were available for adultery, bigamy, desertion of four or more years, and knowledge of sexual incapacity before marriage.[28] In 1838, the Massachusetts legislature added desertion for a period of five years or more to grounds for divorce *a vinculo*, the first time in that state that a divorce decree could be obtained for action that did not carry a criminal sanction.[29] Virginia and Maryland did not enact statutes creating new divorce policies after the Revolutionary War, but their assemblies did begin to grant private bills of absolute divorce. Petitioners applied for such bills directly to the legislatures, who granted such pleas without the benefit of any statutory grounds. Not surprisingly, absolute divorces remained rare in these jurisdictions, although judges did continue a tradition of awarding separations with alimony for wives. By 1842 in Maryland and 1848 in Virginia, chancery courts were granted authority to award absolute divorces.[30]

THE WOMEN'S MOVEMENT AND DIVORCE REFORM

After the Seneca Falls convention, women began to lobby for other statutory changes in the area of marriage reform. In 1853 and 1854, woman's rights advocates led statewide petition drives to persuade the New York legislature to enact liberalized child custody reforms.[31] While there was no immediate reform, by 1860 the legislature did pass a law guaranteeing civil rights for married women, giving them control of their inheritances and wages and allowing them to make contracts and sue in their own names. Moreover, for the first time women were given joint custody of their children, and a widow was entitled to a third of her husband's estate, regardless of whether he left a will to the contrary.

There was, however, remarkably little activism regarding changes in the divorce laws. While Elizabeth Cady Stanton attempted to link the demand for marriage reform with the temperance movement, supporters of the latter feared their goals would be more difficult to achieve if they were allied with such "extreme" requests. Many women's leaders, such as Lucy Stone, believed divorce was too controversial to mix with other reforms. That reluctance, coupled with the war effort between 1861 and 1865, eased the pressure on legislators. Thus, for instance, in 1862 the New York legislature amended or repealed many of the laws that women had campaigned for, including the statute giving men and women joint guardianship of their children and guaranteeing widows control of their property and care of their minor children.

It was not until the second half of the twentieth century that any new reforms appeared in the area of marriage and divorce. Throughout the first half of the century, a married woman was primarily a wife, homemaker, and mother; her husband supported the family and was legally responsible for providing material necessities.

Even though the Married Women's Property Acts had removed most of the restrictions regarding property division in the event of divorce, in order for a divorce to be granted one of the parties had to demonstrate that the marital "bargain" between the dependent woman and the male provider had been violated in some fundamental way. Similar to the legal conventions of the eighteenth and nineteenth centuries, divorce laws were based on the concept of "fault," or moral wrongdoing. To establish grounds for a divorce, there had to be proof that one partner had seriously transgressed against the other—evidence of adultery, cruelty, or desertion by one party had to be provided to the court. If the husband was the one at fault, his financial responsibility endured in the form of alimony and child support. However, if the wife was found guilty of adultery, cruelty, or desertion, she was often denied alimony, and sometimes custody and property as well.

In 1970, California launched a "divorce revolution" when the state legislature abolished the fault requirement in divorce proceedings. Aiming to alleviate the financial and emotional hardships of traditional fault-based divorce proceedings, the no-fault law provided for a divorce upon an assertion that "irreconcilable differences have caused the irremediable breakdown of the marriage." Thus, there was no longer any need to demonstrate moral wrongdoing by either spouse. Rather, the main objective of the proceedings was the just division of marital assets and properties. And "justice" required, according to feminists, along with a new breed of lawyers specializing in family law, that the traditional roles of breadwinner/husband and homemaker/wife be abolished for purposes of determining what was to happen after a divorce. The courts consequently assumed, according to sociologist Lenore Weitzman, that the "new woman" would be able to support herself soon after divorce. The new standards for alimony called for judges to "take into account the spouse's ability to engage in gainful employment."[32]

Adopted in one form or another by almost every state in the nation, this legal innovation has not served, according to Weitzman, the economic and emotional interests of women and children, whom she calls the divorce revolution's victims. In a ten-year study, she found that the no-fault system actually operates in such a way as to punish women financially for time spent as mothers and homemakers and to reward men for leaving their wives and families. Weitzman's data indicate that ex-husbands have considerably more money to spend on themselves (42 percent more), while their former wives and dependent offspring suffer a devastating financial reversal—they are generally 73 percent poorer than they were during the marriage.

Weitzman points out major changes in the patterns of alimony, or "spousal supports" awards:[33] a shift from permanent awards to "transitional," or temporary, awards and a greater reliance on a wife's ability to support herself. The result of these changes is "that the vast majority of divorced women, roughly five out of six divorced, are not awarded alimony." Weitzman goes on to elaborate further results of no-fault divorce, assembling various and numerous data to prove the point. But the bottom line is this: the no-fault model would work in a world where men and women are equals in the marketplace, in which professional skills and career paths of marital partners are similar in most important respects.

In short, no-fault would conform to a certain feminist ideal, where both sexes are socially and economically equal. But the reality, as Weitzman demonstrates, does not correspond to that ideal.

In the early days of the women's movement, and in the rush to embrace equality in all its forms, some feminists thought alimony was a sexist concept that had no place in a society in which men and women were to be treated as equals. . . . But it soon became clear that alimony was a critical mechanism for realizing the goal of fairness in divorce. To a woman who had devoted twenty-five years of her life nurturing a family and who at age fifty had no job, no career, no pension, and no health insurance, alimony was not an insult. It was often her lifeline—her sole means for financial survival. . . . [M]ost of these women not only needed alimony, they had *earned* it.[34]

Indeed, argues Weitzman, the concept of equality and the sex-neutral language of no-fault legislation "are used by some lawyers and judges as a mandate for 'equal treatment' with a vengeance, a vengeance that can only be explained as a backlash reaction to women's demands for equality in the larger society."[35]

There have been criticisms of Weitzman's findings. Using data from Census Bureau surveys conducted since 1968, Herbert Jacob concludes that "the effects of no-fault were either modestly benign or neutral to the economic interests of divorcing women."[36] Jacob finds that the type of divorce granted has a negligible impact on the likelihood of receiving child support and on the incidence of alimony awards.[37] He criticizes Weitzman for failure to distinguish between the effects of no-fault and the new property division laws that accompanied it in California, a situation that held true only for California, Arkansas, Florida, Idaho, and Louisiana. In addition, only fourteen states followed California in making no-fault the exclusive procedure for obtaining divorce; the rest provided fault grounds as an option. Consequently, it is arguable whether one can generalize from Weitzman's study of California law and its consequences.

Weitzman's conclusion that the no-fault divorce system works to the detriment of women has been echoed in several other areas of concern to women, most notably workplace legislation, custody, and abortion rights. In legislation dealing with custody rights, courts have been awarding greater custody rights to fathers while placing lesser emphasis on the presumption that a child naturally belongs with his/her mother. There has been a revival of protective legislation in the work place during the last decade, including policies on maternity leave and "fetal protection" restrictions that exclude fertile women from jobs that could harm their fetuses. In the case of abortion rights, there has been a split among women's groups, some of whom argue that denying a woman the right to choose an abortion also deprives her of the right to pursue employment opportunities on an equal footing with men.[38] Many women's advocates prefer, on the other hand, to avoid this equal protection argument, fearing that the emphasis on equality will lead to the loss of protective legislation designed to improve working conditions for women. The strain running through all of the arguments similar to Weitzman's is that the concept of legal equality is a myth— the fact that women bear children gives them a permanent disadvantage, and protective legislation is necessary to remedy that situation.

Women's groups have worked to improve conditions for divorced women. The National Organization of Women launched a lobbying campaign in the late 1970s to persuade state legislators to pass new divorce laws that would improve the standard of living for a divorced woman and her children. In 1978, Delaware passed a bill that allowed divorced people to collect alimony until they reached financial independence—especially aimed at women who found themselves without the skills necessary to get a job outside the home once they were divorced. But, by and large, courts have retained tremendous discretion in awarding such payments.

Women's rights advocates have also urged courts and legislatures to recognize a homemaker's contribution in assessing the division of property for purposes of alimony awards. NOW has been particularly active in this drive since the mid-1970s, when it appeared that the organization needed to expand its organizational base and appeal to nonworking women who believed that the women's movement was directed only at those who worked outside the home.

The American Bar Association has been sensitive to the arguments made by NOW concerning a homemaker's contribution to a family's economy. Its Uniform Marriage and Divorce Act provides that in allocating property and awarding alimony, courts should consider "the contribution of a spouse as a homemaker of the family unit." Five states have adopted this provision— Arizona, Colorado, Illinois, Kentucky, and Montana.[39]

The call for total equality, which was so prevalent in the late 1960s and early 1970s and which was criticized by Weitzman, is also reflected in the child custody and child support laws and judicial decisions. Until well into this century, most courts held that only fathers were legally obligated to support their children, explaining that women were handicapped by the common law disability of coverture and lacked "pecuniary ability." At the same time, widespread preference was given to mothers when it came to awarding child custody. Using a standard that presumed that "the best interests of the child" were served when a mother was the custodian of young children, courts routinely granted custody of children to their mother.

But in the late 1970s, a majority of states began in some cases to hold fathers primarily liable and mothers secondarily liable for child support. Furthermore, the "best interests of the child" standard was applied in a sex-neutral fashion. "Persons similarly situated, whether male or female, must be accorded even-handed treatment by the law. Legislative classifications . . . may not be premised on unalterable sex characteristics that bear no necessary relationship to the individual's need, ability or life situation."[40] Some courts have gone so far as to hold that the presumption that young children naturally belong with their mothers is an unconstitutional gender-based classification in light of recent Supreme Court decisions.[41]

More recently still, courts have looked at joint or split custody. California has taken the most affirmative stand on this, asserting that joint legal and physical custody is the first preference in custody determinations and establishing a presumption that it is in the best interest of the child in cases where parents agree to such custody.[42]

The most recent battleground in the area of divorce law is the "palimony" issue[43]—whether a valid contract exists when a man and woman live for all intents and purposes as husband and wife, but without having first obtained any formal state or religious sanction to their marriage.

Common-law marriage, for which there are far more stringent legal criteria than for palimony, exists only in thirteen states and the District of Columbia. If a woman wants to prove that she is a common-law wife, she generally has to convince a judge that she and her partner intended to be married and have held themselves out publicly as husband and wife.

Since *Marvin v. Marvin* was filed eighteen years ago, a number of women, most often those who have lived with well-known entertainment figures, have filed palimony suits. They argue that the traditional "trade-off" that wives make at marriage (to give up work in order to be a homemaker) ought to be recognized outside a marriage as well—that "a deal is a deal, even when its terms are spelled out not on paper but in the give and take of daily life."[44] In a landmark decision, the California Supreme Court agreed. Declaring that an unmarried man and woman who live together cannot contract for sex, the court ruled that they can, however, contract for anything else that arises from their relationship, including the financially valuable service of homemaking. Moreover, said the court, the contract does not need to be written or even oral; one could prove that the way a man and woman lived implied a contract, one that entitled the woman to what, according to her, she was promised.[45]

While there have been significant changes in divorce laws during the last twenty years, women's groups have been noticeably absent from the legislative and judicial arenas when it comes to such issues. Perhaps this is because courts have always had such powerful discretion in divorce decrees, custody, alimony, and child support. While NOW has from time to time lobbied in favor of certain innovations in this area, judges have had the primary responsibility for ensuring that divorce laws have been fair and equitable. In contrast to this, the struggles over abortion rights have been carried out "in the street," as well as in legislatures and courtrooms. The next section looks at the role of women's movements in that fight.

ABORTION AND BIRTH CONTROL

There are few issues in the history of women's movements that have aroused such bitter and divisive controversy as abortion. While the political debate revolves around the role the government should play in a woman's decision to terminate her pregnancy, the battle between "prochoice" and "prolife" activists has embraced numerous other social changes and their impact on women's lives: the birth control pill, the urgent need for more child care centers, women's expanding presence in the work place, and the place of motherhood in a woman's life, among others. And the terms in which the arguments are carried out involve questions that go beyond feminism: the relations among religion, morality, and law; the social control of medical technology; the nature of life itself. It is not surprising, therefore that few areas in the history of feminist thought have aroused such deep feelings, such profound thought, and such widespread action.

Abortion was legal in the United States until the middle of the nineteenth century. Patterned after the British common law, U.S. laws did not recognize the existence of a fetus in criminal cases until "quickening"—the first sense of fetal movement felt by the mother, usually in the fourth or fifth month of pregnancy. During the nineteenth century, abortion began to be outlawed in nearly every state in the Union. All the states except Kentucky had an anti-abortion law by 1900. In Kentucky, the state courts outlawed the practice.[46]

Recent analyses suggest that the introduction of antiabortion laws was due, at least in part, to efforts by physicians to regain control from midwives and de facto physicians (known as "irregulars") who often had thriving medical practices. The "irregular" physicians, who were entering medical practice in increasing numbers throughout the first half of the nineteenth century, stood in sharp contrast to physicians who became concerned about losing their practices if women went to irregular doctors for abortions and continued to seek their advice for other medical needs.

Birth Control

In the absence of abortion rights, contraception, not surprisingly, gained increasing approval and acceptance. Middle-class women were able to obtain the pessary (or diaphragm) from private physicians, although doctors were legally required to look for "indications" and prescribe contraceptives only to "cure or prevent disease."

The birth control crusade gained its first real leader in the person of Margaret Sanger. In 1914, she published seven issues of a magazine called *Woman Rebel*, whose purpose was, among other things, to disseminate information about birth control as a tool in the class struggle. Deeply influenced by left-wing ideology and activism, Sanger devoted herself to spreading information about birth control to working-class women. A loose collection of left-wing supporters, including Emma Goldman, joined her in speaking publicly on birth control, but they never organized into a group. On the other hand, middle- and upper-class liberals did form the National Birth Control League (NBCL) in 1915, led by Mary Ware Dennet, a former NAWSA officer and peace activist.

The NBCL rejected radical tactics in favor of campaigning for the repeal of federal and state laws that categorized birth control as obscenity and prevented the free distribution of contraceptive information and devices.

Sanger traveled through the Midwest and the West, speaking to large audiences and encouraging local birth control leagues. In 1916, she opened the first U.S. birth control clinic in the Brownsville neighborhood of Brooklyn, a working-class area. She hoped to achieve publicity by forcing police to arrest her, and thereby to challenge state obscenity laws that prohibited distribution or sale of contraceptive information or devices. Succeeding on all counts, the New York Court of Appeals reviewed Sanger's case in 1919, and though they upheld her conviction, they also opened the way for a broader interpretation of the law. The court decreed that physicians could give help or advice to a married person to cure or prevent disease, meaning the venereal disease clause was extended to cover the provision of contraception to married women as long as it was provided by doctors and under limited conditions.

While Sanger succeeded in attracting a great deal of attention to the cause of contraception and in educating large numbers of women about birth control, it proved to be impossible to involve working-class women in birth control agitation, most of which was carried out by professional people.[47] As in the 1860s, when Elizabeth Cady Stanton and Susan B. Anthony attempted to organize a suffrage movement, reform activism was found largely in the middle and upper classes.

The war era affected the birth control movement more deeply perhaps than Sanger's crusade ever could. The U.S. government distributed condoms to U.S. troops to prevent spread of venereal disease. The government disseminated, without attribution, one of Sanger's articles on venereal disease, "What Every Girl Should Know." The government also targeted left-wing activity for prosecution, effectively dismantling that movement by the end of the war.

Thus, much of Sanger's support had eroded by the 1920s, and the birth control movement was for all intents and purposes rejected by both the working class and by the women's movement. Despite Sanger's attempts to reach women in the stockyards and factories, and despite a reported interest in birth control information by working-class women, the reform movement remained firmly controlled by professional people—as it had been since the 1860s.

The issue of contraception had never been directly addressed by organized feminism before the war. When Sanger had tried to arouse suffragist support, she was told to wait until the vote was won. But in 1927, the National Woman's Party refused to include a birth control plank on its agenda, and three years later the League of Women Voters decided not to study the issue. Carrie Chapman Catt characterized the attitude of women's leaders toward contraception politics when she wrote to Sanger in 1920:

In my judgment you claim too much as the result of one thing. Most reformers do that. Your reform is too narrow to appeal to me and too sordid. When the advocacy of contraception is combined with as strong a propaganda for continence (not to prevent contraception but in the interest of common decency), it will find a more willing sponsor. ... There will come some gains from the program you advocate—and some increase in immorality through safety. The gains will slightly overtop the losses, however, so I am no enemy of you and yours.[48]

Consequently, lacking feminist, working-class, and left-wing support, the birth control movement, including Sanger, directed itself toward the middle class. In 1921, Sanger founded the American Birth Control League (ABCL), which campaigned for the passage of "doctors only" bills, which would allow physicians to provide contraceptive information and devices to all women. The ABCL was a middle-class, highly professionalized reform organization, funded to a large extent by wealthy women. Direct action was replaced by educational campaigns targeted at doctors. By 1926, the ABCL reached a peak membership of 37,000 supporters, mainly from the North and the Midwest. The vast majority of its members were women volunteers who devoted their time to campaigns, education, and birth control clinics. However it was professional men who assumed the managerial, influential roles. Sanger went on lecture tours, speaking at women's clubs and social service groups, and she hired a physician to address medical societies. In short, the once radical birth control movement entered the mainstream in the 1920s. It was not until forty years later that the issue of contraception would reappear in the women's movement—and it was to dominate the national scene for decades to come.

Abortion

The civil rights and antiwar movements in the 1960s, together with the widespread introduction of the birth control pill in the United States, led a number of women's rights advocates to articulate the need to control reproductive capacity for true "liberation." It was a short step to link reproductive and sexual freedom to women's political, economic, and social power.

Prior to 1967, the abortion debate, which began in California, was conducted primarily by professional men and women, including doctors and lawyers, who were bound together by their professional interest in abortion rights. Men and women who supported abortion rights argued that laws prohibiting abortion created problems with both criminal and therapeutic abortions, and they argued that certain kinds of abortions, such as those undertaken to safeguard the health of the woman or to terminate pregnancy after rape or incest, deserved the protection of the law.[49]

There was also a flurry of organized women's activity on behalf of abortion rights, but it was far from instrumental in gaining passage of abortion rights legislation. The Society for Human Abortions (SHA) was established in the 1960s and began to use the language of rights in talking about women and abortion. Their strategy included leafleting, teach-ins, petitions, and civil disobedience. They referred women seeking abortions to illegal abortionists, primarily in Mexico, whom they had inspected for cleanliness and respectability. Gaining in militancy, some SHA members would not give a woman a referral until she had written a letter to her legislator urging the repeal of abortion laws.

SHA based its now-familiar arguments on the assertion that no claims regarding abortion superseded the claims of the pregnant woman, that anyone else's claims had no right to be formally represented in the decision-making process. Therefore, any abortion law at all, any infringement on a woman's ability to opt for an abortion, would be inherently unfair. While proponents of abortion reform declared that there were competing interests in the abortion decision and that some regulation was necessary, SHA members denied the legitimacy of those interests.

Gradually, abortion rights activists began to achieve some victories. In 1967, the Colorado legislature passed a law allowing abortion up to the sixteenth week of pregnancy if a doctor agreed that carrying to term would endanger the physical and emotional health of a woman, or if there was a suspicion of fetal abnormality. Abortion was also allowed for women whose pregnancies resulted from rape or incest. In California, the Therapeutic Abortion Act in 1968 allowed for abortion to be performed for reasons that went beyond simply protecting the physical life of the woman, but physicians would retain effective control over a woman's decision and a significant number of abortion requests would still be denied. Consequently, it was thought by legislators and health professionals that the number of abortions would not rise dramatically. What happened was that in the four years after passage of the new law in 1968, the number of abortions sought and performed in California increased by 2,000 percent; moreover, by late 1970, 99.2 percent of women who applied for an abortion were granted one.[50]

Hawaii was the next state to adopt an abortion statute; in 1970, the legislature legalized abortion, but imposed a ninety-day residency requirement. Later that year, New York liberalized its abortion law without imposing restrictions or a residency requirement. That state soon became a mecca for women seeking to end a pregnancy.

In 1973, the Supreme Court in effect extended this liberalized access to abortion to the rest of the country. In *Roe v. Wade*[51] the Court ruled that women have a constitutional right to an abortion for at least the first six months of pregnancy, invalidating state statutes criminalizing procurement or administration of abortion. But *Roe* was not an unqualified endorsement of a woman's right to have an abortion. While the Court decided that the fetus was not a "person" for constitutional purposes, it recognized only a limited right of a woman to "choose," with the aid of her doctor, to terminate her pregnancy free from unwarranted government interferences. The right that is protected is not that of *having* an abortion, but rather the right *to choose* one—a distinction that would become significant in subsequent cases dealing with government funding of abortion. Indeed, the Court found that the decision to terminate a pregnancy was "in all its aspects—inherently and primarily, a medical decision."

The *Roe* court also found that courts could intervene only when the state placed an "unwarranted" or "unjustified" burden on the abortion decision. This determination was to be made by weighing the state's interest in the regulation against the woman's choice, based on the length of her pregnancy. The state's interest in the "preservation or protection" of "potential human life" becomes compelling, according to *Roe*, once the fetus becomes "viable." Viability was found to occur at around twenty-eight weeks by the Court.

The Court also ruled that the state could interfere in an abortion choice in order to protect maternal health. Although this state interest does not become "compelling" until the end of the first trimester, after that time the Court stated that it would uphold regulations that are reasonably related to maternal health.

There immediately followed a barrage of criticism, from both prolife activists and legal scholars. The latter focused on Justice Blackmun's suggestion that at some point during a pregnancy, the woman's constitutional right to terminate becomes secondary to the rights of the fetus: "The pregnant woman cannot be isolated in her privacy. She carries an embryo and, later, a fetus. . . . [A]t some point in time . . . [t]he woman's privacy is no longer sole and any right of privacy she possesses must be measured accordingly."[52] A frequent criticism of the *Roe* decision is that this passage implies that at some point, as an embryo approaches maturity, it becomes progressively less true that the pregnant woman can exercise the right to abort it. At the point at which the fetus becomes a "viable" entity, recommends Blackmun, it is reasonable for the state to assert an interest in its well-being and withdraw a woman's right to choose abortion. Critics have pointed out, however, that as technology enables scientists to sustain a fetus's life outside the womb earlier and earlier, the point of viability is correspondingly closer to the time of conception. In short, with the rapidly developing technology, *Roe* would become obsolete, argued some constitutional scholars.

While *Roe* opened the door to a flood of criticism and comment from academic quarters, it was the women's movement, the antiabortion movement, and state legislatures that were to take center stage in the post-*Roe* history of abortion rights. With doctors exercising far less control over abortions, the procedure was no longer simply a medical issue, but rather a "women's issue," and with that shift, a new type of women's organization and new forms of political activism came into prominence.

There was a dramatic increase in the number of abortions performed after *Roe v. Wade* became law, provoking a crusade of fierce commitment—a "right-to-life" campaign that was often called the most powerful single-issue force in U.S. politics during the 1980s. Consisting of as many as ten million followers,[53] it has been a loosely knit coalition of religious and right-wing groups, as well as individuals who are committed to the belief that life begins at conception. In general, these prolife adherents feel that abortion contributes to a breakdown of traditional family values and that it is tantamount to genocide. Their goal has been a "Human Life" amendment to the constitution that would reverse *Roe* and guarantee the right to life of the unborn from the moment of fertilization.

The strategies of the prolife activists are carried out at every level of U.S. politics. Capitalizing on their association with religion and moral righteousness, prolife groups have drawn members from a wide variety of sources. For example, the 1975 Bishops' Pastoral Plan called for a sophisticated network of parish committees to carry out antiabortion work, organized along congressional district lines in order to mobilize political action. Activists were directed to work in electoral and party politics and to lobby at the federal and state levels. In the early 1980s, the antiabortion movement came under the aegis of the New Right Conservative groups, who allied themselves with organizations opposed to school busing, the Equal Rights Amendment, sex education in public schools, the ban on public school prayers, tough gun laws, and foreign aid to leftist regimes. One of the main strategists of this coalition was Paul Weyrich, who worked closely with Paul Browne, head of the Life Amendment Political Action Committee and his wife, Judie Browne, of the American Life Lobby.

These groups have been very successful. Two days after he was inaugurated, President Ronald Reagan met with a group of right-to-life advocates. In Congress, until recently, they successfully lobbied for laws like the Hyde Amendment, which prohibited the use of Medicaid funds for abortion for poor women who became pregnant because of rape or incest.[54] Many state legislatures have also prohibited the use of state monies for abortions. Only fourteen states (Alaska, California, Connecticut, Hawaii, Massachusetts, Michigan, New Jersey, New York, North Carolina, Oregon, Rhode Island, Vermont, Washington, and West Virginia) and the District of Columbia still fund abortions. Other legislation has barred municipal hospitals from providing abortion services.

Prolife groups have also raised millions of dollars to contribute to antiabortion political candidates. In the 1980 Senate elections, for example, there was a concerted mobilization effort against prochoice candidates. That campaign helped to defeat Birch Bayh (D-Ind.), George McGovern (D-S.D.), and Frank Church (D-Idaho), among others. The National Conservative Political Action Committee (NCPAC), along with the Life Amendment Political Action Committee and the Moral Majority, poured millions of dollars into the campaign against targeted incumbents. The ninety-eighth Congress saw antiabortion leadership in the Senate Appropriations, Budget, Finance, and Judiciary Committees.[55] The National Conservative Political Action Committee found in its postelection studies that abortion was the most effective single issue to draw Democrats to Republican candidates.[56]

The prolife movement even gained proponents in a surprising and unlikely camp: the feminist movement. The Feminists for Life (FFL) of America was formed in 1972 and claims two thousand members throughout the United

States, including Congresswoman Lindy Boggs of Louisiana. They have held countermarches during marches held by prochoice groups, and they offer an information hotline, coordinate a national newsletter, and organize projects such as radio and television ads aimed at reassuring women that ambivalent feelings about pregnancy are normal. Likening themselves to nineteenth-century women's rights activists who fought for laws that facilitated a woman's role as wife and mother, prolife feminists argue that "in making unfettered sexual satisfaction not just an ideal, but the highest ideal (surpassing even respect for life), mainstream feminists are adopting stereotypically male attitudes."

FFL's twin standards are "equal rights for all women" and "the right of every baby to be born," and its members hold that the two are not contradictory. They support an Inclusive Equal Rights Amendment, a combination of the ERA and the Human Life Amendment, that would forbid "a denial of rights to any person based on biological factors."[57]

Established feminist groups, such as NOW, have rejected the notion of prolife feminism. "A prolife feminist is a contradiction in terms. It's not possible to be a feminist and anti-abortion. We regard pro-life feminism as a public relations ploy by the anti-abortion movement," maintains Jennifer Brown, former head of the New York City chapter of NOW.[58] Antiabortion feminist groups have been banned from ERA rallies, rejected by consortiums of women's groups, and forbidden to meet in campus women's centers. FFL's tactics consist mainly of "educational" activities—counseling, writing articles—rather than lobbying legislators.

In short, then, *Roe* represents a watershed victory in the history of women's rights. But for many years that victory has appeared to be short-lived. Anti-abortion rights groups organized almost immediately after the 1973 Supreme Court decision. They raised money, formed grass-roots organizations, mounted lobbying campaigns, and gained increasing vocal support for their views. Meanwhile, prochoice activists were lulled into complacency, believing they had won both the battle for abortion rights and the war for public support of those rights. The next sections will look at how the women's movement has responded to the prolife campaign and how public opinion has reacted to these events.

Abortion Activism

With the right to choose to terminate a pregnancy firmly entrenched in U.S. law, a host of issues surrounding that right became rallying cries for the women's movement of the 1970s and 1980s. Who has the right to decide to have an abortion? Who, if anyone, should be notified of a woman's decision to terminate her pregnancy? Does a fetus have any rights? Moreover, within nine months of the *Roe* decision, 188 bills to restrict abortion were introduced in forty-one states. Legislatures turned into battlegrounds over laws requiring spousal or parental consent, hospitalization for second trimester abortions, mandatory waiting periods, and funding restrictions.

Women's groups were often militant in their responses to these questions. Feminist theory placed a premium on the interest, claims, and rights of women, emphasizing what motherhood and pregnancy mean for women who may also want careers and "upward mobility." Claims by other interested parties (e.g., fathers, doctors, health care professionals, the fetus) may have a place in a woman's deliberations regarding abortion, but it is the woman who should have the sole *legal* right to decide whether an abortion should be performed.[59]

Many feminists considered the abortion question from the perspective of an involuntarily pregnant woman living in a society that, according to feminist theory, "does not always value highly or support adequately the tasks of child bearing and child rearing."[60] Proponents of abortion rights often refer to "the power wielded by men over women in a patriarchal society [that] tends to see reproductive control as the central issue in the abortion controversy."[61]

Consequently, even with the dramatic liberalization of abortion laws, women's groups continued to organize against any legal restrictions on abortion as part of a perceived fight against the "segregated labor market and the cultural expectations about women's roles."[62] That is, activists wanted to demonstrate that childbearing was not the single most important thing in a woman's life—"and by asserting the right of women to control fertility, it vitiated the arguments of employers that only certain jobs were 'good for a woman.' "[63]

Women's groups, including the Women's Lobby, the National Women's Political Caucus, the American Association of University Women, and NOW began to work together in June 1977 as part of a prochoice coalition along with the National Abortion Rights Action League, Planned Parenthood, and the ACLU to influence legislators. A coalition of twenty-seven women's groups urged President Carter to reconsider his opposition to federal funding for abortion, but with no results. A group of twenty organizations formed the Abortion Information Exchange, and for several years met biweekly to plan strategy.

The first national proabortion rights campaign was the "Abortion Rights Action Week" in 1979 in which groups in over eighty cities participated with various activities such as street meetings, educational programs, and demonstrations. Various demonstrations and rallies were held by prochoice advocates throughout the 1980s.

Unlike the prolife movement, however, the majority of feminist groups have devoted their time and resources to other issues as well as abortion. The National Abortion Rights Action League (NARAL), the only single-issue woman's group to address the abortion issue, concentrated its efforts at the legislative level, combating the hundreds of bills introduced to restrict abortion rights. Their methods have included media campaigns, lobbying, and educational work, as well as challenging abortion laws in the courts. A self-survey in the late 1970s indicated that NARAL membership was primarily white, female, urban, disproportionately Jewish, and relatively young (25–44). A large number of members come from middle Atlantic states, and many are professionally educated and employed.[64]

The problem with the abortion rights movement was that it was barely visible at the local level, especially when compared with the largely local prolife drive.[65] Some groups, such as the Religious Coalition for Abortion Rights and the ACLU-RFP (Reproductive Freedom Project), hired field coordinators, but the focus of the abortion rights movement has been electoral politics.[66] In the late 1970s, NARAL adopted the electoral "hit lists" strategy used by anti-abortion forces and organized a political action committee (PAC) to support prochoice candidates for public office. NARAL claimed victory in two primary races in Massachusetts, when two prochoice candidates won congressional races there. In addition, feminist delegates to the Democratic national convention in 1980 ensured that the party platform would include a prochoice position, including federal abortion funding. In the 1980s, prochoice groups have expanded their use of PACs, but have also attempted to mobilize more support at the grassroots level.

The effort to enlist members and mobilize action at the local level was given an unprecedented push in 1989 with the most significant Supreme Court decision concerning abortion since *Roe v. Wade*—*Webster v. Reproductive Health Services*. In a 5–4 decision written by Chief Justice William Rehnquist, the Court upheld the constitutionality of a Missouri law that sharply restricted the availability of publicly funded abortion services and required doctors to test for the viability of a fetus at twenty weeks, or two-thirds of the way through the second trimester of pregnancy. That ruling gives individual states the opportunity to place restrictions on the ability to obtain an abortion, including the right to prohibit an abortion at any stage of pregnancy.

The *Webster* decision was uniformly regarded as eroding *Roe*, demonstrating that the Rehnquist court no longer endorses the *Roe* standard that a woman's right to choose to have an abortion outweighs any state interest in protecting a fetus until it can survive outside the womb. Moreover, a number of the justices seemed prepared to overturn *Roe* at some future date. Justice Antonin Scalia called for an explicit overruling of *Roe*, while Chief Justice Rehnquist and Justice Byron R. White, both of whom dissented in the *Roe* decision, are widely viewed as prepared to overrule the case. Justice Anthony Kennedy is also considered a likely vote to overrule *Roe*,[67] leaving Justice Sandra Day O'Connor as a possible swing vote.

The likelihood of an eventual Supreme Court decision overturning *Roe* propelled the proabortion rights forces—and the women's movement—to a flurry of activity in 1989 in an attempt to influence state legislatures not to restrict abortion rights. On April 9, 1989, the largest demonstration for women's rights in the history of the women's movement (between 300,000 and 600,000 participants) took place in Washington, D.C., emphasizing abortion rights over all other issues.[68] Overnight, abortion became an issue to be fought at the state level, with two gubernatorial races in 1989 and thirty-six states holding local and senatorial elections in 1990. Prochoice leaders hoped that the *Webster* ruling would convince voters previously lulled into lethargy to vote on the basis of a legislator's stand on abortion.[69]

NARAL assumed a leadership role in the fight against prolife forces. With fifty state grass-roots organizations already in place, NARAL leaders began to concentrate efforts on fund raising and lobbying. A coalition of abortion rights groups decided to protect those rights through legislation, establishing task forces to examine legislative options at the federal and state levels and to analyze political and legislative strategy to determine states on which to concentrate and political candidates to target for defeat because of their opposition to abortion.[70] A conscious decision was made by women's groups, such as the ACLU's Reproductive Freedom Project, not to concentrate the movement's efforts on federal or state supreme courts,[71] but rather to focus on the electoral process.[72]

There was some evidence that the efforts by the prochoice movement were indeed successful. In Florida, the state legislature rejected Republican Governor Bob Martinez's recommendations to restrict abortions in 1989. In the House of Representatives, members reversed a long-standing policy and voted to provide Medicaid funding for abortions in cases of rape and incest. In campaign politics, two gubernatorial candidates, both of whom came out in support of abortion rights, won against candidates who were seen to favor abortion restrictions.[73]

In the past, the abortion rights movement has been far less organized than have abortion adversaries. It remains to be seen whether abortion rights organizations, who after all have little experience in local elections, will be able to support and protect politicians who favor abortion rights. The *Webster* decision has undoubtedly given the women's movement an influx of cash donations and volunteers on the local level.[74] Whether these events will provide a sufficient impetus for the women's movement to revive itself after the complacency of the 1980s remains to be seen. In the next section, we look at the social and societal background against which the women's movement will be working and at public opinion data that will determine how hard the proabortion forces will have to fight in order to sway legislators.

POLL AND CENSUS DATA ON MARRIAGE, CHILDREN, DIVORCE, AND OTHER PERSONAL ISSUES

Given the women's movement's emphasis on careers and abortion rights, its antagonism toward men during the 1960s, and its current struggles to improve the availability of child care, it would not be surprising to find that the incidence of marriage has sharply dropped, while that of divorce has risen dramatically. But one might speculate that the movement has had a more profound impact than simply altering marriage patterns. Do women—and men—expect a different type of marriage today? How do women feel about having children at the expense of interrupting, or even ending, a career for which they had fought long and hard? And, even more controversial, there is the question of abortion, with all the emotional trappings and outrage it has generated on all sides. We report census and public opinion data in order to try to shed additional light on some of these questions.

The most recent population surveys show that the female population in the United States is close to 125 million (children and adults). Of those numbers, 91,483,000 women are fifteen years and older, compared with 83,824,000 men in the same age category. Thus, among the fifteen years and older population, there are some 7.5 million more women than men.

As would seem logical from the recent hype and attention given to women and careers, there has been a significant increase during the last three decades in the percentage of men and women who have never married—and a 250 percent increase in the number of people who have divorced (see Table 4.1). But it is not until the thirty-five to thirty-nine age category that one finds the percent of "never married" showing a decline from earlier decades. Thus, consistent with the women's movement's emphasis on developing careers, the data indicate that women and men have been delaying marriage rather than remaining unmarried for their entire lifetimes.

Once men and women do decide to get married, have there been any changes in the type of marriage they contemplate in the era of "women's liberation?" Do both sexes envisage major changes in the traditional division of labor between husbands and wives? Or has the women's movement made only superficial changes, and do women continue to assume major responsibilities for housekeeping and child care? Between 1974 and 1985, the following item was included four times on national opinion polls: "In today's society there are different lifestyles, some that are acceptable today that weren't in the past. Regardless of what you may have done or plan to do with your life, and thinking just of what would give you *personally* the most satisfying and interesting life, what do you think would be the best as a way of life?"

The responses (see Table 4.2) show that although the traditional division of labor between wives and husbands has lost some support, marriage has not gone out of style. Over 90 percent of men and women still believe it provides the most satisfying and interesting life. But in 1985 as opposed to 1974, a higher percentage of both women and men preferred a more egalitarian marriage over a traditional one in which women carry a greater burden of housekeeping and child rearing.

Further evidence that there have been some changes in both women's and men's ideas about the division of labor between marriage partners may be seen in responses to the items in Tables 4.3 and 4.4, which appeared on national polls three times between 1977 and 1986.

For both men and women, there was an increase in the percentage who did not believe that the traditional arrangement is better for everyone involved. Between 1977 and 1986, the percentages shifted, from 36 to 52 percent for

Table 4.1
Marital Status of Women and Men

Age and Marital Status	Women				Men			
	1950	1960	1970	1980	1950	1960	1970	1980
Total, 30–34 yrs.*	5,897	6,111	5,869	8,954	5,562	5,840	5,608	8,756
Percent:	100.0	100.0	100.0	100.0	100.0	100.0	100.0	100.0
Never married	9.3	6.9	7.4	10.6	13.2	11.9	10.7	14.9
Married, spouse present	82.2	83.9	80.6	72.2	80.5	81.6	81.6	71.8
Separated	2.5	2.9	3.5	4.0	1.7	1.7	1.9	2.8
Spouse absent	1.4	2.0	2.1	1.1	2.2	2.3	2.1	1.6
Widowed	1.6	1.2	1.5	0.9	0.4	0.3	0.3	0.2
Divorced	3.0	3.1	5.0	11.2	2.1	2.2	3.3	8.7
Total, 35–39 yrs.*	5,713	6,419	5,711	7,110	5,433	6,090	5,432	6,863
Percent:	100.0	100.0	100.0	100.0	100.0	100.0	100.0	100.0
Never married	8.4	6.1	5.9	6.7	10.1	8.8	8.2	8.7
Married, spouse present	81.3	83.6	81.2	75.0	82.9	84.4	84.0	78.3
Separated	2.7	2.7	3.4	4.0	1.9	1.7	1.9	2.7
Spouse absent	1.4	1.8	2.0	1.1	2.1	2.2	2.0	1.5
Widowed	2.7	2.2	2.2	1.6	0.7	0.5	0.5	0.3
Divorced	3.5	3.6	5.3	11.6	2.4	2.5	3.4	8.6
Total, 40–44 yrs.*	5125	5918	6150	5958	4970	5649	5830	5708
Percent:	100.0	100.0	100.0	100.0	100.0	100.0	100.0	100.0
Never married	8.3	6.1	5.4	5.3	9.0	7.3	7.5	6.7
Married, spouse present	78.9	81.6	80.3	75.9	83.1	85.4	84.1	80.6
Separated	1.6	2.6	3.2	3.9	1.9	1.7	1.9	2.7
Spouse absent	1.5	1.7	1.7	1.1	2.1	2.0	1.8	1.4
Widowed	5.0	4.0	3.7	2.8	1.2	0.8	0.8	0.5
Divorced	3.7	4.0	5.6	11.1	2.7	2.7	3.8	8.0
Total, 45–49 Yrs.*	4,553	5,554	6,255	5,679	4,444	5,375	5,809	5,346
Percent:	100.0	100.0	100.0	100.0	100.0	100.0	100.0	100.0
Never married	7.9	6.5	5.3	4.7	8.7	7.2	6.6	6.0
Married, spouse present	75.7	78.2	78.8	75.8	81.9	84.7	84.7	81.8
Separated	2.6	2.5	2.8	3.4	2.1	1.8	1.9	2.4
Spouse absent	1.6	1.7	1.6	1.0	2.2	1.9	1.7	1.4
Widowed	8.6	6.7	5.9	5.0	2.1	1.4	1.3	1.0
Divorced	3.6	4.3	5.5	10.1	2.9	3.0	3.8	7.5
Total, 50–54 yrs.*	4,134	4,932	5,741	6,096	4,040	4,765	5,329	5,611
Percent:	100.0	100.0	100.0	100.0	100.0	100.0	100.0	100.0
Never married	7.7	7.6	5.7	4.6	8.3	7.6	6.2	6.0
Married, spouse present	71.1	73.0	74.7	73.7	80.7	83.2	84.3	81.9
Separated	2.3	2.3	2.5	2.9	2.0	1.8	1.8	2.3
Spouse absent	1.7	1.8	1.5	1.0	2.3	2.0	1.7	1.3
Widowed	13.9	11.1	10.0	8.7	3.7	2.3	2.1	1.8
Divorced	3.3	4.2	5.5	9.0	3.0	3.1	3.9	6.8

*In thousands.

Source: S. M. Bianchi and D. Spain, *American Women in Transition* (New York: Russell Sage Foundation, 1986), table 1.a, pp. 41–43.

Table 4.2
Women's and Men's Lifestyle Preferences

	1974		1977*		1979		1985	
	Women	Men	Women	Men	Women	Men	Women	Men
				(Percent)				
Marriage where husband and wife share responsibilities. Both work and share housekeeping and child care responsibilities	46	44	50	46	52	49	57	50
Traditional marriage: husband assumes responsibility for providing for family and wife runs house and taking care of children.	50	48	41	47	42	42	37	43
Living with someone of opposite sex, but not married.	3	3			2	4	2	3
Remain single and living alone.	1	1			2	2	2	1
Remain single and live with others of the same sex.	—	—			—	—	—	—
Live in large family of people with similar interests and in which some are married and some are not.	—	4			--	--	--	--
No opinion / DK	—	4			1	2	1	0

*1977: Only the first two answer categories were included.

Sources: For 1977, CBS News/*New York Times*, Oct. 23–26, 1977, as cited in *Public Opinion*, Jan./Feb. 1979, p. 37; for 1974 and 1985, the Roper Organization for Virginia Slims, as cited in *Public Opinion*, Oct./Nov. 1985, p. 47; and Shirley Wilkins and Thomas A. W. Miller, "Working Women: How It's Working Out," *Public Opinion*, Oct./Nov. 1985, p. 47.

women and from 41 to 51 percent for men. Men seemed more likely than women to favor the traditional arrangement, whereby men are the "outside achievers" and women look after the home and family.

Both men and women were also less likely to agree with the traditional wife's role in 1986 than they were in 1977. But there have been no radical changes in the greater importance that the husband's role is expected to have in defining the family's status, as witness responses to the situations in Table 4.5.

The large majority of women and men believe that it is the wife who should quit her job and relocate with her husband if the husband is offered a more attractive position in another city. There is no quid pro quo on that issue. If

Table 4.3

Percentages of Women and Men Believing Men Should Be the Achievers and Women Should Be the Homemakers

	1977		1985		1986	
	Women	Men	Women	Men	Women	Men
			(Percent)			
Strongly agree	17	19	9	10	11	7
Agree	45	49	37	39	36	40
Disagree	28	27	35	40	37	42
Strongly disagree	8	4	17	8	15	9
No opinion / DK	2	1	2	3	1	2

Source: Charles H. Russell and I. Megaard, *The General Social Survey, 1972–1986: The State of the American People* (New York: Springer-Verlag, 1988).

Table 4.4

Percentages of Women and Men Believing It Is More Important for a Wife to Help Her Husband's Career Than to Have Her Own

	1977		1985		1986	
	Women	Men	Women	Men	Women	Men
			(Percent)			
Strongly agree	15	12	7	6	7	5
Agree	44	39	30	30	30	28
Disagree	31	40	41	49	44	50
Strongly Disagree	7	7	20	11	18	14
No opinion/DK	3	2	2	4	1	3
N	834	690	842	685	848	621

Source: National Opinion Research Center, General Social Survey, 1986.

it is the wife who is offered the better job, the majority of both women and men believe that she should turn it down and stay where she is so that her husband can continue working at his job.

While couples have begun to shed the conventional notions concerning the allocation of responsibilities in a marriage, they have clearly not rejected marriage in favor of other living arrangements. Those radical feminists in the 1960s who urged women to reject the "shackles" of the marriage bond created only a passing fad. In 1970 and 1985, men and women were asked to assess whether

Table 4.5
Opinions on Which Spouse in Childless Couple Should Move for a Better Job

	1980		1985	
	Women	Men	Women	Men
		(Percent)		
Husband should turn down the job	10	18	10	19
Wife should quit and relocate with husband	77	68	72	62
Husband should take new job and move/wife should keep her job and stay	4	4	6	5
No opinion/DK	9	10	12	14
N	3,007	1,004	3,000	1,000

If the wife is offered a very good job in another city?

	1980		1985	
	Women	Men	Women	Men
		(Percent)		
Wife should turn down the job	68	62	55	58
Husband should quit and relocate with wife	17	18	20	22
Wife should take new job and move/husband should keep his job and stay	4	5	8	6
No opinion/DK	11	15	17	14
N	3,007	1,004	3,000	1,000

Source: The Roper Organization, New York, N.Y., 1980–85.

the "institution of marriage" was stronger, weaker, or about the same as it was "ten years ago." As shown in the chart below, for each time period, a majority of men and women believed that the institution was weaker than it was ten years ago. But the percentages were significantly lower in 1985 than they were in 1970, when 71 percent of the men, compared with 59 percent in 1985, and 73 percent of the women, compared with 60 percent in 1985, believed marriage as an institution was weaker than it had been ten years earlier (see Table 4.6). These figures support the notion that the 1960s, a decade of social turmoil in which marriage and the family were targets of attack and derision, quickly gave way to a reemergence of more traditional beliefs.

In contrast to the relative stability of people's attitudes toward the institution

Table 4.6
Opinions on Strength of the Institution of Marriage Compared to Ten Years Earlier (in percentages)

	Women		Men	
	1970	1985	1970	1985
	(Percentage)			
Stronger	5	15	5	16
Weaker	73	60	71	59
Same	19	23	22	24
No opinion/DK	3	2	2	1

Source: Roper Organization of Virginia Slims, March 1985, as cited in *Public Opinion*, Dec./Jan. 1986, p. 25.

of marriage, there has been a dramatic shift in both attitude and behavior concerning the "ideal" number of children a family should have. This shift may be attributed not only to changes in women's roles and perception of their status in society, but also to beliefs about the danger of "overpopulation" and the success of a social movement espousing zero population growth.

The essence of the question regarding ideal family size, which has been phrased slightly differently over the last half century when it has appeared on national polls, is, What do you consider to be the ideal size of a family—a husband and wife and how many children? Between 1941 and 1959, women generally responded that they wanted at least four children. Men's responses varied more than those of women from year to year, but on none of the five polls up to and including 1959 did the level of their responses match those of the women who answered that they wanted four or more children.

As shown in Table 4.7, 1966 marked the emergence of the popularity of the smaller family, reflected in poll data. From 1973 up to 1986, men and women increasingly chose the same answers, with women shifting from their preference for at least four children to a preference for two children.

Women's preferences changed far more than those of men, eventually leading, from 1978 to 1986, to a higher percentage of women than of men who wanted two or fewer children. Men also changed their preferences in the direction of having fewer children from 1973 through 1985, though more women than men selected two children as the ideal family size.

As shown earlier in Table 4.1, the percentage of men and women who have been divorced has gone up over the past thirty years. The increase has been even greater for women than for men. But men's and women's attitudes about divorce have not differed greatly, nor have each gender's views changed much between 1970 and 1985. As shown in Table 4.8, in 1970 slightly more women than men found divorce unacceptable. After that men were more likely to view divorce as an unacceptable alternative.

Table 4.7
Opinions on Ideal Number of Children (in percentages)

	Women (18-39 years)			Men (18-39 years)		
Year	2	3	4 or more	2	3	4 or more
1941	18	20	52	35	30	26
1945	16	23	55	26	35	37
1953	24	26	48	34	32	33
1957	18	36	48	23	44	25
1959	13	21	51	21	33	35
*1966	13	26	41	23	28	29
1973	53	22	17	57	21	11
1974	45	22	20	48	22	17
1978	60	24	11	51	18	16
1980	54	20	15	51	22	16
1983	61	19	11	55	21	13
1985	63	18	10	53	25	11
**1986	67	14	12	61	20	10

*Includes all ages.

*Includes all ages, and figures cited for 2 children include 1 as well. The category is worded "1 or 2."

Sources: For 1941–59, the Gallup Organization, Princeton, N.J.; for 1973 and 1978–85, *Public Opinion*, Dec./Jan. 1986, p. 28.

Table 4.8
Opinions on Acceptability of Divorce

	Women				Men			
	'70	'74	'80	'85	'70	'74	'80	'85
				(Percent)				
Divorce is acceptable if marriage is not working out	52	60	62	57	54	59	58	54
It depends; mixed feelings	20	20	22	23	22	14	16	17
Divorce is unacceptable	26	16	16	19	23	24	25	28

Source: The Roper Organization, New York, N.Y., 1970–85.

Table 4.9
Opinions on Alimony

	Women				Men			
	'70	'74	'80	'85	'70	'74	'80	'85
				(Percent)				
Women should receive alimony	18	19	20	23	8	12	12	14
They should not	62	66	59	54	76	72	69	67
It depends	19	10	19	21	14	11	14	19
No opinion/DK	1	5	2	2	2	5	5	1

Source: The Roper Organization, New York, N.Y., 1970–85.

More women than men believe that women are entitled to alimony even "if a divorced woman can earn a reasonable income," but the majority of men and women do not agree with that premise (see Table 4.9).

Again, proponents of the women's movement might argue that this is a sign of the greater equality between men and women particularly in the work place. However, some women's rights advocates, especially those who espouse the ideas set forth in Lenore Weitzman's work, would maintain that this general belief obscures the fact that the majority of women are not in the same job-earning brackets as men and therefore suffer a disproportionate drop in their standard of living after divorce. Indeed, this debate points to one of the more serious divisions in the women's movement today—those who, on the one hand, believe that men and women should be subject to the same rules, the same treatment, and the same conditions as men, and those who, on the other hand, argue for some type of protective legislation that would take into account such factors as the lesser earning power of women in general and their greater child rearing and housekeeping responsibilities.

As of 1980, there were 80,389,000 households in the United States, of which 73.3 percent were family households, and of those, 60.1 percent involved married couples. Among the family households, 844,000 or 10.5 percent were headed by a woman, and of those, about 58 percent included children. Of the families with children, 46.5 percent of the mothers were divorced and 16.7 percent of the mothers had never married (see Table 4.10).

It is particularly interesting that there has been a significant increase in the number of female-headed households among women under 35 years of age, as opposed to those headed by older women. As of 1970, the increase in households headed by women with children is a function primarily of divorce rather than widowhood.

In summary, the demographic data indicate that in 1990, fewer women are getting married than have married since the end of World War II, and among those who do marry, there is a higher percentage of divorce than has been

Table 4.10
Distribution of Female Family Householders with Children (in thousands)

Age and	Number			Percent Distribution			1960–80 Change	
Marital Status	1960	1970	1980	1960	1970	1980	Number	Percent
Total	1,892	3,017	4,932	100.0	100.0	100.0	1,915	101.2
< 35 yrs.	666	1,274	2,515	35.2	42.2	51.0	1,241	186.3
35–44 yrs.	679	978	1,576	35.9	32.4	32.0	598	88.1
45–64 yrs.	531	743	824	28.1	24.6	16.7	81	15.3
65 yrs. +	16	22	17	0.8	0.7	0.3	(5)	-31.3
Total	1,892	3,017	4,932	100.0	100.0	100.0	1,915	101.2
Separated	454	767	1,047	24.0	25.4	21.2	280	61.7
Spouse Absent	253	251	171	13.4	8.3	3.5	(80)	-31.6
Widowed	606	748	593	32.0	24.8	12.0	(155)	-25.6
Divorced	496	991	2,295	26.2	32.8	46.5	1,304	262.9
Never Married	83	260	826	4.4	8.6	16.7	566	681.9

Source: S. M. Bianchi and D. Spain, *American Women in Transition* (New York: Russell Sage Foundation, 1986), table 3.4, p. 104; U.S. Bureau of the Census, *Census of Population, 1960*, vol. 2. "Families," PC(2)–4A, tables 5 and 6; *Census of Population, 1970*, vol. 2.2, "Family Composition," PC(2)–4A, tables 6 and 8; *Census of Population, 1980*, vol. 1, chap. D, U.S. Summary, tables 267 and 268.

evident in the past four decades. Women are delaying marriage more than they have in previous decades, while birth rates have been declining since the 1950s. These data can plausibly be linked to the impact of the women's movement's emphasis on careers and education at the expense of early marriage and motherhood.

ABORTION

Over the past twenty years, abortion has emerged as the top priority issue of the women's movement, as well as remaining one of the most hotly debated public issues in the country. At least as early as 1966, Gallup has queried the American public about various forms of abortion rights. As with the ERA, public opinion with regard to abortion has changed little over the years. However, unlike opinions about the ERA, differences between men and women

Table 4.11

Opinions on Law That Would Permit First-Trimester Abortion

		Percent Favoring Legality		
		Favor	Oppose	No Opinion
1969:	National	40	50	10
	Men	40	46	14
	Women	40	53	7
1973:	National	46	45	9
	Men	49	?	
	Women	44	?	

Source: The Gallup Organization, Princeton, N.J., 1969, 1973.

Table 4.12

Opinions on Whether Abortion Should Be Legal When Mother's Health Is Endangered, 1966 (in percentages)

	Should	Should Not	Don't Know
Men	77	15	8
Women	77	16	7
National	77	16	7

Source: The Gallup Organization, Princeton, N.J., 1966.

consistently have been rather negligible, albeit with some variation in responses depending on the dimension of abortion rights in question.

Prior to the 1973 Supreme Court decision in *Roe v. Wade,* support for abortion rights had grown among both men and women, but slightly more among men (see Table 4.11).

In 1966, men and women agreed about the desirability of legal abortion in cases where a woman's life was in danger (see Table 4.12).

Men and women also agreed about an abortion decision being a matter between a woman and her doctor (see Table 4.13).

In 1966, women were more decisive than men, however, with regard to the relevance of economic concerns as a criterion upon which to base the legality of the abortion decision (see Table 4.14).

After *Roe,* men were overall slightly more likely than women to support the court's decision on abortion, although by the mid–1980s, there were no differences by gender (see Table 4.15).

In 1988, the public was asked for its views concerning the circumstances under which abortions should be legal. As shown in Table 4.16, with 75 percent expressing disapproval, the family's economic circumstances were not consid-

Table 4.13
Opinions on Decision to Have Abortion Being Made Solely by Women and Their Physicians, 1972 (in percentages)

	Agree	Disagree	No Opinion
Total	64	31	5
Men	63	32	5
Women	64	31	5

Source: The Gallup Organization, Princeton, N.J., 1972.

Table 4.14
Opinions on Whether Abortion for Economic Reasons Should Be Legal, 1966 (in percentages)

	Should	Should Not	Don't Know
Men	20	68	12
Women	17	75	8
National	18	72	10

Source: The Gallup Organization, Princeton, N.J., 1966.

Table 4.15
Opinions on U.S. Supreme Court Ruling Allowing First-Trimester Abortion (in percentages)

	National		Women		Men	
	Favor	Oppose	Favor	Oppose	Favor	Oppose
1974	47	44	43	49	51	38
1981	45	46	43	49	49	44
1983	50	43	46	48	56	37
1986	45	45	45	46	45	43
1988	58	37	58	34	57	38
1989	61	33	58	35	63	32

Source: The Gallup Organization, Princeton, N.J., 1974–89.

ered a legitimate basis for abortion. More women expressed disapproval than men. The circumstances for which abortion received the strongest support from both women and men were if the women's life were endangered, if she was a victim of rape or incest, or if she might suffer severe physical health damage if she were not allowed to abort. Among the 60 percent who favored legalizing abortions if there was a chance that the baby would be born deformed, men were more likely to indicate their approval than women.

Table 4.16
Opinions on Circumstances Under Which Abortion Should Be Legal, 1988 (in percentages)

	National		Women		Men	
	Approve	Disapprove	Approve	Disapprove	Approve	Disapprove
If a woman's life is endangered	94	2	93	2	94	3
If the woman may suffer severe physical health damage	84	11	83	11	86	10
If there is any chance the baby will be born deformed	60	29	56	31	64	27
If the pregnancy is the result of rape or incest	85	11	81	14	89	9
If the family cannot afford to have the child	19	75	15	80	25	69

Source: The Gallup Organization, Princeton, N.J., 1988.

Table 4.17
Opinions on Ruling in *Webster v. Reproductive Health Services*, July 1989 (in percentages)

	Approve		Disapprove		No Opinion
	Strongly	Not Strongly	Strongly	Not Strongly	
National	28	9	44	11	8
Women	28	6	47	11	8
Men	29	12	40	11	8

Source: The Gallup Organization, Princeton, N.J., July 1989.

In July 1989, the Supreme Court ruled in *Webster v. Reproductive Health Services* that states may pass laws restricting abortions. The public expressed disagreement with that ruling when polled days after it was announced (see Table 4.17).

When the public was asked in July 1989 and again in October 1989 for its views on whether *Roe v. Wade* should be overturned, we see in Table 4.18 that almost twice as many respondents favored retaining the *Roe v. Wade* decision, men slightly more than women, on the most recent poll.

By way of conclusion, we look at responses to three general questions about women's status and about the role the women's movement played in family life. In 1977, men and women were asked if they thought the women's move-

Table 4.18
Opinions on Whether U.S. Supreme Court Should Overturn *Roe v. Wade*
(in percentages)

		Should	Should Not	No Opinion
July 1989:	National	34	58	8
	Women	34	58	8
	Men	35	57	8
Oct 1989:	National	33	61	6
	Women	35	58	7
	Men	32	63	5

Source: The Gallup Report, Princeton, N.J., Report 289, October 1989, p. 17; Report 286, July 1989, p. 9.

Table 4.19
Opinions on Impact of Women's Movement on the Family, 1977

	Women		Men	
	High School Graduate or less	College Graduate	High School Graduate or less	College Graduate
	(Percent)			
The women's movement causes families to break down	55	32	51	31
The women's movement creates a better family structure	13	34	7	20
The women's movement makes no difference	33	34	42	49

Source: CBS News/*New York Times*, Oct. 23–26, 1977.

ment influenced family structure. Respondents were divided by educational attainment into two categories: college graduates and those who graduated from high school or had fewer than twelve years of schooling. The results are shown in Table 4.19.

Among the men and women who thought the movement had any impact—and one-third of the women and almost half of the men did not—education was a more important variable than gender. About half of the less-educated women and men, compared with one-third of the male and female college graduates, perceived the movement as hurtful to families.

Table 4.20
Opinions on Respect Given Women Compared with Ten Years Earlier

	1970		1974		1980		1985	
	Women	Men	Women	Men	Women	Men	Women	Men
	(Percent)							
More	38	40	47	48	53	53	60	61
Less	27	25	23	23	22	20	18	15
Same	30	32	23	25	21	24	21	22
No Opinion/DK	5	3	7	4	4	3	1	2

Source: The Roper Organization, New York, N.Y., 1970–85.

Table 4.21
Opinions on Efforts to Strengthen Women's Status

	1970		1972		1974		1980		1985	
	Women	Men	Women	Men	Women	Men	Women	Men	Women	Men
	(in percent)									
Favor	40	44	48	49	57	63	64	64	73	69
Oppose	42	39	36	36	25	19	24	23	17	17
No Opinion/DK	18	17	16	15	18	18	12	13	10	14
N	3,000	1,000	3,000	1,000	3,006	1,002	3,007	1,004	3,000	1,000

Source: The Roper Organization, New York, N.Y., 1970–85.

More than any other category, female college graduates gave the women's movement a positive evaluation for helping to create a better family structure.

Between 1970 and 1985, the following item appeared on four national polls: "On the whole do you feel that, compared with 10 years ago, women are now looked on with more respect as individual human beings, with less respect, or with about the same respect?" The results are shown in Table 4.20.

Men and women started out with much the same views in 1970 and came out in 1985 with similar views. There was a shift on the part of men and women from believing that women were looked upon with less respect to perceiving them as having gained in respect over the past ten years.

And on a subjective note, the American public was asked: "Do you favor or oppose most of the efforts to strengthen and change women's status in society today?"

In 1970, 40 percent women and 44 percent of men said they favored efforts to strengthen women's status. By 1985, 73 percent of women and 69 percent of men favored such efforts (see Table 4.21). That is a big change. Perhaps what is most interesting about the poll data assembled here is that they provide a fairly consistent pattern. The pattern is one that shows the large majority of men and women in this country are not involved in a confrontation about women's rights. Men are as supportive as women themselves are on many of the issues for which the women's movement has struggled. The data also show that the women's movement has not radicalized the American woman: She is still prepared to put marriage and children ahead of her career and to allow her husband's status to determine the family's position in society.

NOTES

1. Personal interviews with Judith Lichtman, executive director, Women's Legal Defense Fund, October 26, 1989.

2. A number of historians have disputed the assertion that women suffered profound discrimination during colonial times, because women were in short supply and therefore more valued and because the vast majority of lawyers were ignorant of certain common law principles. See, for example, Richard B. Morris, *Studies in the History of American Law*, 2d ed. (New York: Octagon Books, 1963); Julia Cherry Spruill, *Women's Life and Work in the Southern Colonies* (New York: Norton, 1972); Mary Beard, *Women as Force in History: A Study in Traditions and Realities* (New York: Octagon Books, 1976); and Herbert Moller, "Sex Composition and Correlated Culture Patterns of North America," *William and Mary Quarterly* 2, no. 2 (April 1945), pp. 124–53.

3. William Blackstone, *Commentaries on the Laws of England*, Edward Christian, ed., vol. 1 (Portland, England, 1807), p. 442.

4. Mary R. Beard, *Women as Force in History*, pp. 117–24.

5. Francis R. Aumann, *The Changing American Legal System: Some Selected Phases* (1940; reprint, Jersey City, N.J.: Da Capo Press, 1969).

6. Marylynn Salmon, *Women and the Law of Property in Early America* (Chapel Hill: University of North Carolina Press, 1986), p. 8.

7. Under common law, a widow was entitled to one-third to one-half of the real property a man possessed at any time during his marriage. These were life interests only, meaning that at the widow's death, these property interests descended automatically to her husband's heirs.

8. See Morton J. Horwitz, *The Transformation of American Law, 1780–1860* (Cambridge: Harvard University Press, 1977), chap. 1, pp. 1–30.

9. Paul S. Reinsch, "English Common Law in the Early American Colonies" (Ph.D. diss., University of Wisconsin, 1899), p. 6.

10. Tapping Reeve, *The Law of Baron and Femme; of Parent and Child; of Guardian and Ward; of Master and Servant; and of the Power of Courts of Chancery* (New Haven, Conn.: 1816), reprinted in R. H. Helmholz and Bernard D. Reams, eds., *Historical Writings in Law and Jurisprudence* (Buffalo, N.Y.: Hein, 1981), pp. 12–17, 63.

11. Ibid., p. 27.

12. These states were Connecticut, Pennsylvania, North Carolina, and Georgia.

13. For a detailed analysis of such a shift and its impact in probate, see Richard H. Chused, "Married Women's Property and Inheritance by Widows in Massachusetts: A Study of Wills Probated between 1800 and 1850," *Berkeley Women's Law Journal*, vol. 3, 1986, pp. 42–88.

14. Linda E. Speth, "The Married Women's Property Acts, 1839–1865: Reform,

Reaction, or Revolution?" in D. Kelly Weisberg, ed., *Women and the Law: A Social Historical Perspective* (Cambridge: Schenkman, 1982), p. 53.

15. See Yuri Shul, *Ernestine L. Rose and the Battle for Human Rights* (New York: Reynal, 1959).

16. "Declaration of Rights and Sentiments, 1848," in Elizabeth Cady Stanton, Susan B. Anthony, and Matilda Joslyn Gage, eds., *History of Woman Suffrage*, vol. 1 (Rochester, N.Y.: Charles Mann, 1881), pp. 70–73.

17. See, for example, Beard, *Women as Force in History*; Beard is one of many to argue that equity allowed room for judges to maneuver the law so that women's rights were protected and even strengthened in some cases.

18. This law did not last long; during the Civil War, the act was amended so that a wife did not have equal guardianship rights with her husband, but did have to give her written consent before her husband could place their child in an apprenticeship or appoint a guardian.

19. Speth, "The Married Women's Property Acts, 1839–1865," pp. 82–83.

20. Ibid.

21. Elizabeth Cady Stanton, *Eighty Years and More: Reminiscences, 1815–1897* (reprint, New York: Schocken Books, 1971). See also Eleanor Flexner, *Century of Struggle: The Woman's Rights Movement in the United States* (Cambridge, Mass.: Belknap Press, 1975), pp. 20–43.

22. Peggy A. Rabkin, "The Silent Feminist Revolution: Women and the Law in New York State from Blackstone to the Beginning of the American Women's Rights Movement" (Ph.D. diss., State University of New York, Buffalo, 1975), and "The Origins of Law Reform: The Social Significance of the Nineteenth Century Codification Movement and Its Contribution to the Passage of The Early Married Women's Property Acts," *Buffalo Law Review* 24 (1974–75), pp. 683–760. See also Kay Ellen Thurman, "The Married Women's Property Acts" (LL.M. diss., University of Wisconsin Law School, 1966).

23. Speth distinguishes between the North and the South, arguing that in the North, growing demands for female equality were a factor in securing the passage of the acts. However, her evidence is limited to an examination of two eminent personalities at the time, Judge Herttell and Ernestine Rose.

24. See Speth, "The Married Women's Property Acts, 1839–1865."

25. Nancy Cott, "Divorce and the Changing Status of Women in Eighteenth-Century Massachusetts," *William and Mary Quarterly* 33, no. 4 (October 1976), p. 586.

26. See Chused, "Married Women's Property and Inheritance," p. 49.

27. Michael S. Hindus and Lynne E. Withey, "The Law of Husband and Wife in Nineteenth Century America: Changing Views of Divorce," in Eugene A. Hechler, ed., *A Short History of Women's Rights* (1914; reprint Westport, Conn.: Greenwood Press, 1971), pp. 133–51.

28. Salmon, *Women and the Law of Property*, p. 67.

29. Hindus and Withey, "The Law of Husband and Wife," pp. 136–37.

30. Salmon, *Women and the Law of Property*, p. 64.

31. Elizabeth Cady Stanton et al., *History of Woman Suffrage*, pp. 536–52.

32. Lenore J. Weitzman, *The Divorce Revolution* (New York: Free Press, 1985), p. 32.

33. Ibid.

34. Ibid., p. 360.

35. Ibid., p. 366.

36. Herbert Jacob, "Another Look at No-Fault Divorce and the Post-Divorce Finances of Women," *Law & Society Review* 23, no. 1 (1989), pp. 95–115.

37. Jacob does, however, agree with Weitzman that no-fault led to more frequent awards of alimony to women after long marriages, while women ending short marriages were less likely to receive it. Ibid., p. 111.

38. See, for example, "Brief of Seventy-Seven Organizations Committed to Women's Equality as Amici Curiae in Support of Appellees," in *Webster v. Reproductive Health Services*, no. 88–605, Supreme Court of the United States, October Term, 1988.

39. Ariz. Rev. State. Section 15–318; Colo. Rev. Stat. Ann. Section 14–10–113; Ill. Rev. Stat. Ann., Ch. 40, Section 503; Ky. Rev. Stat. Ann. 403–190; and Mont. Rev. Codes Section 48–321.

40. *State ex. rel. Watts v. Watts*, 77 Misc.2d 178, 350 N.Y.S.2d 285 (1973).

41. See "Developments in the Law—The Constitution and the Family,"*Harvard Law Review* 93 (1980), 1156, 1334–38.

42. Cal. Cv. Code, Section 4600.5(a).

43. The term "palimony" was coined by reporters covering such cases in 1978, long after the first suit to be identified with that issue had been filed.

44. "Loved and Left: The Palimony Issues," *Washington Post*, January 30, 1989, p. B1.

45. In Michelle Marvin's case, that included a division of their accumulated property (which meant his earnings) and financial support for the rest of her life. But when Michelle Marvin went back to court and presented her evidence, the judges were unconvinced.

46. James Mohn, *Abortion in America, 1800–1900* (New York: Oxford University Press, 1978), pp. 229–30.

47. See Linda Gordon, *Woman's Body, Woman's Right: A Social History of Birth Control in America* (New York: Penguin Books, 1977); and David Kennedy, *Birth Control in America: The Career of Margaret Sanger* (New Haven, Conn.: and London: Yale University Press, 1970).

48. Quoted in Nancy Woloch, *Women and the American Experience* (New York: Knopf, 1984), p. 413.

49. Kristin Luker, *Abortion and the Politics of Motherhood* (Berkeley: University of California Press, 1984), pp. 92–93.

50. Ibid., p. 94.

51. 410 U.S. 113 (1973). The *Roe* plaintiff, "Jane Roe," who was actually Norma McCorvey, had become pregnant as the result of a gang rape. Unable to obtain a legal abortion in Texas, she felt compelled to have the child and give it up for adoption. Her suit alleged that the Texas abortion statutes were unconstitutionally vague and abridged her right of personal privacy protected by the First, Fourth, Fifth, Ninth, and Fourteenth Amendments. Writing for the majority in *Roe*, Justice Harold Blackmun declared that while states may assert a legitimate interest in safeguarding health, maintaining medical standards, and protecting prenatal life, women have a fundamental constitutional right of privacy to decide for themselves in the early stages of pregnancy whether or not to give birth to a child. That right of privacy—choice free of governmental interference— is implicit in the concept of liberty, according to the majority in *Roe*. In a companion case, *Doe v. Bolton*, 410 U.S. 179 (1973), a Georgia statute restricting abortion access was invalidated. Later cases define the limits of *Roe* and *Doe*. See, for example, *Bigelow*

v. Virginia, 421 U.S. 809 (1975) (statutes prohibiting advertisements encouraging or promoting abortion violate the First Amendment); *Planned Parenthood v. Danforth*, 428 U.S. 52 (1976) (statute requiring spousal consent for abortion violates constitutional right of privacy); *Maher v. Roe*, 432 U.S. 438 (1977) (Pennsylvania may limit state assistance to "medically necessary abortions"); *Bellotti v. Baird*, 443 U.S. 622 (1979) (Massachusetts statute requiring parental consent to minor's abortion violates right of privacy); *Akron v. Akron Center for Reproductive Health*, 462 U.S. 416 (1983) (city ordinances requiring that second-trimester abortion be performed in a hospital, that minors obtain written consent from a parent or a court order before having an abortion, and that a women be read a specific list of information and beliefs about abortion are constitutionally invalid); *Thornburgh v. American College of Gynecologists, et al.*, 106 S.Ct. 2169 (1986) (Pennsylvania statute requiring that women seeking abortion be advised of medical assistance programs, of fathers' child support obligations, and of the detrimental risks of abortion are unconstitutional; statutes requiring reporting and requiring the presence of a second physician are unconstitutional; and a statute establishing care appropriate for postviability abortions are invalid).

52. 410 U.S. at 159.

53. Walter Isaacson, "The Battle over Abortion," *Time*, April 6, 1981, p. 21.

54. In October 1989, the House accepted Senate language that would permit federally funded abortions for victims of rape or incest. Previously, the House had only allowed federally funded Medicaid abortions when they were needed to save the woman's life.

55. Joyce Gelb and Marian Lief Pally, *Women and Public Policies* (Princeton, N.J.: Princeton University Press, 1978), p. 143.

56. Tamar Jacoby, "A New Majority Ticks Off the Reagan Agenda," *Newsweek*, July 17, 1989, p. 26.

57. Pamela Erens, "Anti-Abortion, Pro-Feminism?" *Mother Jones*, May 1989, p. 31.

58. As quoted in Maggie Gallagher, "The New Pro-Life Rebels," *National Review*, February 27, 1987, p. 37.

59. Alison Jaggar, "Abortion and a Woman's Right to Decide," in Carol C. Gould and Marx W. Wartofsky, eds., *Women and Philosophy: Toward a Theory of Liberation* (New York: Putnam, 1976), p. 357. See also Nanette Davis, *From Crime to Choice: The Transformation of Abortion in America*, (Westport, Conn.: Greenwood Press, 1985), pp. 125–26.

60. Mary C. Segers, "Abortion and the Culture: Toward a Feminist Perspective," in Sidney Callahan and Daniel Callahan, eds., *Abortion, Understanding Differences* (New York: Plenum Press, 1984), p. 238.

61. Ibid., p. 239.

62. Kristin Luker, *Abortion and the Politics of Motherhood*, pp. 120–21.

63. Ibid., p. 121.

64. Robert Cameron Mitchell, John D. McCarthy, and Kathy Pearch, *Report on a Membership Survey* (Washington, D.C.: NARAL, April 9, 1979).

65. "[I]n nearly every state, abortion rights advocates have failed to equal the opponent's network of dedicated and steady if often modest contributors, or, more often than not, cannot turn out equivalent busloads of demonstrators." *New York Times*, Oct. 23, 1977, p. 24.

66. Gelb and Palley, *Women and Public Policies*, pp. 151–55.

67. "Justices Restrict Right to Abortion, 5–4, Giving States Wide Latitude," *Washington Post*, July 4, 1989, p. A1.

68. "600,000 March for Abortion Rights," *National NOW Times* 21, no. 1 (1989), p. 1. Washington, D.C., officials estimated 300,000 demonstrators.

69. "The New Political Rules," *Newsweek*, July 17, 1989, p. 21.

70. "Abortion Rights Groups Map Strategy to Protect Access," *Washington Post*, July 8, 1989, p. A2.

71. "The Next Battleground on Abortion Rights," *Washington Post*, July 10, 1989, p. A4.

72. See, for example, Rebecca Tillet, *Empower America: Your Campaign and Abortion Rights* (Washington, D.C.: National Women's Political Caucus, 1989).

73. In Virginia, Democrat L. Douglas Wilder won the governorship after a campaign that concentrated heavily on his opponent's position favoring some restrictions on abortion rights. In New Jersey, Congressman Jim Courter (R), running for governor, repeatedly sought to reassure voters that he would not seek sharp restrictions on abortion, but lost anyway to Congressman James A. Florio (D), a pro-abortion-rights candidate.

74. "State Legislators Vent Anxiety over Abortion," *Washington Post*, August 10, 1989, p. A4.

Chapter 5

CONCLUSION

More than a century and a half has gone by since the founding of the first women's movement in the United States. Much has been accomplished as measured by women's status in the occupational, political, and educational spheres; by gains in personal security; and by their increased longevity during that time. How much of each accomplishment women's movements can take credit for is, of course, difficult to assess and subject to political debate. But clearly the women's movement played a central role in obtaining suffrage for women. Women's movements also were instrumental in achieving gains in property rights such as allowing wives to keep the wages they earned rather than placing them under the legal supervision of their husband; in attaining the right to enter into contracts, to control their inheritances, and to sue in their own names; in the child custody debate; and in the passage of an equal pay act and of Title VII of the Civil Rights Act, which prohibits discrimination based on sex in all terms, conditions, or privileges of employment.

In the beginning, of course, there was nothing like a women's movement in the United States despite an egregious lack of rights. In the years before 1848, vocal feminists had raised their voices as individuals. Gradually, women developed an awareness of their disadvantaged status. But they were scattered throughout the states. They had not formed a unified movement. They were a group of highly educated, middle-class, white urban women leaders—with no cohesive, unified following.

The 1848 Seneca Falls convention provided an impetus for the first U.S. women's movement, and its Declaration of Principles included many aspects of women's status that are applicable today. The sixty-nine women (and thirty-two men) who signed the declaration represented the beginning of a feminist movement that recognized itself as such. But their appeal was to their own kind: educated, middle-class, and white urban residents.

Their early successes reflect the backgrounds of their supporters. On issues such as property reform and guardianship rights of married women, along with educational opportunity, they found extensive support. These issues were perceived as serving the interests of conservative wealthy families—fathers who wanted to keep their riches within their family, citizens who prided themselves on the trappings of wealth, which included a particular type of costly education. Indeed, it is debatable how much of the change in property law and the progress in women's education that occurred during the first half of the nineteenth century was at all attributable to these early feminists.

The same trend toward conservative issues that served a particular social stratum can be seen by the end of the nineteenth century. During the 1800s, dozens of inspiring, highly intelligent, committed women had attempted to organize a women's movement—Frances Wright, Susan B. Anthony, Lucretia Mott, Sarah and Angelina Grimke, Elizabeth Cady Stanton, Lucy Stone, to name a few. They were at best only partially successful, as women's rights associations sprang up around the country. But there was no formal organization, no network of female societies, no readily identifiable following, and there were no state or national organizations.

Moreover, any fledgling women's movement was quickly co-opted by the abolitionist movement. While some women's leaders attempted to separate women's rights from those of the blacks, they were largely unsuccessful, and only caused abolitionists to divide into factions over women's roles in the antislavery movement. Until the emancipation of slaves, the women's rights movement was inextricably linked to an antislavery base of support.

After the Civil War, there was a transformation in the women's movement from a concern with a broad set of issues to a movement involved almost exclusively with suffrage. Ideological conservatism became more prominent, as women's leaders departed from an insistence on women's equality with men. Instead, as the radical and mainstream faction of the women's movement reunited after several decades of antagonism, the women's movement became the suffrage movement. It based much of its argument on the moral superiority of women and on their need to defend the home. Suffrage advocates emphasized women's traditional roles as mothers and housewives, and presented suffrage as a tool with which to pursue such traditional values, as well as a means by which to improve the moral tone of national life.

Having restricted its pronouncements to those espousing traditional values and having focused its efforts on one specific goal, the organized women's movement was successful. But at what cost? Once suffrage had been achieved, the women's movement remained identified with the same sterotypes valued by early nineteenth-century society. Moreover, what was left of the women's movement splintered into numerous factions after suffrage had been gained.

While the movement had for all intents and purposes petered out by 1930, the conservative values so widely embraced in the name of suffrage lived on.

The women's movement's emphasis on women as mothers and house-keepers, so apparent in the suffrage campaigns, found a logical extension in its views of protective legislation. After the turn of the century, women's leaders increasingly shifted their attention to measures that would give women special "advantages" in the work place, enabling them to fulfill their familial obligations as well as their job-related responsibilities. This was one of the few instances in history when a coalition of groups—feminist, suffrage, and working class—successfully lobbied for changes in the law. From the vantage point of a later generation, however, such protective legislation was perceived as "protecting" women from employment opportunities as well as from harsh working conditions.

Thus, women's positions were perceived as mainly those of child rearing and hearth keeping for the first half of the twentieth century. While there were periodic attempts to break that mold, especially by women in political and academic life, women continued to be relegated to secondary positions even during the 1960s civil rights movement.

In many ways, not much had changed for women since the abolition movement of the previous century—except for one thing. There had been a radical increase in the number of educated women, the bedrock of nearly all women's movements to date. Like their forerunner, the new feminists were almost always white, middle-class, and well educated. Raised in economic security, they believed that jobs meant more than economic security. They began to participate in the civil rights and student movements of the 1960s, but discovered they were expected to do service jobs, traditional "women's work" like typing, filing, housekeeping; meanwhile, leadership remained a male pre-rogative. The eventual outrage felt by many of these women gave birth to the women's liberation movement of the 1960s, which emphasized equal rights and the concept of the oppression of women by men.

Reminiscent of the radical women's leaders in the era preceding the Civil War, feminists during the 1960s alienated large segments of potential constituents with their extremist pronouncements. The Equal Rights Amendment and lesbian rights were hot topics for years, overshadowing any attention on the more mundane concerns of child care and flexible work schedules. During its heyday, many of the more prominent feminist leaders eschewed so-called special privileges, such as maternity leave. They argued that women would never attain equality with men if they demanded such treatment. For close to two decades, many people identified the women's movement with some version of such egalitarian feminism. After decades of fighting for protective legislation, the women's movement had shifted to the other side.

The 1960s and 1970s were a time of tremendous accomplishment for the women's movement. Numerous sex-related barriers for women in society eroded. Gender-based job classifications were found to be unconstitutional in *Reed v. Reed*[1] and *Frontiero v. Richardson*.[2] Mandatory termination of employment for pregnant women was held unconstitutional in *Cleveland Board of Education v. La Fleur*.[3] Title VII's sex-discrimination provisions were the subject of considerable litigation in federal courts. In *Phillips v. Martin Marietta Corporation*,[4] a refusal to hire women with preschool-age children was held unconstitutional. And in *Dothard v. Rawlinson*,[5] the Supreme Court found that a seemingly neutral job qualification relating to height and weight actually denied equal opportunity to women. These cases, coupled with the abortion rights encompassed by *Roe v. Wade*, made for heady days for the women's movement.

But key problems remained, including wage differentials and continuing sex-related occupational segregation. And, most significantly, despite increased social acceptance of work and careers for women, the position of women in the home and family remained essentially the same: they were expected to adapt to dual roles—economic and domestic—unmitigated by any dramatic social transformation.

As young women entered the 1980s, they took advantage of the gains made by the women's movement in the previous two decades. As they did in the 1920s—when there was a surge in the number of women pursuing higher education—women pursued college degrees and professional qualifications in record numbers and went on to enter the work force. Moreover, with the comprehensive legislation that barred discrimination, these women were able to hold jobs and begin careers in a host of fields that had hitherto been closed to them. Rather than assume the burden of maintaining a family as well as a career, they gradually decided to delay marriage until their careers were well established.

In the meantime, however, the women's movement was slowly drained of its energy as it splintered once more among a variety of issues and failed to mobilize the younger generation. While the National Organization for Women may have been popularly identified as the dominant voice of the women's movement, there were also signs that it was having difficulty setting priorities that would attract popular support. It was criticized for neglecting the concerns of poor women, minority women, working women in unskilled jobs, and women with traditional beliefs in motherhood and the family.[6]

By the mid-1980s, younger women took many of their rights for granted. If they belonged to groups at all, it was to professional women's networks or to organizations grouped around career goals rather than social change. *Time* magazine dubbed these new women the "No, but . . . " generation:[7] women who reject the feminist label, but who take certain rights as a matter of course. To this mass of women, mostly young and well educated, the term "women's movement" connotes an outdated, strident image. The fight for the ERA means nothing to them because they assume equality.

Time also identified another body of women, the "Yes, but . . . " generation, who are mostly in their thirties and forties and who still may consider themselves feminists, but for whom things have not turned out the way they had anticipated in the 1960s. They have achieved career success to a greater or lesser extent, but are now juggling child care, elderly parent care, and increasing work-place stress. They blame "the movement" for emphasizing issues that today seem, at best, of secondary importance, if not outright irrelevant.

In short, the same flaws that were evident in women's movements in the first and second half of the nineteenth century and in the first part of the twentieth are surfacing yet again: narrowness of vision, alienation of large segments of potential supporters, self-absorption. What the women's movement has accomplished is that it no longer functions as an isolated entity, unwilling to join forces with other groups to gain passage of a particular piece of legislation. Nor does it stand in the shadow of other social movements as it did in the past in relation to slavery, antiwar movements, and civil rights. There is clearly a coherent set of beliefs that could serve to identify the women's movement today: work-place equality, abortion rights, and participation in electoral politics, among others.

But in the past, women's movements have been most successful when they have been most conservative, hewing to a traditional moral stance and generally accepted views of women's position in society. What are the generally accepted views of women's position in society? Has the women's movement affected perceptions of women's roles? If we can answer these questions, we may be able to discern whether the above-mentioned beliefs represent areas for further reform and new directions for a women's movement. Are they susceptible to legislative change, or do they require more subtle change than can be provided by an organized women's movement? In short, what, if any, are the causes that a women's movement might seize upon in the coming decades to avoid the alienation and irrelevance that has plagued it so often in the past?

The availability of national poll data since the mid-1930s allows us to examine and track, in systematic fashion, changes in both men's and women's attitudes on issues the women's movement has deemed important or essential, as well as to compare perceptions held by women and men of the appropriate roles for women in society and of the "rights" to which they are entitled.

Even over a relatively short time span of fifty years, there have been major changes in both men's and women's attitudes on many issues. For example, in 1937, 34 percent of the American public (40 percent of the women and 27 percent of the men) said they would vote for a woman for president of the United States. In 1987, 82 percent of the American public (83 percent of the women and 81 percent of the men) said they would vote for a woman for president. Women have also become more involved in the political process. In the first presidential election in which they were eligible to vote, only 26 percent of them exercised their newly won and hard-fought-for right. By 1952,

60 percent of women compared with 64 percent of men voted in the presidential election; from that time forward, the percentage of women voters has matched or slightly exceeded that of men.

Beginning in the mid-1970s, a woman's view began to emerge on substantive public issues. The woman's voice contained many of the qualities that the early nineteenth-century leaders of the women's movement predicted it would. Women were more likely to support programs that would reduce the income gap between rich and poor, to oppose the death penalty, to favor greater protection for the environment. They were less likely to support increased spending for the military and less likely to favor a military draft.

What is most striking about the national poll results in the "family, marriage, divorce, children, abortion" areas are the lack of differences in the opinions held by men and women. For example, in response to items that asked whether they favored or opposed efforts to strengthen and change women's status in society, from 1970 on, over 80 percent of both women and men said they favored such efforts. Over a fifteen-year time span, men and women responded almost identically to an item that asked whether women were looked upon with more respect than they had been ten years earlier. In 1970, some 40 percent thought they were; in 1985, 60 percent of men and women thought they were. Men and women also responded in similar fashion on the abortion issue. Where there are differences, men are more "prochoice" than women. Men and women also agree that the institution of marriage is weaker "today" (in 1970 and 1985) than it was ten years previously; they share a preference for smaller families; they accept divorce if the marriage is not working out. Although a majority of women and men believe women should not receive alimony, a higher percentage of men as opposed to women hold that view. That is an issue about which the women's movement is currently divided.

On matters pertaining to women in the labor force, there have been big shifts in men's and women's opinions. On most issues, the shifts have been in the same direction or have been such as to bring men's and women's views closer together. On the former pattern, we reported that in 1936, 18 percent of the women polled and 12 percent of the men approved of married women working outside their homes. In 1986, 76 percent of the women and 78 percent of the men approved. Over 90 percent of the men and women polled approved of paying women the same salary as men for equal work. In 1970, 40 percent of the women and 44 percent of the men said they favored most of the efforts to strengthen women's status; in 1985, 68 percent of the men and 73 percent of the women said they favored such efforts. And over a ten-year period from 1975 through 1984, in responses on seven national polls, men have been more supportive than, or as supportive as, women of the ERA.

Using demographic data, we also reported other changes in women's status over the past four decades. From the 1970s, a pattern emerged showing that both men and women have been delaying marriage and that the percentage of divorced women has increased two-and-a-half-fold. Family size has also declined from an average of three or more to fewer than two children per couple.

In 1987, 55.4 percent of the women were in the labor force. Of married women, 56 percent worked outside their homes, and of those women, 56.9 percent had children under six years of age. In 1950, only 24 percent of the college graduates were women. In 1985, women comprised 49.4 percent of those who earned baccalaureate degrees. In 1985, 50 percent of all master's degrees were earned by women compared with 29 percent in 1950, and 34 percent of all doctorates were held by women as opposed to 9 percent in 1950. Even more dramatic have been the inroads made by women in what a few decades ago had been almost exclusively male professions. In 1960, women held 5.5 percent of the M.D. degrees and 2.5 percent of the J.D.'s or LL.B.'s. In 1985, 30 percent of the M.D.'s and 39 percent of the J.D.'s were conferred on women. The increases have been as great for dentistry and engineering over the same time period, but the percentages are much smaller because in 1960, women received fewer than 1 percent of the dentistry and engineering degrees.

The area in which there is the greatest dissatisfaction on the part of the women's movement is the income ratio between men and women. Over slightly less than the past three decades, the ratio that indicates that women earn 64 percent of men's earning has never been higher. When the data are disaggregated, we noted that among college-educated workers, women earned 75 percent of men's earnings and among younger workers (those aged 25 to 34) women's earnings were 72 percent of men's.

Today, the problem confronted by women and the women's movement is that while they are enjoying the success resulting from the legal equality for which women's movements fought long and hard, they are also struggling to accommodate women's more traditional roles. Sylvia Anne Hewlett, a Harvard sociologist, writes in *A Lesser Life: The Myth of Women's Liberation in America*,[8] that instead of organizing women to work for the social programs that would help them cope with the double burden in the home and in the work place, the modern feminists have encouraged women to avoid both marriage and children. She recommends that political feminists form new alliances with existing organizations such as professional groups, formal political parties, church groups, labor unions, and grass-roots volunteer associations that are already involved in social reform programs aimed at bolstering the family through tangible assistance to mothers.

Betty Friedan argues in her 1981 book, *The Second Stage*,[9] that the women's movement must change its focus from achieving success in a man's world on a man's terms to achieving a balance between the professional roles and women's traditional roles as mother and housewife. In order to attain this balance, she says, the structure of the work place and the home must change.

However, both of these suggestions run the risk of leading to the further weakening, if not dissipation, of the women's movement. Alliances with other groups were followed in the mid-nineteenth century by dire consequences for the fledgling suffrage movement when it was co-opted by the abolitionists. Could not the same fate await women's groups who identify themselves too closely with other groups? And Friedan's argument raises the question of how far a women's movement per se can change the social structure without alienating large segments of people who do not agree with such transformation.

Poll data show that the majority of Americans agree that women are entitled to equal opportunity and pay equity. The mistake that women's movements have made in the past is in thinking that legal equality also means parity with men. Current women's groups are shifting from an emphasis on equal opportunity legislation to the kind of protectionist arguments that were adopted by women's groups not quite one hundred years ago. Women and women's groups claim the right to assistance in such areas as parental leave, adequate child care, and financial aid to mothers who are unable to afford child care. They are doing this through the legislative process, lobbying state legislatures for comprehensive parental leave laws or maternity leave bills.

There are areas, however, where the women's movement remains invisible, perhaps irrelevant. In the area of work-place structure, for instance, many women's professional groups (but not the traditional women's movement) are battling the glass ceiling, pushing for child care benefits, recommending and implementing the flexibility that is needed by women who want to take care of families as well as careers.

Can an organized women's movement help implement such change, or is the work-place structure something that must be changed from within? Examples from the past, such as the suffrage campaign, indicate that women's movements often outlive their usefulness once they have generated the legislation that has resulted in such social change. What is more, one might argue, there is historical evidence that demonstrates that once basic legislation has been passed, further attempts by women's groups to force through more extreme measures, such as legislation that grants women greater work-place "protection," results in divisiveness and social backfire. For the past century, women's groups have been torn over the question of whether special treatment reinforces sexual stereotyping and whether it would result in a backlash of employers who will refuse to hire women of childbearing age.

The women's movement has already accomplished a great deal in the cause of working women: educational opportunities, equal employment opportunity, and professional opportunity. It remains questionable whether, once it has opened the doors for women, a women's movement can address the more subtle problems that arise from the resulting complexity of women's lives.

Many women's groups view the abortion issue as the salvation of the moribund women's movement. Membership in NOW, which was 160,000 in 1988 (from a peak of 220,000 in 1982), jumped almost 100,000 in the aftermath of *Webster v. Reproductive Health Services.* Women's groups argue that the Supreme Court, by allowing states to restrict the availability of abortion services, has provided the women's movement with a prime opportunity to move its core agenda into the mainstream of U.S. politics. A considerable number of the mainstream women's groups are narrowing their agendas to concentrate on abortion rights.

But again, the specter of the past's failures looms. It is the young, well-educated women who have nearly always been the primary beneficiaries of the women's movement's pioneering efforts. As more moderate elements in the women's movement recognize, these are the women who must be mobilized if the abortion rights movement is to progress beyond the street demonstration stage to the job of influencing state legislatures. The risk is that extremist tactics, such as those adopted by NOW president Molly Yard, who calls for the formation of a third political party, could fragment the abortion rights movement just as it faces the tough task of persuading voters and legislatures to reject abortion restrictions.

The agenda facing the current women's movement involves public education and lobbying for abortion rights legislation on a grass-roots level, while at the same time avoiding the abrasive, alienating quality assumed by some radical women's groups in the past two hundred years. If the women's movement is to regenerate itself via an abortion rights campaign, it will have to overcome the obstacle faced by many women when confronted with membership in so-called feminist organizations: women today do not focus their concerns or cast their votes on the basis of "women's issues." Their lives and concerns are intertwined with the interests of their husbands, children, and colleagues, and with the larger community.

A number of women's groups are indeed returning to grass-roots mobilization, both in support of abortion rights and improvements in the child care situation. States have proven willing to allocate funds for domestic violence and maternal and child health care projects and to provide support for affirmative action and comparable worth legislation. This increasing focus on local action, along with the entry of more and more women into local, state, and national politics and the blurring of distinctions between women's interests and those of society at large, may signal a new type of women's movement in U.S. history. Indeed, the term "movement" may no longer be applicable. Instead, there may be a loose conglomeration of groups who are working in support of women's rights and interests, but who do not answer to or owe allegiance to any central organization. History demonstrates that in order to succeed, a women's movement in any form must make a cause, such as abortion rights or pay equity or child care support, an issue that appeals to both men and women, while separating it from the rhetoric so often adopted by feminists in the past.

NOTES

1. 404 U.S. 71 (1971).
2. 411 U.S. 677 (1973).

3. 420 U.S. 535 (1975).

4. 400 U.S. 542 (1971).

5. 97 S.Ct. 2720 (1977).

6. At its 1989 annual convention, NOW pushed for an expanded Bill of Rights that would guarantee access to abortions, protect sexual preferences, established a variety of economic and environmental standards, and explore the possibility of creating a third political party.

7. "Women Face the '90's," *Time,* December 4, 1989, p. 80.

8. Sylvia Ann Hewlett, *A Lesser Life: The Myth of Women's Liberation in America* (New York: Morrow, 1986).

9. Betty Friedan, *The Second Stage* (New York: Summit Books, 1982).

BIBLIOGRAPHY

PRIMARY SOURCES

Addams, Jane. *Why Women Should Vote*. National American Woman Suffrage Association. New York, 1912.

American Women. Report of the President's Commission on the Status of Women. Washington, D.C.: Government Printing Office, 1963.

Austin, Mary, and Anne Martin. *Suffrage and Government: The Modern Idea of Government by Consent and Woman's Place in It*. New York: National Woman Suffrage Association, 1914.

Ballintine, Eveline P. "Women Physicians in Public Institutions." Radcliffe College Library, Woman's Archives. Paper read before the Women's Medical Society of the State of New York, Rochester, March 11, 1908.

Barnhouse, Robert B., and Donald F. Burke. *EEO—Preventive Action*. Baltimore: Maryland Institute for Continuing Professional Education of Lawyers, 1980.

Beedy, Mary E. *The Joint Education of Young Men and Women in the American Schools and Colleges*. London: The Sunday Lecture Society, 1873.

Bennett, Sarah Clay. *Report of the Federal Suffrage Committee of the National American Suffrage Association*. Grand Rapids, Michigan, 1899.

Blackwell, Alice Stone. "Jane Addams Testifies." *Woman's Journal*, Boston, 1915.

———. *Liquor Against Suffrage*. Boston: Grimes, 1915.

Blackwell, E. "Address on the Medical Education of Women." New York: Baptist and Taylor, 1864.

Blackwell, Henry B. "Objections to Woman Suffrage Answered." *Woman Suffrage Leaflet*, Boston, March 1896.

Blake, Lillie Devereux. "Legislative Advice." *Woman Suffrage Leaflet*, Boston, May 1895.

Bradford, Mary C. C. *Equal Suffrage in Colorado From 1908 to 1912*. Denver: Colorado Equal Suffrage Association, 1912.

Brehm, Marie C. *Suggestion for Franchise Superintendents*. Boston: Woman's Christian Temperance Union, Franchise Department, 1900.

Bronson, Minnie. *The Wage-Earning Woman and the State: A Comparison of the Laws for Her Protection in Various States of the Union*. Boston: The Massachusetts Association Opposed to the Further Extension of Suffrage to Women, September 1910.

Brown, Olympia, Charlotte F. Daley, Marietta M. Bones, and Matilda Joslyn Gage. *A Statement of Facts*. New York: National Woman Suffrage Association, 1889.

Brown, William Symington, "The Capability of Women to Practice the Healing Art." Boston: Ripley, 1859. Lecture given before the Ladies' Medical Academy, Boston, 1859.

Cameron, Robert Mitchell, John D. McCarthy, and Kathy Pearch. *Report on a Membership Survey*. Washington, D.C.: NARAL, April 9, 1979.

"Campaigning in a Different Voice." Prepared for the Majority Project, EMILY's List, by Celinda Lake. Washington, D.C.: Greenberg-Lake: Analysis Group, 1988.

Catt, Carrie Chapman. *President's Annual Address*. Washington, D.C.: National American Woman Suffrage Association, 1904.

Compensation in Certain Occupations of Women Who Have Received College or Other Special Training. Boston: Wright and Potter Printing, 1896.

Corbin, Caroline F. *Woman's Rights in America; A Retrospect of Sixty Years, 1848–1908*. Chicago: The Illinois Association Opposed to Woman Suffrage, 1908.

Delzell, Ruth. *The Early History of Women's Trade Unionists of America*. Chicago: National Women's Trade Union League, 1914.

Dorr, Rheta Childe. *Women's Demand for Humane Treatment of Women Workers in Shop and Factory*. New York: The Consumer's League of the City of New York, 1909.

Effect of Vote of Women on Legislation: An Investigation in the Equal Suffrage States Made in December, 1913, by "The Evening Sun" of New York City. New York: The National Woman Suffrage Publishing Company, April 1914.

Fairchild, Rev. James H. *Coeducation of the Sexes as Pursued in Oberlin College*. Oberlin College, July 10, 1867.

Fay, Clement K. *Municipal Woman Suffrage*. Brookline, Mass.: The Chronicle Press, 1887.

Fifth Annual Announcement of the Female Medical College of Pennsylvania. Philadelphia: The Female Medical College of Pennsylvania, 1854.

Fussle, Edwin. *Valedictory Address of the Graduating Class of the Female Medical College of Pennsylvania*. Philadelphia: The Female Medical College of Pennsylvania, March 13, 1861.

Gannett, William C. *Putting a Smile Into Politics: A Reply to Ex-Senator Root's Objections to Woman Suffrage*. The Hanford Collection, Library of Congress. New York, 1914.

Goodell, Lavinia. "Women in the Legal Profession." Papers read at the Fourth Congress of Women at St. George's Hall, Philadelphia, October 4–6, 1876.

Gregory, Samuel, M.D. *Circular*. Boston: New England Female Medical College, 1853.

Harper, Ida Husted. *History of the Movement for Woman Suffrage in the United States*. New York: Interurban Woman Suffrage Council, 1907.

———. *How Six States Won Woman Suffrage*. New York: National Woman Suffrage Association, 1912.

Harris, W. T. "Why Many Women Should Study Law." *The Ohio Educational Monthly*, July 1901.

Holmes, James H. *A Report on the Condition of the Cause of Woman Suffrage*. Washington, D.C.: Universal Franchise Association, 1868.

Jordan, Joan. *Amend the Equal Rights Amendment to Extend the State Protective Laws to Men*. San Francisco: Women Incorporated and San Francisco Women's Liberation Intergroup Council, 1970.

Laidlaw, H. B. *Organizing to Win by the Political District Plan*. New York: National Woman Suffrage Publishing Company, 1914.

Nestor, Agnes. *The Working Girl's Need of Suffrage*. Chicago: Women's Trade Union League of Chicago, 1910.

Peterson, Celia F. Osgood. "The Effect of the Woman Vote in Colorado." New York: National American Woman Suffrage Association, 1899.

Pollard, Edward Bagby. "Women, Home and Government." New York: National Woman Suffrage Publishing Company, 1915.

Pope, Emily F. "The Practice of Medicine by Women in the United States." Paper read before the American Social Science Association, Saratoga, New York, 1881.

Potter, Frances Boardman. *Women, Economics, and the Ballot*. Youngstown, Ohio: Vindicator Press, 1909.

Pregnancy Discrimination: A Case Study of the Impact of Public Policy on Families and Work. Washington, D.C.: Women's Legal Defense Fund, 1986.

"Present Mode of Female Education Reconsidered." *The Lady's Weekly Miscellany*, June 11, 1808, pp. 100–104.

Referendum Policy of the Women's Political Union. New York: The Women's Political Union, 1914.

"Remarks on Female Politicians." *The Lady's Monitor*, May 29, 1802, pp. 324–25.

Robins, Margaret Dreier. "Need of a National Training School for Women Organizers: The Minimum Wage Industrial Education." Chicago: National Women's Trade Union League of America, 1913.

Rush, Benjamin. "Thoughts upon Female Education." *New England Quarterly Magazine*, April–June 1802, pp. 146–53.

Thompson, Daniel Greenleaf. "Woman's New Opportunity." New York: Longmans, Green, and Co., 1894. Address delivered at the closing exercises of the Woman's Law Class of the University of the City of New York, 1894.

Tillet, Rebecca. *Empower America: Your Campaign and Abortion Rights*. Washington, D.C.: National Women's Political Caucus, 1989.

Van Kleeck, Mary. *Storage Bulletin on the Employment of Women in the Storage and Warehousing Depots of the U.S. Army*. Washington, D.C.: War Industries Board, 1917.

Votes for Women on the Home Stretch. Proceedings of the National American Woman Suffrage Association. New York, February 17, 1913.

Willard, Frances E. *The Ballot for the Home*. Boston: The Woman's Journal, March 1898.

Woman Suffrage: Facts and Opinions. Edited by the King County Franchise Committee. Seattle, 1887.

Women's Bureau. *Women's Bureau Conference*. Washington, D.C., February 1948.

Women's Educational and Industrial Union. Boston: Todd, 1919.

The Work of the Consumers' League of the City of New York. New York: Consumer's
   League, 1916.

BOOKS

Allen, Anita L. *Uneasy Access: Privacy for Women in a Free Society*. New York: Rowman
   and Littlefield, 1987.
Andrews, John B. *History of Women in Trade Unions*. New York: Arno, 1974.
Aumann, Francis R. *The Changing American Legal System: Some Selected Phases*. 1940;
   reprint, Jersey City, N.J.: Da Capo Press, 1969.
Babcock, Barbara E. *Sex Discrimination and the Law: Causes and Remedies*. Boston:
   Little, Brown, 1975.
Baehr, Ninea. *Abortion without Apology: Radical History for the 1990s*. Boston: South
   End Press, 1990.
Baer, Judith A. *The Chains of Protection: Judicial Response to Women's Labor Legis-
   lation*. Westport, Conn.: Greenwood Press, 1978.
Baxter, Sandra, and Marjorie Lansing. *Women and Politics: The Visible Majority*. Ann
   Arbor: University of Michigan Press, 1983.
Beard, Mary R. *Women as Force in History: A Study in Traditions and Realities*. New
   York: Octagon Books, 1976.
Becker, Susan. *The Origins of the Equal Rights Amendment: American Feminism
   between the Wars*. Westport, Conn.: Greenwood Press, 1981.
Berg, Barbara J. *The Remembered Gate: Origins of American Feminism: The Woman
   and the City, 1800–1860*. New York: Oxford University Press, 1978.
Bernard, Jessie. *The Female World*. New York: Free Press, 1981.
Blackstone, Henry. *Commentaries on the Laws of England*. Oxford, 1765–1769.
Boles, Janet A. *The Politics of the Equal Rights Amendment: Conflict and the Decision
   Process*. New York: Longman, 1979.
Brownlee, W. Elliot, and Mary M. Brownlee. *Women in the American Economy: A
   Documentary History, 1675 to 1929*. New Haven, Conn.: Yale University Press,
   1976.
Bureau of National Affairs. *Equal Pay for Equal Work: Summary, Analysis, Legislative
   History and Text of the Federal Equal Pay Act of 1963, with Summaries of
   Applicable State Laws*. Washington, D.C.: Bureau of National Affairs, 1963.
Cahn, Anne Foot, ed. *Women in the U.S. Labor Force*. New York: Praeger, 1979.
Callahan, Sidney, and Daniel Callahan, eds. *Abortion: Understanding Differences*. New
   York: Plenum, 1984.
Caplan, Patricia, and Janet Bujra, eds. *Women United, Women Divided*. Bloomington:
   Indiana University Press, 1980.
Carroll, Berenice. *Liberating Women's History*. Urbana, Ill.: University of Illinois Press,
   1976.
Chafe, William H. *The American Woman: Her Changing Social, Economic, and Political
   Role, 1920–1970*. New York: Oxford University Press, 1972.
———. *Women and Equality: Changing Patterns in American Culture*. New York:
   Oxford University Press, 1977.
Clarke, Edward. *Sex in Education; or, a Fair Chance for the Girls*. Reprint of 1873
   edition. Salem, N.H.: Ayer, 1972.

Clinton, Catherine. *The Other Civil War: American Women in the Nineteenth Century.* New York: Hill & Wang, 1984.

Cott, Nancy F. *The Bonds of Womanhood: "Woman's Sphere" in New England, 1780–1825.* New Haven: Yale University Press, 1977.

———. ed. *Root of Bitterness: Documents of the Social History of American Women.* New York: Dutton, 1972.

Cummings, Bernice, and Victoria Schuck, eds. *Women Organizing: An Anthology.* Metuchen, N.J.: Scarecrow Press, 1979.

Davis, Nanette J. *From Crime to Choice: The Transformation of Abortion in America.* Westport, Conn.: Greenwood Press, 1985.

Davis, Susan E., ed. *Women Under Attack.* Boston: South End Press, 1988.

Deckard, Barbara Sinclair. *The Women's Movement: Political, Socioeconomic and Psychological Issues.* New York: Harper and Row, 1975.

Delzell, Ruth. *The Early History of Women Trade Unionists of America.* Chicago: National Women's Trade Union League of America, 1914.

DePauw, Linda Grant, and Conover Hunt. *Remember the Ladies: Women in America, 1750–1815.* New York: Viking Press, 1976.

Dexter, Elizabeth Anthony. *Career Women of America, 1776–1840.* Boston: Houghton Mifflin, 1950.

DuBois, Ellen C. *Feminism and Suffrage: The Emergence of an Independent Women's Movement in America, 1848–1860.* Ithaca, N.Y.: Cornell University Press, 1978.

Evans, Sara. *Personal Politics: The Roots of Women's Liberation in the Civil Rights Movement and the New Left.* Cambridge, Mass.: Belknap Press, 1975.

Flexner, Eleanor. *Century of Struggle: The Woman's Rights Movement in the United States.* Cambridge: Harvard University Press, 1975.

Fogel, Walter. *The Equal Pay Act: Implications for Comparable Worth.* New York: Praeger, 1984.

Foner, Philip S. *Women and the American Labor Market: From World War I to the Present.* New York: Free Press, 1980.

———. ed. *Frederick Douglass on Women's Rights.* Westport, Conn.: Greenwood Press, 1976.

Friedan, Betty. *The Feminine Mystique.* New York: Dell, 1974 [1963].

———. *The Second Stage.* New York: Summit Books, 1982.

Friedman, Jean E., and William G. Shade. *Our American Sisters: Women in American Life and Thought.* Boston: Allyn and Bacon, 1976.

Friedman, Lawrence M., Roger H. Davidson, G. Calvin Mackenzie, John E. Jackson, Maris A. Vinovskis, and Cynthia E. Harrison. *The Abortion Dispute and the American System.* Washington, D.C.: Brookings Institution, 1983.

Fulenwider, Claire Knoche. *Feminism in American Politics: A Study of Ideological Influence.* New York: Praeger, 1980.

Gelb, Joyce, and Marian Lief Palley. *Women and Public Policies.* Princeton, N.J.: Princeton University Press, 1987.

George, Carol V. R. *"Remember the Ladies": New Perspectives on Women in American History.* Syracuse, N.Y.: Syracuse University Press, 1920.

Ginsburg, Faye D. *Contested Lives: The Abortion Debate in an American Community.* Berkeley: University of California Press, 1989.

Githens, Marianne, and Jewel L. Prestage, eds. *A Portrait of Marginality: The Political Behavior of the American Woman.* New York: Longman, 1977.

Goldstein, Leslie Friedman. *The Constitutional Rights of Women*. Madison: University of Wisconsin Press, 1988.

Gordon, Linda. *Woman's Body, Woman's Right: A Social History of Birth Control in America*. New York: Penguin Books, 1977.

Gould, Carol C., and Marx W. Wartofsky, eds. *Women and Philosophy: Toward a Theory of Liberation*. New York: Putnam, 1976.

Greer, Germaine. *Sex and Destiny: The Politics of Human Fertility*. New York: Harper and Row, 1984.

Grimke, Sarah M. *Letters on the Equality of the Sexes and the Condition of Woman*. New York: Lennox Hill, 1838.

Groneman, Carol, and Mary B. Norton, eds. *To Toil the Livelong Day: America's Women at Work, 1780–1980*. Ithaca, N.Y.: Cornell University Press, 1987.

Harris, Barbara J. *Beyond Her Sphere: Women and the Professions in American History*. Westport, Conn.: Greenwood Press, 1978.

Harrison, Cynthia. *On Account of Sex: The Politics of Women's Issues, 1945–1968*. Berkeley: University of California Press, 1988.

Hechler, Eugene A., ed. *A Short History of Women's Rights*. 1914; reprint, Westport, Conn.: Greenwood Press, 1971.

Helmholz, R. H., and Bernard D. Reams, eds. *Historical Writings in Law and Jurisprudence*. Buffalo, N.Y.: Hein, 1981.

Hersh, Blanch G. *"The Slavery of Sex": Feminist-Abolitionists in Nineteenth-Century America*. Chicago: University of Illinois Press, 1978.

Hewlett, Sylvia Ann. *A Lesser Life: The Myth of Women's Liberation in America*. New York: Morrow, 1986.

Hole, Judith, and Ellen Levine. *Rebirth of Feminism*. New York: Quadrangle Books, 1971.

Horwitz, Morton J. *The Transformation of American Law, 1780–1860*. Cambridge: Harvard University Press, 1977.

Hymowitz, Carol, and Michaele Weissman. *A History of Women in America*. New York: Bantam Books, 1978.

Irwin, Inez Haynes. *The Story of the Woman's Party*. New York: Harcourt Brace, 1921.

James, Edward T. *Notable American Women, 1607–1950: A Biographical Dictionary*. Cambridge, Mass.: Belknap Press, 1971.

————. ed. *Papers of the Women's Trade Union League and Its Principal Leaders*. Woodbridge, Conn.: Research Publications, 1981.

Jaquette, Jane S., ed. *Women in Politics*. New York: Wiley, 1974.

Jaquith, Cindy. *Surrogate Motherhood, Women's Rights, and the Working Class*. New York: Pathfinder Press, 1988.

Johansen, Elaine. *Comparable Worth: The Myth and the Movement*. Boulder, Colo.: Westview Press, 1984.

Kanowitz, Leo. *Woman and the Law: The Unfinished Revolution*. Albuquerque: University of New Mexico Press, 1975.

Kelley, Mary, ed. *Woman's Being, Woman's Place: Female Identity and Vocation in American History*. Boston: G. K. Hall, 1979.

Kelly, Rita Mae, and Mary Boutilier. *The Making of Political Women: A Study of Socialization and Role Conflict*. Chicago: Nelson Hall, 1978.

Kennedy, David. *Birth Control in America: The Career of Margaret Sanger*. New Haven, Conn., and London: Yale University Press, 1970.

Keynes, Edward. *The Court v. Congress: Prayer, Busing, and Abortion*. Durham, N.C.: Duke University Press, 1989.

Kirkpatrick, Jean J. *Political Woman*. New York: Basic Books, 1974.

——. *The New Presidential Elite: Men and Women in National Politics*. New York: Russell Sage Foundation, 1976.

Klein, Ethel. *Gender Politics*. Cambridge: Harvard University Press, 1984.

Kraditor, Aileen. *The Ideas of the Woman Suffrage Movement, 1890–1920*. Garden City, N.Y.: Doubleday, 1971.

——. ed. *Up from the Pedestal: Selected Writings in the History of American Feminism*. Chicago: Quadrangle Books, 1968.

Leet, Rebecca K. *Republican Women Are Wonderful: A History of Women at Republican National Conventions*. Washington, D.C.: National Women's Political Caucus, 1980.

Lemons, J. Stanley. *The Woman Citizen: Social Feminism in the 1920's*. Urbana: University of Illinois Press, 1973.

Lerner, Gerda. *The Majority Finds Its Past: Placing Women in History*. New York: Oxford University Press, 1979.

——. *The Woman in American History*. Menlo Park, Calif.: Addison-Wesley, 1971.

Lovenduski, Joni, and Jill Hills, eds. *The Politics of the Second Electorate: Women and Public Participation*. London: Routledge and Kegan Paul, 1981.

Luker, Kristin. *Abortion and the Politics of Motherhood*. Berkeley: University of California Press, 1984.

Lundberg, Ferdinand, and Marynia Farnham. *Modern Woman: The Lost Sex*. 1947; reprint, Philadelphia: West, 1977.

MacKinnon, Catherine A. *Sexual Harassment of Working Women: A Case of Sex Discrimination*. New Haven, Conn.: Yale University Press, 1979.

Mandel, Ruth B. *In the Running: The New Woman Candidate*. New Haven, Conn.: Ticknor and Fields, 1981.

Mansbridge, Jane. *Why We Lost the ERA*. Chicago: University of Chicago Press, 1986.

McGlen, Nancy E., and Karen O'Connor. *Women's Rights: The Struggle for Equality in the Nineteenth and Twentieth Centuries*. New York: Praeger, 1983.

McPherson, James M. *Battle Cry of Freedom*. New York: Oxford University Press, 1988.

Melder, Keith. *Beginnings of Sisterhood: The American Woman's Rights Movement, 1800–1850*. New York: Schocken Books, 1977.

Mohn, James. *Abortion in America, 1800–1900*. New York: Oxford University Press, 1978.

Morgan, Robin. *Sisterhood Is Powerful: An Anthology of Writings from the Women's Liberation Movement*. New York: Vintage Books, 1970.

Morris, Richard B. *Studies in the History of American Law*. 2d ed. New York: Octagon Books, 1963.

Omilian, Susan M. *Sexual Harassment in Employment*. Wilmette, Ill.: Callaghan, 1987.

O'Neill, William L. *Everyone Was Brave: The Rise and Fall of Feminism in America*. Chicago: Quadrangle Books, 1969.

Papachristou, Judith. *Women Together: A History in Documents of the Women's Movement in the United States*. New York: Knopf, 1976.

Parsons, Alice Beal. *Women's Dilemma*. 1926; reprint, Salem, N.H.: Ayer, 1974.

Pease, Jane H., and William H. Pease. *Bound with Them in Chains: A Biographical History of the Antislavery Movement.* Westport, Conn.: Greenwood Press, 1972.

Peck, Mary Gray. *The Rise of the Woman Suffrage Party.* Chicago: Myra Strawn Hartshorn, 1911.

Reeve, Tapping. *The Law of Baron and Feme, of Parent and Child, of Guardian and War, of Master and Servant, and of the Powers of Courts of Chancery.* New Haven, Conn., 1816.

Rix, Sara E. *The American Woman, 1990–91: A Status Report.* New York: Norton, 1990.

Rossi, Alice S. *The Feminist Papers, from Adams to de Beauvoir.* New York: Bantam Books, 1973.

Rothman, Sheila M. *Woman's Proper Place: A History of Changing Ideals and Practices, 1870 to the Present.* New York: Basic Books, 1978.

Rupp, Leila, and Verta Taylor. *Survival in the Doldrums: The American Women's Rights Movement, 1945 to the 1960's.* New York: Oxford University Press, 1987.

Salmon, Marylynn. *Women and the Law of Property in Early America.* Chapel Hill: University of North Carolina Press, 1986.

Scharf, Lois. *To Work and to Wed: Female Employment, Feminism, and the Great Depression.* Westport, Conn.: Greenwood Press, 1980.

Schneir, Miriam. *Feminism: The Essential Historical Writings.* New York: Random House, 1972.

Sheeran, Patrick J. *Women, Society, the State, and Abortion: A Structural Analysis.* New York: Praeger, 1987.

Showalter, Elaine, ed. *These Modern Women: Autobiographical Essays from the 1920s.* Old Westbury, N.Y.: Feminist Press, 1978.

Simmons, Adele, Ann Freedman, Margaret Dunkle, and Francine Blau. *Exploitation from 9 to 5: Report of the Twentieth Century Fund Task Force on Women and Employment.* Lexington, Mass.: Lexington Books, 1975.

Snyder, Eloise C., ed. *The Study of Women: Enlarging Perspectives of Social Reality.* New York: Harper and Row, 1979.

Spruill, Julia Cherry. *Women's Life and Work in the Southern Colonies.* New York: Norton, 1972.

Stanton, Elizabeth Cady. *Eighty Years and More: Reminiscences, 1815–1897.* Reprint, New York: Schocken Books, 1971.

Stanton, Elizabeth Cady, Susan B. Anthony, and Matilda Joslyn Gage, eds. *History of Woman Suffrage.* New York: Charles Mann, 1881.

Stern, Madeleine B., ed. *The Victoria Woodhull Reader.* Weston, Mass.: M & S Press, 1974.

Stevens, Doris. *Jailed for Freedom.* New York: Boni and Liveright, 1920.

Suhl, Yuri. *Ernestine L. Rose and the Battle for Human Rights.* New York: Reynal, 1959.

Thompson, Roger. *Women in Stuart England and America: A Comparative Study.* London: Routledge and Kegan Paul, 1974.

Tinker, Irene, ed. *Women in Washington: Advocates for Public Policy.* Beverly Hills, Calif.: Sage, 1983.

Tolcin, Susan, and Martin Tolcin. *Clout: Womanpower and Politics.* New York: Coward, McCann and Geoghegan, 1974.

U.S. Commission on Civil Rights. *The Federal Civil Rights Enforcement Effort—1974.* Washington, D.C.: 1975.
Van Horn, Susan H. *Women, Work, and Fertility, 1900–1987.* New York: New York University Press, 1987.
Weisberg, D. Kelly, ed. *Women and the Law: A Social Historical Perspective.* Cambridge: Schenkman, 1982.
Weitzman, Lenore J. *The Divorce Revolution: The Unexpected Social and Economic Consequences for Women and Children in America.* New York: Free Press, 1985.
Willborn, Steven L. *A Comparable Worth Primer.* Lexington, Mass.: Lexington Books, 1986.
Woloch, Nancy. *Women and the American Experience.* New York: Knopf, 1984.

JOURNAL ARTICLES

Abbott, Edith, and Sophronia P. Breckenridge. "Employment of Women in Industries, Twelfth Census Statistics." *Journal of Political Economy*, Vol. 14, January and February 1906, pp. 14–40.
Aiegler, Harmon, and Keith Pole. "Political Woman: Gender in Difference." *Public Opinion*, Aug.-Sept. 1985, p. 55.
Allen, Jodie T. "Not NOW—It's Time for Consensus, Not Conflict." *Washington Post Outlook*, July 30, 1989, p. C1.
Andersen, Kristi. "Working Women and Political Participation, 1952–1972." *American Journal of Political Science*, Vol. 19, August 1975, pp. 439–53.
Andrews, Lori. "Surrogate Motherhood: The Challenge for Feminists." *Law, Medicine & Health Care*, Vol. 16, Spring 1988, pp. 72–80.
Annas, George J. "Fairy Tales Surrogate Mothers Tell." *Law, Medicine & Health Care*, Vol. 16, Spring 1988, pp. 17–33.
Anter, Joyce. "After College, What? New Graduates and the Family Claim." *American Quarterly*, Vol. 32 (Fall 1980), pp. 409–35.
Avery, Patricia. "For Women, a Slow Climb up the Political Ladder." *U.S. News & World Report*, October 8, 1984, pp. 76–78.
Basch, Norma. "Invisible Women: The Legal Fiction of Marital Unity in Nineteenth Century America." *Feminist Studies*, Vol. 5, Summer 1979, pp. 346–66.
"Battle of the Gender Gap." *Ms.*, April 1988, p. 79.
Berger, Caruthers Gholson. "Equal Pay, Equal Employment Opportunity and Equal Enforcement of the Law for Women." *Valparaiso University Law Review*, Vol. 5 (1971), pp. 326–73.
Biskupic, Joan, "States Move to Curb Abortion, Stir Concern in Congress." *Congressional Quarterly Weekly Report*, Vol. 48, March 31, 1990, pp. 1003–1004.
Bouton, Katherine. "Women and Divorce: How the New Law Works against Them." *New York*, October 8, 1984, pp. 34–40.
Bromley, Dorothy Dunbar. "Feminist—New Style." *Harper's*, Vol. 155 (Oct. 1927), pp. 552–60.
Brown, Adelaide. "The History of the Development of Women in Medicine in California." *California and Western Medicine*, May 1915.
Brown, Barbara A. "The Equal Rights Amendment: A Constitutional Basis for Equal Rights for Women." *Yale Law Journal*, Vol. 80, April 1971, pp. 871–985.

Budiansky, Stephen. "The New Rules of Reproduction." *U.S. News & World Report*, April 18, 1988, pp. 66–68.

Callahan, Sidney. "Abortion and the Sexual Agenda: A Case for Pro-Life Feminism." *Commonweal*, April 26, 1986, pp. 232–38.

Capron, A. M., and M. J. Radin. "Choosing Family Law over Contract Law as a Paradigm for Surrogate Motherhood." *Law, Medicine & Health Care*, Vol. 16, Spring 1988, pp. 34–43.

Caudle, Sheila. "Abortion Rights Rescued: The Triumph of Coalition Politics." *Ms.*, January 1983, pp. 40–44.

Chapman, Fern Schumer. "Taking Time Out to Have a Baby: What It Means to Companies . . . and to Women's Careers." *Washington Post Health Magazine*, September 22, 1987, pp. 13–18.

Chused, Richard H. "Married Women's Property and Inheritance by Widows in Massachusetts: A Study of Wills Probated between 1800 and 1850." *Berkeley Women's Law Journal*, Vol. 3, 1986.

———. "Married Women's Property Law: 1800–1850." *Georgetown Law Journal*, Vol. 72, 1983, pp. 1359–1412.

Conover, Pamela Johnston. "Feminists and the Gender Gap." *Journal of Politics*, Vol. 50, November 1988, pp. 985–1006.

Cook, Beverly B. "Women Judges: A Preface to Their History." *Golden Gate University Law Review*, Vol. 14, Fall 1984, pp. 573–610.

Cott, Nancy F. "Divorce and the Changing Status of Women in Eighteenth Century Massachusetts." *William and Mary Quarterly*, Vol. 33, October 1976, pp. 586–614.

———. "Feminist Politics in the 1920s: The National Woman's Party." *Journal of American History*, Vol. 71, June 1984, pp. 43–68.

Decrow, Karen. "The Man and the Woman Are One." *Law in American Society*, Vol. 3, September 1974, pp. 18–24.

Donovan, Beth. "Early Campaigning Tests Abortion Foes' Muscle." *Congressional Quarterly*, Vol. 48, March 10, 1990, pp. 765–75.

DuBois, Ellen. "The Radicalism of the Woman Suffrage Movement: Notes toward the Reconstruction of Nineteenth Century Feminism." *Feminist Studies*, Vol. 3, Fall 1975, pp. 63–71.

Ehrenreich, Barbara. "Comment on Feminism, Family and Community." *Dissent*, Vol. 30, Winter 1983, pp. 103–6.

Ehrenreich, Barbara, and Deirdre English. "Blowing the Whistle on the 'Mommy Track.' " *Ms.*, July/August 1989, pp. 56–58.

Ehrlich, Elizabeth. "The Mommy Track." *Business Week*, March 20, 1989, pp. 126–34.

Eisenstein, Zillah R. "Antifeminism in the Politics and Election of 1980." *Feminist Studies*, Vol. 9, Summer 1981, pp. 187–205.

English, Deirdre. "The War against Choice: Inside the Anti-Abortion Movement." *Mother Jones*, February-March 1981.

Erens, Pamela. "Anti-Abortion, Pro-Feminism?" *Mother Jones*, May 1989.

Esbeck, Carl. "Employment Practices and Sex Discrimination: Judicial Extension of Beneficial Female Protective Labor Laws." *Cornell Law Review*, Vol. 59, November 1973, pp. 133–57.

Evans, Judith. "The Good Society? Implications of a Greater Participation by Women in Public Life." *Political Studies*, Vol. 32, December 1984, pp. 618–26.

Farnham, Marynia. "Women's Opportunities and Responsibilities." *Annals of the American Academy of Political and Social Science*, Vol. 63, May 1947, p. 251.

Fosu, Augustin Kwasi. "Trends in Relative Earnings Gains by Black Women: Implications for the Future." *Review of Black Political Economy*, Vol. 17, no. 1 (Summer 1988), pp. 31–45.

Fraser, Arvonne S. "Women: The New Image." *Vital Speeches*, July 15, 1971, pp. 599–605.

Fryburger, L. Bruce. "Maternity Leave Policies under Title VII." *Labor Law Journal*, Vol. 26, March 1975, pp. 163–73.

Gallagher, Maggie. "The New Pro-Life Rebels." *National Review*, February 27, 1987, pp. 37–39.

———. "Womb to Let." *National Review*, April 24, 1987, pp. 27–30.

Gilman, Charlotte Perkins. "The New Generation of Women." *Current History*, Vol. 18 (Aug. 1923), pp. 735–36.

Ginsburg, Ruth B. "Gender and the Constitution." *University of Cincinnati Law Review* 44, no. 1 (1975), pp. 1–42.

Glazer, Penina M. "Organizing for Freedom." *Massachusetts Review*, Vol. 14, Winter/Spring 1972, pp. 29–44.

Glover, Jonathan. "Matters of Life and Death." *New York Review of Books*, May 30, 1985, pp. 19–23.

Goldwin, Robert. "Why Blacks, Women, and Jews Are Not Mentioned in the Constitution." *Commentary*, May 1987, p. 28.

Hacker, Andrew. "The Divorce Revolution." *New York Review of Books*, August 14, 1986, pp. 26–30.

Hely, Barbara Sherman. "Commercial Contracts and Human Connectedness." *Society*, Vol. 25, March-April 1988, pp. 11–17.

Hodes, W. William. "Women and the Constitution: Some Legal History and a New Approach to the Nineteenth Amendment." *Rutgers Law Review* 25, no. 1 (1971), pp. 26–53.

Isaacson, Walter. "The Battle over Abortion." *Time*, April 6, 1981, pp. 20–28.

Jacob, Herbert. "Another Look at No-Fault Divorce and the Post-Divorce Finances of Women." *Law & Society Review* 23, no. 1 (1989), pp. 95–115.

Jacoby, Tamar. "A New Majority Ticks Off the Reagan Agenda." *Newsweek*, July 17, 1989, p. 26.

Johnson, Marilyn. "Women and Elective Office." *Society*, Vol. 17, May-June 1980, pp. 63–70.

Karst, Kenneth L. "Woman's Constitution." *Duke Law Journal*, Vol. 33, June 1984, pp. 447–508.

Kelley, Florence. "Women in Trade Unions." *The Outlook*, New York, 1906.

Krauss, Wilma Rule. "Political Implications of Gender Roles: A Review of the Literature." *American Political Science Review*, Vol. 68, December 1974, pp. 1706–1723.

Kugler, Israel. "The Trade Union Career of Susan B. Anthony." *Labor History*, Vol. 2 (Winter 1961), pp. 90–100.

Kunin, Madeleine M. "Lessons from One Woman's Career." *Journal of State Government*, Vol. 60, September-October 1987, pp. 209–13.

Lady's Magazine 2 (December 1792), p. 69.

Lear, Martha Weinman. "The Second Feminist Wave." *New York Times Magazine*, March 10, 1968.

Lee, Marcia Manning. "Why Few Women Hold Public Office: Democracy and Sex Roles." *Political Science Quarterly*, Vol. 91, Summer 1976, pp. 297–314.

Lemons, J. Stanley. "Social Feminism in the 1920s: Progressive Women and Industrial Legislation." *Labor History*, Vol. 14, Winter 1973, pp. 83–91.

Long, Huey B. "The Education of Girls and Women in Colonial America." *Journal of Research and Development in Education*, Vol. 8, Summer 1975, pp. 66–82.

Mahoney, Joan. "An Essay on Surrogacy and Feminist Thought." *Law, Medicine & Health Care*, Vol. 16, Spring 1988, pp. 81–88.

"Management Women and the New Facts of Life." *Harvard Business Review*, January–February 1989, pp. 65–76.

Martin, Elaine. "Men and Women on the Bench: Vive la Difference?" *Judicature*, Vol. 72, December–January 1989, pp. 204–9.

Martin, Philip L. "Equal Rights Amendment: An Overview." *St. Louis University Law Journal*, Vol. 50, Fall 1972, pp. 1–16.

McDaniel, Ann. "The Future of Abortion in America." *Newsweek*, July 17, 1989, pp. 14–16.

Meyer, Howard N. "Women, 'Big Fourteen' and Equal Rights." *New Politics*, Vol. 10, Fall 1972, pp. 50–60.

Moller, Herbert. "Sex Composition and Correlated Culture Patterns of Colonial America." *William and Mary Quarterly*, Vol. 12, April 1945, pp. 122–53.

Moran, Robert. "Reducing Discrimination: Role of the Equal Pay Act." *Monthly Labor Review*, Vol. 93, June 1970, pp. 30–34.

Murphy, Thomas E. "Female Wage Discrimination: A Study of the Equal Pay Act, 1963–1970." *University of Cincinnati Law Review*, Vol. 39, Fall 1970, pp. 615–49.

Murray, Judith Sargent. *The Gleaner* 1, Boston, 1798, pp. 70–71.

"The New Political Rules." *Newsweek*, July 17, 1989, p. 21.

Noah, Timothy. "The Right-to-Life Split. *New Republic*, March 21, 1981, pp. 7–9.

"On Female Authorship." *The Lady's Magazine and Repository of Entertaining Knowledge*, Dec. 1792, pp. 69–71.

"On Female Universities and Academies." *The Lady and Gentleman's Pocket Magazine of Literary and Polite Amusement*, Aug. 15, 1796, pp. 116–18.

"On the Adoption of the Male Costume by Women." *The Lady's Weekly Miscellany*, Sept. 5, 1807, pp. 364–66.

"On the Mental Endowments of Women." *The Lady's Miscellany*, Nov. 29, 1806, pp. 37–39.

Palmieri, Patricia. "Patterns of Achievement of Single Academic Women at Wellesley College, 1880–1920." *Frontiers*, Vol. 5 (Spring 1980), pp. 63–67.

Perlez, Jane. "Women, Power, and Politics." *New York Times Magazine*, June 24, 1984.

Rabkin, Peggy. "The Origins of Law Reform: The Social Significance of the Nineteenth-Century Codification Movement and Its Contribution to the Passage of the Early Married Women's Property Acts." *Buffalo Law Review*, Vol. 24, 1975, pp. 683–760.

Rush, Benjamin. "Thoughts upon Female Education." *New England Quarterly Magazine*, Boston, April-June 1802, p. 146.

Salholz, Eloise. "Voting in Curbs and Confusion." *Newsweek*, July 17, 1989, pp. 16–20.

Sassower, Doris L. "Women in the Law: The Second Hundred Years." *American Bar Association Journal*, Vol. 57, April 1971, pp. 329–32.

Schwartz, Felice N. "Management Women and the New Facts of Life." *Harvard Business Review*, Vol. 89, January-February 1989, pp. 65–76.

Shapiro, Laura. "Revering Motherhood, Not Mom." *Nation*, October 8, 1983, pp. 309–11.

Sherill, Robert. "The Equal-Rights Amendment—What, Exactly, Does It Mean?" *New York Times Magazine*, September 20, 1970.

"600,000 March for Abortion Rights." *National NOW Times* 21, no. 1 (1989), p. 1.

Spake, Amanda. "Women Can Be Power Brokers, Too." *Washington Post Magazine*, June 5, 1988.

Spivack, Miranda S. "Political Compromise Afoot?" *Ms.*, July 1988, pp. 68–69.

Steinbock, Bonnie. "Surrogate Motherhood as Prenatal Adoption." *Law, Medicine & Health Care*, Vol. 16, Spring 1988, pp. 44–50.

Steinem, Gloria. "A Basic Human Right." *Ms.*, July/August 1989, pp. 38–41.

"Symposium—Women's Rights." *Hastings Law Journal*, Vol. 23, November 1971.

Takas, Marianne. "Divorce: Who Gets the Blame in "No Fault"? *Ms.*, February 1986, pp. 48–50.

Thompson, Carol. "Women and the Anti-Slavery Movement." *Current History*, Vol. 23, May 1976, pp. 198–201.

Trecker, Janice L. "Suffrage Prisoners." *American Scholar*, Vol. 42, Summer 1972, pp. 409–23.

Triedman, Kim. "A Mother's Dilemma." *Ms.*, August 1989, pp. 62–63.

Wallis, Claudia. "Onward, Women!" *Time*, December 4, 1989, pp. 80–89.

Wein, Roberta. "Women's Colleges and Domesticity, 1875–1918." *History of Education Quarterly*, Vol. 14 (Spring 1974), pp. 31–47.

Weisberg, D. Kelly. "Barred from the Bar: Women and Legal Education in the United States." *Journal of Legal Education* 28, no. 4 (1977), pp. 484–507.

Wolfe, A. B., and Helen Olson. "War-Time Industrial Employment of Women in the United States." *Journal of Political Economy*, Vol. 27, October 1919.

"Women and the Law—A Symposium." *Rutgers Law Review*, Vol. 25, Fall 1970.

"Women Face the '90's." *Time*, December 4, 1989, p. 80.

NEWSPAPER ARTICLES

"Abortion Divides Democrats in Iowa Primary as Activists from Washington Leap into the Fray." *Wall Street Journal*, April 30, 1990, p. 16.

"Abortion Molds Pennsylvania Politics." *New York Times*, May 14, 1990, p. B8.

"Abortion Rights Groups Map Strategy to Protect Access." *Washington Post*, July 8, 1989, p. A2.

"Abortion-Rights Strategy: A Move to Thwart States." *Washington Post*, January 23, 1990, p. 23.

"Are Working Mothers a Trend That's Peaked?" *Wall Street Journal*, November 2, 1988, p. B1.

"As Abortion-Rights Groups Rally Support, Foes Set Legislative Drive in Four States."
     Washington Post, July 5, 1989, p. 10.
"Connecticut Acts to Make Abortion a Statutory Right." *New York Times*, April 28,
     1990, p. 1.
"Court Upholds Pregnancy Leave Laws." *Washington Post*, January 14, 1987, p. 1.
"Crown and Scepter." *Washington Post*, March 1, 1989, p. D1.
"Day Care Spreading in Industry." *Los Angeles Times*, September 16, 1986, p. 1.
"Discrimination Case against SEC Finishes." *Washington Post*, July 3, 1987, p. G1.
Goodman, Ellen. "Employing Women: A Price Worth Paying." *Washington Post*, January
     24, 1989, p. A23.
"House Votes to Relax Medicaid Abortion Rule." *Washington Post*, October 12, 1989,
     p. 1.
"Justices Restrict Right to Abortion, 5–4, Giving States Wide Latitude." *Washington
     Post*, July 4, 1989, p. A1.
Kunin, Madeleine M. "Politics: Still a Man's World." *Washington Post*, February 3,
     1989, p. A25.
"Legislatures Set to Struggle with Abortion." *Washington Post*, September 24, 1989,
     p. 4.
"Loved and Left: The Palimony Issues." *Washington Post*, January 30, 1989, p. B1.
" 'Mommy Track' Author Answers Her Many Critics." *Washington Post*, March 19,
     1989, p. 1.
"Mommy Track—Right to the Top." *Washington Post*, March 19, 1989, p. C1.
"The Next Battleground on Abortion Rights." *Washington Post*, July 10, 1989, p. 4.
"NOW Renews Equal Rights Battle." *New York Times*, July 1, 1988, p. B6.
"Parental Leave: Women's Ranks Break on Issue." *Wall Street Journal*, September
     24, 1986, p. 1.
" 'Politics of Fear' Quelled in Abortion Debate." *Washington Post*, October 13, 1989,
     p. 1.
"Pro-Choice Coalition Fields Massive Protest." *Women's Political Times*, September/
     October 1989, p. 1.
"SEC Agrees to Outside Review in Sexual Harassment Case." *Washington Post*, June
     17, 1988, p. A1.
"State Bar to Jobless Pay after Pregnancy Is Upheld." *New York Times*, January 22,
     1987, p. B17.
"State Legislators Vent Anxiety over Abortion." *Washington Post*, August 10, 1989,
     p. A4.
"Supreme Court, 6–3, Extends Preferences in Employment for Women and Minorities."
     New York Times, March 26, 1987, p. 1.
"Victims of Sexual Harassment Face Long Fight." *Los Angeles Times*, August 9, 1986,
     p. 23.
"Women Finding Hope in Quest for Judgeships." *Los Angeles Daily Journal*, May 25,
     1989, p. 1.
"Women, Jobs and Children: A New Generation Worries." *New York Times*, November
     27, 1988, p. 1.
"Women Lawyers in Survey Report Bias, Harassment." *Washington Post*, December
     4, 1989, p. 1.
"Women Winning Locally, but Higher Office Is Elusive." *New York Times*, April 1,
     1989, p. L29.

"Women's Groups to Press for Parental Leave." *New York Times*, May 8, 1987, p. 19.
"Women's Place in the House." *Washington Post*, March 6, 1990, p. C4.
"Working Mother Is Now Norm, Study Shows." *New York Times*, June 16, 1988.

DISSERTATIONS

Bland, Sidney R. "Techniques of Persuasion: The National Woman's Party and Woman Suffrage, 1913–1919." Ph.D. dissertation, George Washington University, 1972.

Cassell, Joan M. "A Group Called Women: Recruitment and Organization in Contemporary American Feminism." Ph.D. dissertation, Columbia University, 1975.

Florer, John Harmon. "NOW: The Formative Years. The National Effort to Acquire Federal Action on Equal Employment Rights for Women in the 1960s." Ph.D. dissertation, Syracuse University, 1972.

McCreesh, Carolyn D. "On the Picket Line: Militant Women Campaign to Organize Garment Workers, 1880–1917." Ph.D. dissertation, University of Maryland, 1975.

Rabkin, Peggy A. "The Silent Feminist Revolution: Women and the Law in New York State from Blackstone to the Beginnings of the American Women's Rights Movement." Ph.D. dissertation, State University of New York, Buffalo, 1975.

Reinsch, Paul S. "English Common Law in the Early American Colonies." Ph.D. diss., University of Wisconsin, 1899.

Schott, Linda Kay. "Women against War: Pacifism, Feminism and Social Justice in the United States, 1914–1941." Ph.D. dissertation, Stanford University, 1985.

Thurman, Kay Ellen. "The Married Women's Property Acts." LL.M. dissertation, University of Wisconsin Law School, 1966.

Warbasse, Elizabeth Bowles. "The Changing Legal Rights of Married Women, 1800–1861." Ph.D. dissertation, Radcliffe College, 1960.

Zelman, Patricia. "Development of Equal Employment Opportunity for Women as National Policy, 1960–1967." Ph.D. dissertation, Ohio State University, 1980.

INDEX

ABOUT THE AUTHORS

RITA J. SIMON is a sociologist and University Professor in the School of Public Affairs and the Washington College of Law at the American University. Her recent publications include *The Crimes Women Commit and the Punishments They Receive* (1990), *Intercountry Adoption: A Multinational Perspective* (Praeger, 1990), and *The Insanity Defense: A Critical Assessment of Law and Policy in the Post-Hinckley Era* (Praeger, 1988).

GLORIA DANZIGER is an attorney and freelance writer in Washington, D.C. She specializes in immigration law and international law and has written extensively on civil rights, politics, and the law.